language testing

Palgrave Advances in Linguistics

Consulting Editor:
Christopher N. Candlin,
Macquarie University, Australia

Titles include:

Mike Baynham and Mastin Prinsloo (*editors*)
THE FUTURE OF LITERACY STUDIES

Noel Burton-Roberts (*editor*)
PRAGMATICS

Susan Foster-Cohen (*editor*)
LANGUAGE ACQUISITION

Monica Heller (*editor*)
BILINGUALISM: A SOCIAL APPROACH

Martha E. Pennington (*editor*)
PHONOLOGY IN CONTEXT

Barry O'Sullivan (*editor*)
LANGUAGE TESTING: THEORIES AND PRACTICES

Ann Weatherall, Bernadette M. Watson and Cindy Gallois (*editors*)
LANGUAGE, DISCOURSE AND SOCIAL PSYCHOLOGY

Forthcoming:

Charles Antaki (*editor*)
APPLIED CONVERSATIONAL ANALYSIS: CHANGING
INSTITUTIONAL PRACTICES

Palgrave Advances
Series Standing Order ISBN 978–1–4039–3512–0 (Hardback) 978–1–4039–3513–7 (Paperback)
(*outside North America only*)

You can receive future titles in this series as they are published by placing a standing order.
Please contact your bookseller or, in the case of difficulty, write to us at the address below
with your name and address, the title of the series and one of the ISBNs quoted above.

Customer Services Department, Macmillan Distribution Ltd, Houndmills, Basingstoke,
Hampshire RG21 6XS, England

language testing

theories and practices

edited by

barry o'sullivan

First published 2011 by
PALGRAVE MACMILLAN

Palgrave Macmillan in the UK is an imprint of Macmillan Publishers Limited,
registered in England, company number 785998, of Houndmills, Basingstoke,
Hampshire RG21 6XS.

Palgrave Macmillan in the US is a division of St Martin's Press LLC,
175 Fifth Avenue, New York, NY 10010.

Palgrave Macmillan is the global academic imprint of the above companies
and has companies and representatives throughout the world.

Palgrave® and Macmillan® are registered trademarks in the United States,
the United Kingdom, Europe and other countries.

ISBN: 978-0-230-23062-0 hardback
ISBN: 978-0-230-23063-7 paperback

This book is printed on paper suitable for recycling and made from fully
managed and sustained forest sources. Logging, pulping and manufacturing
processes are expected to conform to the environmental regulations of the
country of origin.

A catalogue record for this book is available
from the British Library.

Library of Congress Cataloging-in-Publication Data

Language testing : theories and practices / edited by Barry O'Sullivan.
p. cm
Includes index.
ISBN 978-0-230-23063-7 (pbk.)
1. Language and languages – Ability testing. 2. Language and languages – Examinations.
3. Language and languages – Study and teaching. I. O'Sullivan, Barry, Dr.

P53.L3647 2011
402.8'7—dc22
2011004150

10   9   8   7   6   5   4   3   2   1
20 19 18 17 16 15 14 13 12 11

Printed and bound in Great Britain by
CPI Antony Rowe, Chippenham and Eastbourne

to my family

contents

series preface

christopher n. candlin

The *Advances in Linguistics* Series is part of an overall publishing programme by Palgrave Macmillan aimed at producing collections of
original, commissioned articles under the invited editorship of distinguished scholars.

The books in the Series are not intended as an overall guide to
the topic or to provide an exhaustive coverage of its various sub-
fields. Rather, they are carefully planned to offer the informed
readership a conspectus of perspectives on key themes, authored by
major scholars whose work is at the boundaries of current research.
What we intend the Series to do, then, is to focus on salience and
influence, move fields forward and help to chart future research
development.

The Series is designed for postgraduate and research students, including advanced-level undergraduates seeking to pursue research work
in Linguistics, or careers engaged with language and communication study more generally, as well as for more experienced researchers
and tutors seeking an awareness of what is current and in prospect in
research fields adjacent to their own. We hope that some of the intellectual excitement posed by the challenges of Linguistics as a pluralistic
discipline will shine through the books!

Editors of books in the Series have been particularly asked to put their
own distinctive stamp on their collection, to give it a personal dimension, and to map the territory, as it were, seen through the eyes of their
own research experience.

As with other volumes in the *Advances in Linguistics* Series, whose significance for future research developments extends beyond their particular disciplinary focus, so in *Language Testing: Theories and Practices* we recognise an engagement, not just with language testing *per se*, but with a much more broadly canvassed sweep across contemporary applied linguistic research. The mutualities between research and practice (what we may term *praxis*) invoked by the title speak to a much more generally relevant concern in Applied Linguistics for *interrelationality*; a construct which, as Barry O'Sullivan's imaginative and future-focused volume makes clear, calls forth a richly textured weaving of practices and participants engaging new sites, new populations, new and different research traditions, innovatively displayed expertise and practical relevancies.

Take, for example, the three themes Barry O'Sullivan identifies in his Introduction as criterial for future research and practice in Language Testing: validation, professionalisation and localisation. These are not just criterial themes for language testing: they engage all applied linguistic research and practice. *Validation* matters to us all in terms of the warranting of claims, the making transparent of research processes, the interpretations we and others place on evidence, and in particular the need we share to engage with the practical relevance of research as a central imperative for the discipline. Equally critical, as Barry O'Sullivan argues for test development, is the requirement to keep key stakeholders, whose languages, discourses and practices give rise to our research, at the centre of the research exercise: this is important not only for honouring considerations of ethical practice but as the mainspring for authenticating the joint problematisation of issues of communication central to Applied Linguistics. *Professionalisation*, in terms of the legitimisation of testing practices and the concurrent need for training and professional development for a widening cadre of all those engaged in the language testing enterprise (designers, administrators, researchers and, indeed, marketers), is, again, a theme of importance not just to language testing. Increasingly, it is incumbent on all those involved in applied linguistic research not only to maintain their own professional standards of practice but to connect with, and to understand, the codes and conventions in place among those research and practice participants from other fields and professions with whom they engage. Inter-professionalisation, as an aspect of interrelationality, is now an imperative, certainly a challenge, and one not only directed at the practices of language testing, as heralded in this volume. Finally, it is necessary to take into account that the exigencies and circumstances of the *localisation* of language testing, in terms of test design, test processes, test participants and, perhaps most critically, the consequential effects of test performance, all have their reflexive implications for applied linguistics as a discipline. Such factors go far beyond matters of guaranteeing the authenticity of sociolinguistic evidence for test item design; they engage with social–psychological issues of the identities, attitudes and self-worth of test takers, with socio-political agendas concerning access to rights, freedoms and futures, and above all, as Barry O'Sullivan makes amply and clearly plain for language testing, addressing the imperative that *all* applied linguistic research should be locally validated and contextualised to the conditions of those participants with whom it is engaged, and, most important of all, should constitute a research and practice which is identified as being *with*, not *on* or *for*. In this book, as quite generally, interrelationality matters.

Christopher N. Candlin
Consultant Editor
Advances in Linguistics Series

acknowledgements

I would very much like to thank all of the contributing authors and also the consulting editor, Christopher Candlin, for his support and advice throughout this project.

list of tables and figures

tables

figures

list of contributors

Teresa De Jesus Romero Barradas
Lecturer and test developer at EXAVER Examinations at Universidad Veracruzana, Mexico

Annie Brown
Associate Director (Assessment & Professional Development) Ministry of Higher Education, United Arab Emirates

Deirdre Burrell
Lecturer, Institute of Education, University of Reading, UK

Carmen Sanchez Chavez
Lecturer and test developer at EXAVER Examinations at Universidad Veracruzana, Mexico

Alan Davies
Emeritus Professor of Applied Linguistics at the University of Edinburgh, UK

Roger Anthony Dunne
Lecturer and Senior Editor, EXAVER Examinations at Universidad Veracruzana, Mexico

Adriana Abad Florescano
General Coordinator, EXAVER Examinations at Universidad Veracruzana, Mexico

Suzanne Graham
Professor of Education at the Institute of Education, University of Reading, UK

Anthony Green
Reader in Language Testing, Centre for Research in English Language Learning and Assessment (CRELLA), University of Bedfordshire, UK

Patricia Evelyn Grounds
Senior Projects Manager, British Council Mexico, Mexico

Mary Maxwell Hart
Lecturer and test developer at EXAVER Examinations at Universidad Veracruzana, Mexico

Paul Jaquith
Chair of Assessment, Higher Colleges of Technology, United Arab Emirates

Paul Joyce
Assistant Professor at J. F. Oberlin University, Tokyo, Japan

Elif Kantarcioğlu
Researcher and Test Developer, Bilkent University School of English Language (BUSEL), Ankara, Turkey

Richard Kiely
Head of the Centre for International Language Teacher Education (CILTE) at University College of St Mark and St John Plymouth, UK

Esperanza Zamora Lara
Lecturer and test developer at EXAVER Examinations at Universidad Veracruzana, Mexico

Maria Isabel Gonzalez Macias
Lecturer and test developer at EXAVER Examinations at Universidad Veracruzana, Mexico

Luis Alejandro Santana Martinez
Lecturer and test developer at EXAVER Examinations at Universidad Veracruzana, Mexico

Dominique Medley
Lecturer, Institute of Education, University of Reading, UK

Fumiyo Nakatsuhara
Researcher, Centre for Research in English Language Learning and Assessment (CRELLA), University of Bedfordshire, UK

Brian North
Head of Academic Development at Eurocentres, Switzerland and of EAQUALS (European Association for Quality Language Services), Budapest, Hungary

John O'Dwyer
Director of the Bilkent University School of English Language (BUSEL), Ankara, Turkey

Barry O'Sullivan
Professor of Applied Linguistics and Director of the Centre for Language Assessment Research (CLARe) at Roehampton University, UK

Spiros Papageorgiou
Researcher, Michigan University, Ann Arbor, MI, USA

Abdul Halim Abdul Raof
Associate Professor at the University of Technology, Johor Bahru, Malaysia

Pauline Rea-Dickins
Professor of Applied Linguistics and Director of the Institute for Educational Development, Eastern Africa, Aga Khan University, Tanzania and Visiting Professor at the University of Bristol, UK

Brian Richards
Professor Emeritus at the Institute of Education, University of Reading, UK

Jon Roberts
Visiting Research Fellow at the Institute of Education, University of Reading, UK

David Ewing Ryan
Lecturer and test developer at EXAVER Examinations at Universidad Veracruzana, Mexico

Patricia Reidy Ryan
Lecturer and test developer at EXAVER Examinations at Universidad Veracruzana, Mexico

Toshihiko Shiotsu
Professor of Language Education at Kurume University, Japan

Cyril J. Weir
Powdrill Chair in English Language Acquisition and Director of the Centre for Research in English Language Learning and Assessment (CRELLA), University of Bedfordshire, UK

Guoxing Yu
Senior Lecturer at the Graduate School of Education, Bristol University, UK

introduction

barry o'sullivan

the birth of modern testing

In the nineteenth century Galton was already using the "new" science of psychometrics, which he defined as the "the art of imposing measurement and number on the operations of the mind" (Galton, 1879: 1). Following Galton, people such as Edgeworth (1888, 1890) began to introduce ideas of scientific enquiry to the study of essay marking in higher education. These early scholars were not to have the sort of impact on assessment in the UK we might have imagined, and by the time the Cambridge Proficiency in English examination, the first formal international language test, was administered in the UK in 1913 the focus had moved from measurement to content, where it was to remain for most of the rest of the century.

However, the situation in the United States was quite different. Here, techniques were devised which offered a solution to dealing with the sheer number of people to be examined across that country. Examples of such techniques include the standardisation of tests of handwriting (Thorndike, 1910) and of composition marking (Hillegas, 1912), which led to the first formal standardised tests (Courtis, 1914). These developments paved the way for a very different approach from that adopted in the UK. The development of the final part of the puzzle, the multiple choice format (Kelly, 1915), meant that very large numbers of people could now be tested across the country, with no compromise on test accuracy. The "modern" tests which emerged from the standardisation movement were perceived to be more scientifically based than the more subjective tests (such as essays or translation into and out of L1) that preceded them (and which remained strong throughout the twentieth century in the UK), and as such their strength was seen to be derived from their accuracy and consistency.

Over the coming half century, the "science" of measurement grew in influence, particularly in the USA, while the "art" of assessment held sway in the UK.

more recent events

The changes that have occurred in language testing over the past three decades have seen the area move from a relatively atheoretical, psychometrically driven (in the United States) and practice-led position to one of growing academic success and reach. A number of significant developments in our understanding of language and language development were driven by language testers in this period, the most obvious example being Bachman's model of language ability, which, though based on earlier work in SLA by Hymes (1972) and Canale and Swain (1980), has had an impact on both language testing and SLA research. In this period, also, the subject has come to be seen by the mainstream of applied linguistics as representing a distinctive field of study, which represents a true "application" of the research findings of linguistics and applied linguistics alike.

Having gone through a revolutionary change in the late 1980s and early 1990s, with the growth in our understanding of the importance of explicit theoretical values to language test design and delivery (driven most obviously by scholars such as Lyle Bachman, J. D. Brown and Adrian Palmer in the United States and Alan Davies, Don Porter, Arthur Hughes, Cyril Weir and Charles Alderson in the UK), there was a general feeling among testers at the turn of the century that things had begun to stagnate. This is, however, not a uniform opinion, as I have felt for some years now that this perception is actually quite wrong. Instead of stagnating, the area has seen the beginnings of a great change, which I see as the "new" revolution, and as a positive force. The major change I am referring to is the dismantling of the old hegemony in which the two dominating centres of language testing, the United States and the UK, provided the dominating theories and practices. This fragmentation has led to the growth in "local" confidence to place the individual test taker, and with this the test context, at the heart of the language testing agenda. One key impact of this change in focus is the recognition that the contextual parameters of test task delivery (e.g. task purpose, timing, knowledge of how task performance will be assessed) should not simply satisfy the predicted demands of the cognitive processes employed in task performance. Instead, if we are to truly place the test taker at the heart of test development, then both the contextual parameters and the underlying cognitive processes (i.e. the stages of cognition that under-lie performance) and resources (e.g. language competence, background knowledge etc.) must be taken into consideration from the perspective of the test taker. This concept forms the basis of the theory of validation discussed by O'Sullivan and Weir in this book.

Half a century ago, when we were first presented with systematic theories of validity (e.g. Cronbach and Meehl, 1955), developers were typically expected to demonstrate the validity of a test by providing evidence related to any one of what were then seen as three distinct types of validity (content, criterion or construct). Within 30 years, Messick (1975, 1980 1989) and Anastasi (1986) had changed the way we viewed validity, arguing that it was a unitary concept. By this they meant that we needed to move away from the position where a single type of evidence would be sufficient to establish the validity of a test to one in which the developer put together a validation argument, to which evidence of various types contributed. In effect, this change meant that we were moving from a position that saw validity as a dichotomy (a test either had it or didn't have it) to a position of degree (to what extent is it possible to demonstrate the validity of a test?). The unitary theory of validity remains the dominant view to this day, and is interesting not least because it has tended to bring together the two sides of the testing world, the United States, where standardisation and measurement dominated for many years, and the UK, where test content as a reflection of the underlying construct dominated.

This volume offers, I believe for the first time, a coherent overview of some of the key issues currently dominating the profession, bringing together a large group of authors from across the world who are actively engaged in language testing in different ways, from the practitioner to the academic, evidencing, for example, the issue of "joint problematisation" (Sarangi and Roberts, 1999) and the "thick participation" of practitioners with researchers and with consumers and sponsors. The book highlights a number of central ideas, the interpretation of which is coming to be seen as crucial to modern testing (validation, localisation, professionalisation, reflexivity and politicisation).

The book is located in the present, but its main focus is on the future. Each chapter is designed to offer the reader an opportunity to glimpse how language testing researchers and practitioners envisage the discipline developing in the coming years. To achieve the goals set out in this book we need to look beyond present boundaries to embrace the opportunities presented to us by other disciplines and methodologies. This will bring with it a whole new raft of issues and levels of complexity to testing research and practice, which we will be compelled to deal with in our theories and in the way we conceive, deliver and evaluate assessments. The ongoing contribution of language testing to applied linguistics theory will hinge on our ability to meet these new opportunities.

current issues

The themes that surface through the chapters in this book are those that are currently emerging as the central issues that will come to dominate the area of language testing over the coming years. The issues are primarily those of validation, localisation and professionalisation, together with parallel issues of reflexivity and politicisation.

validation

Theories of validity have been with us now for over half a century and have moved in a series of stages from a view in which validity was primarily seen as a matter of presenting evidence that the test was accurately testing what it claimed to test, with only a limited expectation of the breadth of evidence required to substantiate any claim. When Messick (1975, 1980, 1989) extended his conceptualisation of validity to include test consequence and the unitary nature of validity (in which a validation argument was constructed from a number of sources of validity evidence), the time seemed right for a major breakthrough from academic theorising (validity) to operational evidence gathering and reporting (validation). However, this failed to happen.

One reason for this situation is the complexity and lack of clarity in Messick's model of validity. The lack of exemplars in Messick's writing has meant that just how specific elements relate to other elements has never been satisfactorily demonstrated, rendering the model at best difficult, and at worst impossible, to operationalise. This is perhaps most clearly exemplified by the recent perception of test consequence as a source of validity evidence (i.e. *consequential validity*). In fact, test developers should consider the impact on performance of all decisions made during the development process. While undertaking so-called *impact* studies to look back (typically) on how the test affects, or is affected by, society where there is no direct or indirect effect on performance may soothe our collective conscience, it is unlikely to offer us any meaningful understanding of *how* that performance should be interpreted. This suggests that test consequence should not be marginalised, as in my view it currently is (i.e. seen as a separate element of the post validity argument), but instead should be recognised as a central aspect of all test development decisions. In doing so, we acknowledge that consequence drives an ethical and informed test development process by keeping the most important stakeholder (the test taker) at the centre of every decision taken during the process. This is, I believe, how Messick intended consequence to be interpreted.

The reluctance of test developers to commit necessary resources, and the apathy and lack of knowledge among test stakeholders, has meant that there is little or no perceived need for large-scale tests to demonstrate evidence of validity for use in particular contexts. Over the past few decades, however, the atmosphere has begun to change. The push across Europe, in particular (though also seen from Asia to Australia to the Americas and beyond), for transparency and evidence-based proof of the value of test outcomes has stemmed, in my opinion, from the growing and widening professionalism of scholars and practitioners in the field.

professionalisation

One major impact of the development of language testing as an area of academic study in its own right over the past 30 years has been the growth of a cadre of professionals with a deepening awareness of theories of language knowledge, use and measurement. One interesting example of this is the Language Testing Forum, an annual meeting of UK testing professionals. When the first group met, in late 1980, there were hardly more than half a dozen participants. The 30th anniversary meeting planned for November 2010 is expected to attract over 40 specialists – a number only limited by the organisers to try to maintain the gathering's original "feel". Another interesting aspect of the two events is the profile of the attendees. In the original meeting almost all were British and male; now this is changing, with more women than men, who tend to be younger and more highly academically qualified (either with a doctorate or in the process of gaining one) and from a wider international background.

In the same period, organisations such as the International Language Testing Association (ILTA) and the Association of Language Testers in Europe (ALTE) began to develop professional identities around systematised codes of practices and ethics and offered testers a forum in which theoretical and practical issues could be debated and developed. This has, in turn, led to a more sophisticated understanding of the importance and relevance of test validation. One aspect of this sophistication has been the realisation by testing professionals, particularly in the academy, that, by truly placing the individual at the centre of the development process, we are recognising the importance of the *local* in the process.

localisation

By localisation, I mean the practice of taking into account those learner-focused factors that can impact on linguistic performance. While this can be seen as an attempt to facilitate the individualising of assessment, it can also be understood as an attempt to take into account character-istics (individual, linguistic, cultural and social) of the learners from a particular population when developing tests for use with that popula-tion. Another aspect of localisation is the understanding that by look-ing primarily to the test taker when developing our tests we are actually taking into consideration aspects of test consequence. This awareness of consequence reinforces the argument presented above, that the current conceptualisation of consequential validity should be rejected in favour of the view that it is an essential aspect of all elements of a validation argument.

Yet another implication of localisation is the recognition of the importance of test context on test development and, by implication, the calling into question of the use of international tests in local con-texts without first careful screening (i.e. validation) to establish that they are likely to offer the sort of information required for that context at an acceptable level of accuracy. The example below offers an insight into my argument.

The developers of iBT (Educational Testing Services – ETS) state that:

> TOEFL iBT test scores are interpreted as the ability of the test taker to use and understand English as it is spoken, written, and heard in college and university settings. The proposed uses of TOEFL iBT test scores are to aid in admissions and placement decisions at English-medium institutions of higher education and to support English-language instruction. ETS (2008: 1)

The IELTS Test (designed to allow users to draw inferences on a learner's ability to cope with the linguistic challenges of academic or non-academic training contexts in UK higher and further education institutions) is described by its developers with the broader claim that:

> IELTS is a secure, valid and reliable test of real-life ability to com-municate in English for education, immigration and professional accreditation. IELTS (2010)

Both of these claims must be seen as problematic: the former in assuming that there is no difference in the contexts of English-medium institutions (i.e. where English is the language of communication of the society in which the institution is based, or where another language takes that role); the latter in offering no significant evidence of its suitability for use beyond the original intentions of its developers (academic study or training). Moreover, using either of these tests as a benchmark in a context where learners share a common L1 (which is not English) is clearly problematic, since, without a substantial body of evidence to support this usage, neither test is likely to be demonstrably valid (i.e. for use in that particular context or domain).

Another challenge facing the developers of large-scale international examinations is their accuracy (or internal consistency) in different contexts. Many major examination boards make public internal consistency and standard error of measure estimates based on actual or experimental data. The fact that the ability level of the very large candidature for these examinations is typically very varied means that the reported internal consistency is quite high. When local tests are compared with these figures they often fail to meet the high standards set by their international competitors. However, if we were to make like-for-like comparisons (i.e. the internal consistency figures for the same candidates on both examination papers) it is quite likely that similar estimates would be reported – suggesting that the gulf between the two is probably quite small, if it exists at all. Indeed, the lack of systematic double or multiple marking in some international examinations (such as IELTS speaking and writing papers, for example) means that many local examinations (certainly those employing multiple markers) are likely to be significantly more accurate.

In the past, local examinations were typically seen as being of poorer quality and accuracy than major international examinations. We have seen that this situation is changing as we work together to develop clearer and more transparent validation theories. These theories have highlighted our awareness of the centrality of the test taker and the test context, which, when combined with the spreading professionalism of test developers, has led to the fragmentation of the language testing industry. We are now beginning to understand that tests developed for use in a particular domain or context with a particular population are far more likely to work if the population and domain are taken into account at all stages of design and development.

the organisation of the book

The book is presented in four sections, each of which is dedicated to a different aspect of assessment. In the first section of this book (Test theories, evidence and our understanding of language) we begin as any book that takes as its focus the future of language testing must begin, in my opinion, with the most current thinking on validation.

The opening chapter of the first section offers a look at the area of test validation by **O'Sullivan and Weir**. In this chapter, the focus is on the growing influence on test development practice across the world of a set of test validation frameworks, first proposed by Weir (2005). The chapter revisits these frameworks in the light of their continued application, arguing that validation must be placed at the centre of all test development and should not be seen as an optional research issue. One very important aspect of test validity to emerge in recent years is the notion of test level. While the focus in the past tended to be on defining level in relation to other measures of the ability being tested, the development of the Common European Framework of Reference for Languages (commonly referred to as the CEFR) and the positive impact it has had on assessment, particularly, but not exclusively, in Europe, has changed the area dramatically.

In the second chapter of this section, **North** stresses the significant difference between levels seen as stages of a process, and levels seen as a distinction master/non-master. He moves on to outline the significant recognition the CEFR levels are having in Europe and beyond before discussing the issue of developing descriptors for levels. In this part of his chapter he offers an original and interesting overview of the influence of the different styles/schools of thought on the development of language standards, and sketches out possible development approaches. He also provides an argument for the validity of the CEFR descriptors.

In the third chapter of this section, **Davies** examines the Linguistic Relativity Principle (also known as the Sapir–Whorf Hypothesis) and seeks to explain how, if at all, it relates to the wider concerns of applied linguistics and the narrower concerns of language testing. This interesting and original piece explores current language testing debates, in particular that of testing English for Specific Purposes (ESP) from an LSP perspective.

The final chapter in the section moves away from the description of test and candidate level to look at a different aspect of test validation, the componentiality of the listening skill. The importance of applying a theoretically sound understanding of the cognitive aspects of a language skill or ability to the development of a test in that area, stressed by Weir (2005) and Weir and O'Sullivan in Chapter 1 of this book, is revisited here by Joyce. The study reported on in this chapter used a componential research methodology to explore the area of L2 English listening. The findings, that syntactic knowledge is the key component of listening, are discussed here in relation to theories of listening as well as to the practice of test development and the learning and teaching of the skill. This is particularly relevant in that it highlights a limitation of many benchmark descriptors, in which the underlying view of language competence is not supported by a clear theoretical perspective of each language sub-skill.

The second section of the book contains four chapters which look at the application of theory to practice. In the first of these chapters, **Kantarcıoğlu and Papageorgiou** return to the CEFR and in particular to its use as a benchmark for describing test (and candidate) level. This chapter, which links the earlier chapters by O'Sullivan and Weir and North and reviews the theoretical and practical aspects of standard setting and benchmarking, looking to the authors' own projects (in Turkey and the UK respectively) for exemplification of the issues involved in engaging in such a process. This paper also explores the interface between the socio-cognitive perspective on validation offered by O'Sullivan and Weir and the process of establishing empirical evidence of a link between a particular test and a language benchmark such as the CEFR.

The second chapter in this section looks at the area of wordlist development. In a departure from the current practice of basing wordlists on analysis of large corpora (see, for example, the work of Nation (e.g. 1990, 2001), Schmitt (e.g. 2000, 2010) and Meara (e.g. 1980, 1996)), **Shiotsu** employs a sophisticated use of Rasch modelling to develop wordlists from learners' self-assessment of their own word knowledge. The methodology devised for this project has clear applications for future research in the area.

Abdul Raof then looks to the use of content specialists in the development of what he calls "indigenous" rating scales for assessing conference presentations in the area of civil engineering. The approach taken is founded on earlier quantitative scale development methodologies but offers a unique take on these, and proposes a very practical and user-friendly, yet valid, scale.

In the final chapter in the section, **O'Sullivan and Nakatsuhara** highlight the need to understand how test takers interact with each other, particularly in terms of how they initiate and ratify topics. This is of real importance, since it is at these junctures in the interaction that co-construction of discourse (a significant issue in testing speaking using pairs or small groups but also in our broader understanding of spoken interaction) is most likely to be manifested. They outline the development of a set of empirically based measures to quantify conversational styles in groups and then apply these measures to describe conversational styles in group oral tests.

The third section of the book contains four chapters which are devoted to the practice of language testing, all looking at different issues relating to test purpose. The first of these chapters is by **Green**, who describes the development of the reading component of suite of placement tests for use in English language teaching centres around the world. The constraints implied by the tests' purpose and candidature and the solutions that emerged during the project are described and discussed, along with the implications for future placement testing projects.

The second chapter in the section looks to the area of diagnostic testing. **Burrell, Graham, Medley, Richards and Roberts** suggest a model for the development of such an instrument, and exemplify this by describing its application in projects where the resulting instrument was incorporated into a programme of formative assessment in a teacher-training environment. The authors also explore the possibility of using this type of test as a tool for research.

The tendency of international tests to systematically avoid the kind of local traditions and customs in favour of "own-country" culture (e.g. a UK-based international test including elements of UK culture), when combined with the very high costs of these tests, leads to a potentially critical situation for learners in what are often less well off and less "international" communities. **Abad Florescano, O'Sullivan, Sanchez Chavez, Ryan, Zamora Lara, Santana Martinez, Gonzalez Macias, Maxwell Hart, Grounds, Reidy Ryan, Dunne and Romero Barradas** discuss a suite of tests developed by Universidad Veracruzana in Mexico with the support of a number of UK-based organisations, which marks a first systematic attempt to create a "local", affordable, and sustainable language test system. The chapter itself is unique in that it was written by the entire team who worked on the development project, and not just by the leaders and/or consultants on that project, thus offering a practical and realistic overview of the process, rather than the filtered narrative such descriptions often present.

In the final chapter in this section **Brown and Jaquith** return to the general topic of Green's chapter, that of placement testing. The two papers differ in that, while Green looks at the placement test from a mainly theoretical perspective, Brown and Jaquith focus on the way in which technology can influence how a large-scale test is managed. In this chapter, they describe the on-line essay marking system that allows them to return test scores for approximately 38,000 candidates in the space of a few days. The chapter first discusses the development of the system before going on to describe the sophisticated rater calibration system put in place, based on multifaceted Rasch analysis of rater performance.

In the first chapter of the final section of the book, **Rea-Dickins, Kiely and Yu** examine the area of language test use. Using data from a study of a major international test used for language-related university entrance decisions in the UK and other English-speaking countries, they investigate how admissions officers in international programmes interpret test scores in relation to test content and purpose. They also explore the challenges of communication between test theorists, developers and stakeholders, suggesting a need to involve test users, in particular those of high-stakes tests, in the research and development of high-stakes tests.

In the final chapter of the volume, **O'Dwyer** describes a major curriculum reorganisation in a large pre-university language centre and the various attempts made to develop a formative assessment system to complement the resulting learning system. By learning system, O'Dwyer means the broad triangle of curriculum, delivery and assessment, which together form an integrated whole without which learning is unlikely to be facilitated. The approach taken in the analysis of the situation, namely, to focus on organisational learning and information management, offers a unique and informative perspective that differs from traditional analyses of test washback.

references

Anastasi, A. (1986). Evolving concepts of test validation. *Annual Review of Psychology, 37*, 1–15.

Canale, M. and Swain, M. (1980). Theoretical bases of communicative approaches to second language teaching and testing. *Applied Linguistics, 1*, 1–47.

Courtis, S. A. (1914). Standard tests in English. *The Elementary School Teacher, 14*(8), 374–392.

Cronbach, L. J. and Meehl, P. E. (1955) Construct validity in psychological tests. *Psychological Bulletin, 52*, 281–302.

Edgeworth, F. Y. (1888). The statistics of examinations. *Journal of the Royal Statistical Society, 51*, 599–635.

Edgeworth, F. Y. (1890). The element of chance in competitive examinations. *Journal of the Royal Statistical Society, 51*, 460–475, 644–663.

Educational Testing Services (2008). *Validity Evidence Supporting the Interpretation and Use of TOEFL iBT Scores.* Available at http://www.ets.org/Media/Tests/TOEFL/pdf/TOEFL_iBT_Validity.pdf (accessed 11 March 2010).

Galton, F. (1879). Psychometric Experiments. *Brain, 2*(2), 149–162.

Hillegas, M. B. (1912). *A Scale for the Measurement of Quality in English Composition by Young People.* New York: Teachers College.

Hymes, D. H. (1972). On communicative competence. In J. B. Pride and J. Holmes (Eds), *Sociolinguistics: Selected Readings.* Harmondsworth: Penguin, pp. 269–293.

IELTS. (2010). What is IELTS? Available at http://www.ielts.org/institutions/about_ielts.aspx (accessed 11 March 2010).

Kelly, F. J. (1915). *Kansas Silent Reading Test.* Topeka, KS: Kansas State Printing Plant.

Meara, P. (1980). Vocabulary acquisition: a neglected aspect of language learning. *Language Teaching and Linguistics: Abstracts, 14,* 221–246.

Meara, P. (1996). The dimensions of lexical competence. In G. Brown, K. Malmkjaer and J. Williams (Eds), *Performance and Competence in Second Language Acquisition.* Cambridge: Cambridge University Press, pp. 35–52.

Messick, S. (1975). The standard program: meaning and values in measurement and evaluation. *American Psychologist, 30,* 955–966.

Messick, S. (1980). Test validity and the ethics of assessment. *American Psychologist, 35,* 1012–1027.

Messick, S. (1989). Validity. In R. L. Linn (Ed.) *Educational Measurement* (3rd edition). London/New York: McMillan.

Nation, I. S. P. (1990). *Teaching and Learning Vocabulary.* New York: Newbury House.

Nation, I. S. P. (2001). *Learning Vocabulary in Another Language.* Cambridge: Cambridge University Press.

Sarangi, S. and Roberts, C. (Eds). (1999). *Talk, Work and Institutional Order: Discourse in Medical, Mediation and Management Settings.* Berlin: Mouton de Gruyter.

Schmitt, N. (2000). *Vocabulary in Language Teaching.* New York: Cambridge University Press.

Schmitt, N. (2010). *Researching Vocabulary: A Vocabulary Research Manual.* Basingstoke: Palgrave Macmillan.

Thorndike, E. L. (1910). The measurement of the quality of handwriting. In E. L. Thorndike. Handwriting. *Teachers College Record, 11,* 86–151. Available at http://www.brocku.ca/MeadProject/Thorndike/1910/Thorndike_1910_1.html (accessed 11 January 2010).

Weir, C. J. (2005) *Language Testing and Validation: An Evidence-Based Approach.* Oxford: Palgrave.

1
test development and validation

barry o'sullivan and cyril j. weir

introduction

Stakeholders increasingly expect explicit evidence of how developers are meeting the demands of validity in their tests. More specifically, stakeholders want to know how developers operationalise and validate criterial distinctions between the tests they offer at different levels on the proficiency continuum or establish the cut scores they claim are indicators of specific levels. There is a growing awareness in the stakeholder community of the need for a sound theoretical model that underlies a test (validity) and the generation of evidence concerning the operationalisation and interpretation of the model in practice (validation).

In presenting our thinking on language test validity and validation, we first look to recent attempts to model language use, identifying their benefits and limitations. We then turn to some current frameworks to see whether they offer test developers and stakeholders a more comprehensive and systematic means for generating and interpreting validity evidence. This review leads us to present what we see as a viable and practical model for conceptualising test validity and carrying out validation.

modelling communicative language ability

The fact that L2 has been recognised for some time as a multi-componential construct (see, for example, Kunnan, 1998) masks concerns that these components are not fully grounded, nor is their interaction with each other understood (Skehan, 1988; Douglas, 2000: 25; Milanovic and Weir, forthcoming). The most influential multi-componential model of

13

Communicative Language Ability (CLA), that of Bachman (1990), provided test developers with a wide ranging account of CLA and useful theoretical questions to ask in the design of language tests. However, a critical weakness of the model is that it proved to be extremely difficult if not impossible to operationalise, not least because of its daunting breadth and depth, but also due to its lack of clear prioritisation as to what might constitute criterial parameters for language testing purposes (Kunnan, 1998; McNamara, 2003; Chalhoub-Deville and Deville, 2005). As such, Bachman's model (1990) has contributed less than might have been hoped to empirical test validation. This point is emphasised by McNamara (2003: 468), who argued that "those who have used the test method facets approach have found it to be difficult to use, and it has in fact been implemented in relatively few test development projects...."

McNamara (2003) also criticises the Bachman model as being:

> essentially psychological, seeing communicative language ability as a mental ability, while the context of use is increasingly understood theoretically as a social arena, as in virtually all current work in discourse analysis...The idea of a general a priori competence is increasingly questioned in studies of language use in context, and it is being found to be problematic in practical language testing contexts too.

McNamara questions the value of the model in so far as it lacks an interactional/social dimension (see Kramsch, 1986, 1998; Chalhoub-Deville, 1997, 2003; Young, 2000; Chalhoub-Deville and Deville, 2005), arguing that it needs to take into account social theories of language use, and directs the reader to O'Sullivan (2000) for an example of how this might be done in speaking tests.

In a similar vein, Chalhoub-Deville (2003: 369) argues that "individual ability and contextual facets interact in ways that change them both". This view of the L2 construct as being "socially and culturally mediated" (Ibid.: 371), argues Chalhoub-Deville, should result in our representation of the construct as being "primarily social" since it implies "the language use situation primarily as a social event in which language ability, language users and context are inextricably linked" (Ibid.: 372). And, of course, in one sense we have also come to see testing as also primarily a "social phenomenon" – in which test scores, test score users and score use contexts are "inextricably linked". Chalhoub-Deville and Deville (2005: 822) is supportive of Bachman's model to the extent that it addresses "issues related to language use", but she agrees with McNamara's view that it represents an essentially psycholinguistic view of performance and is largely missing important interactional and sociolinguistic elements.

We broadly share these reservations and would add that the inadequacy of the treatment of the cognitive processing dimensions (as versus metacognitive) of the various skills components in the Bachman model is also a disadvantage when considering its use for test development purposes, especially where attempts are made to define different levels of language proficiency.

Bachman's model offered an impressive theoretical model of CLA, albeit with limitations in both its cognitive and social dimensions, which was potentially useful for academics in testing research, but it suffered in terms of its suitability for use as an operational framework by language testing practitioners. At the same time work was being carried out on the Common European Framework of Reference for Languages (CEFR), which aimed to be directly useful to both testers and teachers as a descriptive framework of language ability over a series of distinct levels (Council of Europe, 2001). This framework was certainly usable, but, as we shall see, it was to fall a long way short in terms of its underlying theory and descriptive adequacy.

the common european framework of reference for languages (CEFR)

The Common European Framework of Reference (CEFR) offers a broad and valuable perspective on language proficiency and illustrates this through a group of scales composed of ascending level descriptors couched in terms of outcomes (Council of Europe, 2001). However, in the final version of the CEFR these scales, previously intended as illustrative appendices only, had found their way into the main body of the text and have subsequently assumed a far greater degree of importance to users than was ever intended (Milanovic, 2009). They are now reified as benchmarks in many eyes rather than being merely useful examples of practice (lacking, in many cases, robust empirical test validation) from the field. These descriptor scales are supplemented by a broad compendium of useful information on consensus views regarding language learning, teaching and assessment. In relation to testing, the following strong claims are made for the CEFR:

...the Framework can be used

1) for the specification of the content of tests and examinations;

2) for stating the criteria to determine the attainment of a learning
objective;
3) for describing the levels of proficiency in existing tests and examinations thus enabling comparisons to be made across different systems of qualifications. (Council of Europe, 2001: 178)

Over the past decade, test developers across Europe (and outside the
continent) have used the CEFR in attempting to establish meaningful
levels of language ability that are readily interpreted by stakeholders.
Organisations such as the Association of Language Testers in Europe
(ALTE) have promoted a move towards test score interpretation that
is more transparent, through the development of functional descriptors (Can Dos). Additionally, through the attempts of ALTE and the
European Association for Language Testing and Assessment (EALTA)
to support an evidence-driven approach to establishing the quality
and level of language tests, much work has gone into linking their
examinations with the CEFR (see Alderson 2002; Council of Europe
2003, 2009; Morrow, 2004; and Martyniuk, 2011). This work has
resulted in the promotion of better communication about test purpose and use between stakeholders such as government agencies, test
developers and the wider public, something we see as perhaps the
greatest contribution of the CEFR to date; see Taylor (2000) for an
extensive listing of the different types of stakeholders in language
testing.
    However, while the CEFR has had a significant and positive impact
on the practice and discourse of language testing since its publication, we should also acknowledge that it has a number of inherent
limitations and has been used on occasion for purposes for which it
was not suitable, for example as a basis for detailed test specification.
In addition to the limitations acknowledged by its original authors
(see North in this book), others have pointed to its lack of "sufficient
theoretical and practical guidance to enable test specifications to be
drawn up for each level" (Alderson et al., 2004: 1); its use to support
"the political agenda in standardising the language of assessment
across Europe" (Fulcher, 2004); and the danger that it will become
what Weir (2005b: 298) calls "a prescriptive device," a point also made
by Fulcher (2004).
    While agreeing that the CEFR contains valuable descriptions of lan-
guage proficiency levels, Weir (2005b: 281) argues that "in its present
form the CEFR is not sufficiently comprehensive, coherent or transparent for uncritical use in language testing." Weir goes on to point out

two significant limitations to using the CEFR as a basis for developing or comparing tests; these are:

- The CEFR does not recognise the impact on task performance of variations in contextual parameters (e.g. planning time, knowledge of assessment criteria, etc).
- There is no recognition of the need to establish clearly what cognitive processes are undertaken by an individual when responding to a language elicitation task, neither is there any recognition of the impact this might have on establishing equivalent tasks (i.e. two tasks may appear to be equivalent, but if candidates tend to use different cognitive processes to respond to the tasks then they are not the same).

Since its introduction, the CEFR has become more and more influential in the areas of learning and assessment, with important initiatives such as the European Language Portfolio and the publication of a draft and later final Manual for establishing a link between a particular examination and the CEFR (Council of Europe, 2003, 2009). The Manual advocates a four-stage approach to linking: Familiarisation (of those involved in test development or the linking process); Specification (of how the test to be linked relates to the CEFR); Standardisation (establishing cut scores based on the CEFR); and Validation (presenting evidence of the quality of the linking claim). The notion of establishing strong links between language tests and the CEFR has become widely accepted across Europe and beyond, for instance in Taiwan (Wu and Wu, 2010), despite some very obvious shortcomings in both the CEFR itself and the approach advocated in the Manual. These latter shortcomings have been pointed out by O'Sullivan (2009a, b, c) in his reports to the City & Guilds examining board on the projects designed to establish evidence of a link between their International ESOL suite of examinations and the CEFR, and can be summarised as:

- Limitations in the CEFR itself are not recognised, meaning that if a test developer does not deploy considerable additional resources to more comprehensively define the level as described in the CEFR then any claimed link is likely to be very weak.
- There is an assumption that the process is linear (i.e. that a developer can neatly progress from stage to stage with no evaluative monitoring of the process).
- It is assumed that the test being linked is satisfactory from a quality perspective, although there is little advice available on this in

the Manual. O'Sullivan (2009a) introduced an additional stage to the process advocated by the Manual's authoring group – that of a critical review of the test in question by an expert panel comprised of experts internal and external to the developer.

- The relevance of the Specification phase to the process is never rationalised, probably because the authoring group failed to see the necessity of a link between this phase and the Validation phase. The Specification phase, therefore, is in danger of becoming a meaningless box-ticking exercise.
- The view of Validation in the Manual is both limited and outdated. By this we mean that the Manual fails to acknowledge advances in theoretical or practical validation from Messick to Weir.
- The process advocated in the Manual is atheoretical, in that it comprises a static description of independent parts rather than a dynamic interconnected model.
- There is a real danger that organisations will see linking projects as a one-off activity. The Manual fails to highlight the need for test developers to embed the test levels (as defined by the CEFR or any other set of language benchmarks) in their development system at all stages of the development cycle in the same way as they should be embedding a culture of quality, transparency and validity in these processes.

In order to make the process tenable, O'Sullivan (2009a, b, c), in addition to the introduction of a critical review phase to the process, used the Weir validation frameworks, described below, to inform both the Specification and Validation phases, thus creating a sounder theoretical basis for the linking process than is currently provided in the Manual.

Bachman's model failed to offer us a comprehensive model of L2 and the ready means for operationalising it in a testing context. The CEFR offers a useful but imprecise and theoretically limited framework. Test developers have always had to start from a practical perspective, informed by theory, which tries to identify and operationalise the performance conditions and language operations that offer an adequate description of the most important components of language use in particular contexts (see, for example, the work of Alderson and Hughes, 1981; Skehan, 1988 and Weir, 1993). By developing tasks around clearly defined parameters such as these, we can begin to more closely replicate the reality of language use situations, and by ensuring that our tests address a number of distinct contexts (e.g. to include dialogic as well as monologic discourse in a test of speaking) we can be more fully assured that the claims we make related to the ability of candidates to use language appropriately in context are more justified and valid.

building a model of test validation

It is clear from the above sections that the models of language ability and frameworks for description that currently dominate our profession are not as comprehensive, transparent and useful as they might be. On their own they are insufficient to meet the needs of language testers, who need a comprehensive model that enables them to consider and incorporate criterial social, cognitive and evaluative parameters at the test design and development stage, and, more importantly, one that guides them in generating evidence of the successful operationalisation of these features at the test implementation stage. In other words, language testers need a comprehensive, appropriate and accessible theory of test validity, which can additionally underpin an effective and efficient model of validation. This distinction is important, as we see the model of validity as the underlying theory and the model of validation as the manifestation or operationalisation of this theory.

We now turn to the theories of validity upon which we might rely to support the systematic gathering of validity evidence to support the claims we make for our tests.

Significant advances in our conceptualisation of test validity have been happening since as long ago as the late nineteenth century, with Edgeworth's (1888) early consideration of rater reliability and the later breakthrough by Spearman (1904), seen by Brennan (2001: 297) as the paper that "launched measurement as a distinct field of inquiry." By the 1950s theories of the kind of evidence needed to support test-based claims were beginning to form and were set out in Cronbach and Meehl's (1955) seminal paper. Just a couple of years later, Loevinger (1957) was arguing that "since predictive, concurrent, and content validities are all essentially ad hoc, construct validity is the whole of validity from a scientific point of view" (p. 636). This thinking was built upon by others (most notably Messick, 1975, 1980; Anastasi, 1986) and led to the recognition of validity as a unitary concept. Messick's work, in particular his 1989 "Validity" paper, was to bring the various strands of thought together in a single all-encompassing theory, which included recognition of the social consequence of test usage, an idea that had, in fact, been around since Cureton's (1950) paper on test validity.

In the same way as the CEFR has, in recent years, come to dominate European approaches to language learning and assessment, the work of

Messick has come to be seen as the pre-eminent theory of test validity. This pre-eminence is obvious in the work of Bachman (in particular his 1990 work) and Weir, which is explored below. However, while Messick's work in bringing together various strands of thinking has been important to test developers, it has yet to inform a significant and practical model of validation. An example of this is his influence on theorists such as Kane (1992), Mislevy et al. (2002 and 2003) and Chapelle et al. (2008), who have contributed significantly to our broad conceptualisation of the need for a coherent validation argument but have, to date, failed to offer a workable specification outlining the nature and source of evidence required for such an argument. Their diminution of the importance of a comprehensive descriptive framework (social, cognitive and evaluative) in favour of a more abstract, argumentative, logical framework means that there is a real danger that some test developers will, just as happened in the 1960s and 1970s, focus on types of evidence that show their test in a good light, leading to a weakening of validation practice at best and systematic dissembling at worst.

We believe that the approach taken by Weir (2005a) offers the beginning of a way forward in that it marks the first systematic attempt to incorporate the social, cognitive and evaluative (scoring) dimensions of language use into test development and validation. The approach also identifies the nature of the evidence required to develop a transparent and coherent validity argument, while at the same time it starts to address an area essentially ignored by earlier theorists, that of the interaction between the different types of validity evidence. Another strength of the approach is the temporal factor implied in the framework (identifying which aspects of validity should be considered at which stage of the testing cycle), detailed versions of which are presented by Weir (2005a) for each of the four skills (see also Shaw and Weir, 2007, for writing; Khalifa and Weir, 2009, for reading; Taylor (Ed.), 2011, for speaking). A graphical representation of the approach to construct definition, building on Weir (2005a), is shown in Figure 1.1.

In this figure, we can see that there are a number of elements, each of which should be attended to by the test developer, who, Weir (2005a: 48) argues, must generate sufficient evidence to answer all of the following questions if they are to offer an acceptable validity argument to stakeholders:

- How are the physical/physiological, psychological and experiential characteristics of candidates catered for by this test? Is the test likely to be appropriate for the candidates? (Test-taker)

- Are the characteristics of the test tasks and their administration fair to the candidates who are taking them? (Context validity)
- Are the cognitive processes required to complete the tasks appropriate? Are candidates likely to use the same cognitive processes as they would if performing the task in a "real world" context? (Cognitive validity)
- To what extent can we depend on the scores on the test? What do the numbers or grades mean? (Scoring validity)
- What effects does the test have on its various stakeholders? (Consequential validity)
- What external evidence is there outside the test scores themselves that the test is doing a good job? (Criterion-related validity)

For descriptive purposes, the elements of the model are presented as being independent of each other. However, Weir argues that there is a "symbiotic" relationship between the context, cognitive and scoring aspects of validity, a relationship that is seen by Weir as representing a unified approach to establishing the overall construct validity of a test. The epiphenomena of consequential and criterion-related validity necessarily derive their value from the successful realisation by the

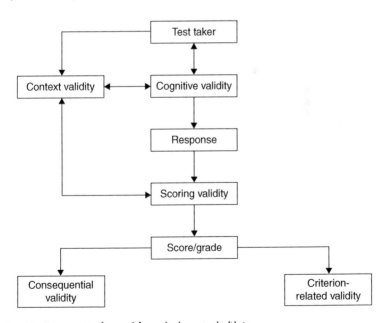

Figure 1.1   A socio-cognitive framework for test development and validation

test developer of construct validity. We will return to this observation briefly after we have discussed the various validity components.

The Test-taker and Cognitive validity elements of the model shown in Figure 1.1 together represent the candidate in the test event. Weir (2005a: 51) believes that "individual characteristics will directly impact on the way the individuals process the test task" as defined by the parameters contained in the description of the test context (i.e. Context validity). By working to a clearly defined descriptive model of the candidate we can consider in a systematic way the various ways in which the individual might interact with the task. Meanwhile, a priori evidence (typically person-driven) when combined with a posteriori evidence (typically data-driven) on the cognitive processing involved in the performance of the task helps us establish evidence of the cognitive validity of the test.

Context validity refers, as indicated above, to the knowledge base relating both to task input and expected output and to the physical conditions or parameters that define the event. These latter parameters include those related to the demands of the setting (i.e. planning time in speaking, etc.) and to the administrative settings (i.e. security, etc.). Where context validity is clearly and comprehensively defined, this helps in identifying criterial parameters that distinguish vertically across different proficiency levels or horizontally across domains (e.g. English for Specific Purposes (ESP) vs. English for Economic Purposes (EAP) vs. general English).

Scoring validity forms the third core element in the test system. By clearly establishing links between all decisions taken in developing the scoring system to the other elements of the model, we are ensuring that the system will result in outcomes (scores or grades) that are fair and meaningful. Figure 1.2 asks the core questions central to the process, and, unless we can demonstrate empirically that our responses to all of these are complete and that they demonstrate a link between the underlying concepts, our test is unlikely to allow us to make valid inferences about the candidature.

As we noted above, the need to consider the consequences of our tests for stakeholders has been recognised for over half a century. The current understanding of test consequence as "consequential validity", which emerged from interpretations of Messick's validity theory, has seen a growth of interest in how tests impact on stakeholders by exploring whether the social consequences of test interpretation support the intended testing purpose(s) and are consistent with other social values. This notion of impact also includes washback (i.e. the impact of a test on the learning and teaching that precedes it from social, educational and institutional perspectives).

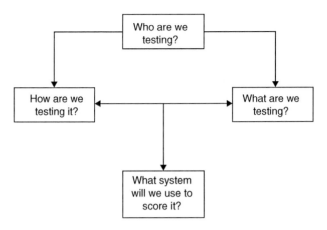

Figure 1.2 The "core" of construct validity

While the idea of consequence is clearly central to a validity argument, it is not at all certain that the concept of consequential "validity" is useful in the way it is currently interpreted. Alderson (2004), in his introduction to Cheng et al.'s *Washback in Language Testing: Research Contexts and Methods*, questions the notion of consequence as a unique form of validity, although, while he makes his doubts clear, he does not offer an alternative perspective on the matter. The fact is, we can look at consequence in a number of ways. On the one hand, it is valuable to perform a posteriori research to review the impact a test has had in order to gain insights into the way in which the scores are actually interpreted and used (looking at intended and unintended consequence). The aspect of consequence that does not share this temporal sequence is the notion of consequence as ethical approach. By this we mean that an ethical approach to test development is a reflection of an understanding of the consequences of decisions made during the process of development. Unless we have a clear definition of the construct (in terms of the candidate, the context, the cognitive demands and the scoring system), such an ethical approach is probably impossible. We should, therefore, see this aspect of awareness of consequence as impacting on all elements of validity and as forming a guiding principle for the development process from the very beginning of the cycle.

Finally, we look at Criterion-Related Validity, which focuses on the extent to which test scores reflect a suitable external criterion of performance or demonstration of the same abilities as are included in the test (see Anastasi, 1988: 145; Messick, 1989: 16). This type of validity evidence is very much dependent on selecting appropriate criteria with which to compare or contrast a test. One such contrast, of course, is to compare a test, or different forms of a test, with itself, an activity that offers us a measure of test reliability. We can also interpret other criterion-related comparisons, with a language benchmark, for example, or with another measure of the same ability, as relating to test level and accuracy respectively; two other elements of scoring validity. This implies that there is an argument to be made for considering criterion-related evidence as an aspect of scoring validity.

We can look at the elements of the model in a number of ways. One of these is the tendency of the "core" elements of construct validity to be essentially inward-looking, in that they are focused on aspects of the test itself. Those aspects of consequence that impact on candidate performance can be included in this view, as they too are looking into the test itself (while taking outside elements into account). The other elements of the model (consequence and criterion-related) are primarily outward-focused. By this we mean that they can be seen as looking outside the immediate world of the test for some verification of the value and interpretation of the inferences drawn from test performance and the decisions that these lead to.

However the elements of Weir's socio-cognitive framework are viewed, it seems clear that, in the words of Taylor (forthcoming), it:

> looks like being the first model/framework which allows for serious theoretical consideration of the issues but is also capable of being applied practically; it therefore has direct relevance and value to an operational language testing/assessment context – especially when that testing is taking place on a large, industrial scale such as in Cambridge ESOL...other frameworks (e.g. Bachman 1990) were helpful in provoking us to think about key issues from a theoretical perspective but they generally proved very difficult for practitioners to operationalise in a manageable and meaningful way.

We now look to how the framework has already begun to be used across a range of test validation and development projects.

using the framework

The examination board most involved in applying the framework to its examinations has been Cambridge ESOL. The main focus of the work undertaken at Cambridge ESOL has been the gathering of validity evidence for the tests in its main suite English examinations. This work has led to the publication of two volumes in the *Studies in Language Testing* series, one on the Cambridge ESOL approach to examining writing (Shaw and Weir, 2007) and the other on its approach to examining reading (Khalifa and Weir, 2009). Within the context of the modification projects for the First Certificate in English (FCE) and the Certificate of Advanced English (CAE), Angela ffrench and Anne Gutch (2006) present a table of validity evidence based on the parameters outlined in Weir's model and the timescale for completion of this work, along with reference to activities that support the decisions made (see also Hawkey, 2009). The framework has also been applied to other Cambridge ESOL tests with considerable success, for example in the International Legal English Certificate (see Corkhill and Robinson, 2006; Thighe, 2006; Green, 2009; Galaczi and Vidakovic, 2010), the Teacher's Knowledge Test (see Ashton and Khalifa, 2005; Harrison, 2007; Novakovi'c, 2006), Asset languages (Ashton, 2006; Jones, 2005), the Surveylang project (SurveyLang, 2008), the Business English Certificates (BEC) and BULATS (see O'Sullivan, 2006).

O'Sullivan has also applied the framework in multiple international contexts and for a number of purposes. One very interesting application of the framework has been in building test specifications. Starting off with the QALSPELL project (QALSPELL, 2004), O'Sullivan, working with partners in Estonia, Latvia and Lithuania, based the specifications for a generic test of English for specific purposes aimed at tertiary institutions in the Baltic states on the frameworks. The experience of the participants in this project, in taking the framework for each skill area and responding to each parameter to describe the test tasks in great detail, was very positive and led to further applications of the approach. The most notable of these was the Exaver project, which is described in detail in Chapter 11 of this book. In this project we were faced with the problem of specifying not just one test, but a series of three, each at a specific CEFR level (A2, B1 and B2). The solution in this project was to create the specifications initially on a single template (by making a table of the parameters to be addressed from the framework and then adding columns for each examination). This approach was replicated, though this time for the six levels of the Zayed University preparatory English programme, in the United Arab Emirates (O'Sullivan, 2005) and proved to be an efficient and practical way of ensuring systematic changes in the tests across all levels. Ongoing work with institutions as far apart as Saudi Arabia (at the pre-university level) and Malaysia (at the pre- and exit university levels) continues to demonstrate the value of basing test specifications on a clearly defined model of validation, which will then drive the formal collection of evidence for a later validity argument. This is an important point to make, as it is a weakness in other published approaches to test specification (e.g. Bachman and Palmer, 1996; Davidson and Lynch, 2002; Fulcher and Davidson, 2009), where it is not made clear that such a link to validity and validation is necessary.

Another valuable use of the framework has been its use as a theoretical basis for the CEFR linking projects carried out by O'Sullivan (2009a, b, c, 2011) and reported above in the section 'The common European framework of reference for languages (CEFR)' of this chapter, as well as linking projects in Turkey (see Chapter 5 in this book), Mexico (again see the report on the Exaver project in Chapter 11) and the UK (as part of the recently completed British Council International Language Assessment project and the Password development project; see Green, this volume).

conclusions

Bachman's theoretical model of CLA was of considerable value to theoreticians but of less practical use to those responsible for test development and implementation. The CEFR, on the other hand, has been welcomed by governments and practitioners as a suitable tool for communicating about language proficiency, but unfortunately it lacks the theoretical rigour, coverage and explicitness necessary for its confident use by language testers to develop tests to determine levels of language proficiency. The CEFR is based on teachers' perceptions of language use (which can contribute to a useful understanding of language use) rather than empirically derived, grounded distinctions of language proficiency levels arising from learner performance data. Similarly, Bachman's theory suffers from a lack of a broad empirical base or subsequent validation.

A theory of validity is only of practical value if it is translatable into a coherent theory or "model" of validation, which can then be operationalised through a set of validation procedures. For a test developer to make strong claims of the validity of inferences based on performance on their tests, they must ensure that all aspects of the test development process reflect the model of validation. It is, therefore, obvious that, unless the model of validation clearly accounts for the evidence that needs to be collected in support of a validity claim, one is left with the form and not the substance.

The theoretical validity framework we have proposed in this paper benefits from its original grounding in the practice of language testing. The coverage of the framework goes beyond the linguistic description of the language in use to take account of both the social context in which the language is used and the psycholinguistic processing that is involved in performance. It adds the further dimension of the quality of the output that is produced. It thus allows the test developer to define focal language objectives and to collect evidence on their attainment in a more comprehensive and satisfactory fashion than earlier models such as the CLA or frameworks such as the CEFR. It is a model developed by language testers for use by practising language testers in actual language testing.

In addition to its growing influence on language testing practice, a clear indication of the true value of the framework is the fact that adaptations have been used in a range of areas outside language testing, for example for assessment of art at tertiary level in Portugal (Torres Pereira de Eça, 2005), as the basis for physics examinations in Sri Lanka (Selvaruby, 2006; Selvaruby et al., 2008), and more recently as the basis for specifying and validating a new high-level examination in ophthalmology (Taylor et al., 2009). These uses of the framework suggest that the underlying theory of validity and the conceptualisation of the validation model are robust. This is because the whole approach truly places the individual at the centre of the process and forces the test developer to acknowledge the relevance of what is happening inside the head of the individual during the process of responding to a test task or item, including how that individual reacts to characteristics of any interlocutor or audience (either actual or perceived) where this is a feature of the task.

future directions

The metaphor of a journey is an important one, and it is salutary to remember we are still on it. Widdowson (2003: 169–170) reminds us of the lack of dynamic coherence in communicative competence models:

> The essential problem with these different models of communicative competence is that they analyse a complex process into a static set of components, and as such cannot account for the dynamic interrelationships which are engaged in communication itself. As a consequence, when you make such models operational in language teaching and testing, you can only deal with the separate parts as

discrete features, since the essential interrelationships that make the whole are missing.

As we mentioned above, the various elements of the model in Figure 1.1 are presented as being separate from each other for descriptive purposes only. There is undoubtedly a close relationship between these elements; for example, even small changes to parameters of context validity are likely to impact significantly on cognitive validity and subsequently on the score or grade a candidate receives in a test. For us to more fully understand the whole process, we will need to explore the interactions between, and especially within, these different aspects of validity. Doing so may well eventually offer further insights into a closer definition of different levels of task difficulty.

So, some considerable distance still to go. The current work of Chalhoub-Deville encourages us in the direction of exploring these interrelationships in future language testing research. She argues (2003: 369) convincingly that we need to accept that "individual ability and contextual facets interact in ways that change them both". How they do this will keep testers occupied for the foreseeable future and will constitute an important chapter in a similar volume to this in a few decades' time.

references

Alderson, J. C. (Ed.) (2002). *Common European Framework of Reference for Languages: Learning, Teaching, Assessment: Case Studies*. Strasbourg: Council of Europe.

Alderson, J. C. and Hughes, A. (Eds) (1981). *Issues in Language Testing ELT Documents 111*. London: The British Council.

Alderson, J. C., Figueras, N., Kuijper, H., Nold, G., Takala, S. and Tardieu, C. (2004). *The Development of Specifications for Item Development and Classification within the Common European Framework of Reference for Languages: Learning, Teaching, Assessment Reading and Listening. Final Report of The Dutch CEF Construct Project*. Lancaster: Lancaster University.

Anastasi, A. (1986). Evolving concepts of test validation. *Annual Review of Psychology, 37*, 1–15.

Anastasi, A. (1988). *Psychological Testing* (6th edition). New York: Macmillan.

Ashton, K. (2006). Can do self-assessment: investigating cross-language comparability in reading. *Research Notes, 24*, 10–14.

Ashton, M. and Khalifa, H. (2005). Opening a new door for teachers of English: Cambridge ESOL teaching knowledge test. *Research Notes, 19*, 5–7.

Bachman, L. F. (1990). *Fundamental Considerations in Language Testing*. Oxford: Oxford University Press.

Bachman, L. F. and Palmer, A. (1996). *Language Testing in Practice*. Oxford: Oxford University Press.

Brennan, R. L. (2001). An essay on the history and future of reliability from the perspective of replications. *Journal of Educational Measurement, 38*(4): 295–317.

Chalhoub-Deville, M. (1997). Theoretical models, assessment frameworks and test construction. *Language Testing, 14*(1), 3–22.

Chalhoub-Deville, M. (2003). Second language interaction: current perspectives and future trends. *Language Testing, 20*(4), 369–383.

Chalhoub-Deville, M. and Deville, C. (2005). A look back at and forward to what language testers measure. In E. Hinkel (Ed.), *Handbook of Research in Second Language Teaching and Learning*. Mahwah, NJ: Lawrence Erlbaum, pp. 815–831.

Chapelle, C. A., Enright, M. K. and Jamieson, J. (2008). *Building a Validity Argument for the Test of English as a Foreign Language*. New York: Routledge.

Corkhill, D. and Robinson, M. (2006). Using the global legal community in the development of ILEC. *Research Notes, 25*, 10–11.

Council of Europe (2001). *Common European Framework of Reference for Languages: Learning, Teaching, Assessment*. Cambridge: Cambridge University Press.

Council of Europe (2003). *Relating Language Examinations to the Common European Framework of Reference for Languages: Learning, Teaching, Assessment (CEF). Manual: Preliminary Pilot Version. DGIV/EDU/LANG 2003, 5*. Strasbourg: Language Policy Division.

Council of Europe (2009). *Relating Language Examinations to the Common European Framework of Reference for Languages: Learning, Teaching, Assessment: Manual*. Strasbourg: Council of Europe, Language Policy Division.

Cronbach, L. J. and Meehl, P. E. (1955). Construct validity in psychological tests. *Psychological Bulletin, 52*, 281–302.

Cureton, E. E. (1950). Validity. In E. F. Lingquist (Ed.) *Educational Measurement*. Washington, DC: American Council on Education.

Davidson, F. and Lynch, B. K. (2002). *Testcraft: A Teacher's Guide to Writing and Using Language Test Specifications*. New Haven, CT: Yale University Press.

Douglas, D. (2000). *Assessing Language for Specific Purposes*. Cambridge: Cambridge University Press.

Edgeworth, F. Y. (1888). The statistics of examinations. *Journal of the Royal Statistical Society, 51*, 599–635.

ffrench, A. and Gutch, A. (2006). *FCE/CAE Modifications: Building the Validity Argument: Application of Weir's Socio-Cognitive Framework to FCE & CAE*. Cambridge ESOL Internal Report.

Fulcher, G. (2004). Are Europe's tests being built on an unsafe framework? *Guardian Weekly*, EFL Supplement, 18 March. Available at http://www.guardian.co.uk/education/2004/mar/18/tefl2 (accessed 29 November 2009).

Fulcher, G. and Davidson, F. (2009). Test architecture, test retrofit. *Language Testing, 26*(1), 123–44.

Galaczi. E. D. and Vidakovic, I. (2010). Testing legal English: Insights from the international legal English test. *Professional and Academic English, 35*(March).

Green, A. (2009). *A Review of the International Legal English Certificate (ILEC)*. Unpublished report submitted to Cambridge ESOL Examinations, April 2009.

Harrison, C. (2007). Teaching knowledge test update – adoptions and courses. *Research Notes, 29*, 30–32.

Hawkey, R. A. (2009). *Examining FCE and CAE: Key Issues and Recurring Themes in Developing the First Certificate in English and Certificate in Advanced English Exams. Studies in Language Testing 28.* Cambridge: Cambridge University Press.

Jones, N. (2005). Raising the languages ladder: constructing a new framework for accrediting foreign language skills. *Research Notes, 19,* 15–19.

Kane, M. T. (1992). An argument-based approach to validity. *Psychological Bulletin, 112*(3), 527–35.

Khalifa, H. and Weir, C. (2009). *Examining Reading: Research and Practice in Assessing second language reading, Studies in Language Testing 29.* Cambridge: Cambridge University Press.

Kramsch, C. (1986). From language proficiency to international competence. *Modern Language Journal, 70*(4), 366–72.

Kramsch, C. (1998). *Language and Culture.* Oxford: Oxford University Press.

Kunnan, A. (1998). Approaches to validation in language assessment. In A. Kunnan (Ed.) *Validation in Language Assessment.* Mahwah, NJ: Lawrence Erlbaum. pp. 1–16.

Loevinger, J. (1957). Objective tests as instruments of psychological theory. *Psychological Reports, 3*(Monograph Supplement), 635–94.

McNamara, T. (2003). Looking back, looking forward: rethinking Bachman. *Language Testing, 20*(4), 466–473.

Martyniuk, W. (Ed.) (2011). *Relating Language Examinations to the Common European Framework of Reference for Languages: Case Studies and Reflections on the Use of the Council of Europe's Draft Manual.* Cambridge: Cambridge University Press.

Messick, S. (1975). The standard program: meaning and values in measurement and evalu-ation. *American Psychologist, 30,* 955–66.

Messick, S. (1980). Test validity and the ethics of assessment. *American Psychologist, 35,* 1012–1027.

Messick, S. (1989). Validity. In R. L. Linn (Ed.) *Educational Measurement* (3rd edition). London/New York: McMillan.

Milanovic, M. (2009). Cambridge ESOL and the CEFR. *Research Notes, 37,* 2–5.

Milanovic, M. and Weir, C. J. (forthcoming). *Measured Constructs: English Language Testing Constructs Underlying Cambridge ESOL Examinations 1913–2013.* Cambridge: Cambridge University Press.

Mislevy, R. J., Steinberg, L. S. and Almond, R. G. (2002). Design and analysis in task-based language assessment. *Language Testing, 19*(4), 477–496.

Mislevy, R. J., Steinberg, L. S. and Almond, R. G. (2003). On the structure of educational assessments. *Measurement: Interdisciplinary Research and Perspectives, 1*(1), 3–62.

Morrow, K. (Ed.) (2004). *Insights from the Common European Framework.* Oxford: Oxford University Press.

Novakovi'c, N. (2006). TKT – a year on. *Research Notes, 24,* 22–24.

O'Sullivan, B. (2000). *Towards a Model of Performance in Oral Language Testing,* Unpublished PhD thesis, University of Reading.

O'Sullivan, B. (2005). *Levels Specification Project Report.* Internal report, Zayed University, United Arab Emirates.

O'Sullivan, B. (2006). *Issues in Testing Business English: The BEC Revision Project, Studies in Language Testing 17.* Cambridge: Cambridge University Press.

O'Sullivan, B. (2009a). *City & Guilds Communicator Level IESOL Examination (B2) CEFR Linking Project Case Study Report*. City & Guilds Research Report. Available at http://www.cityandguilds.com/documents/ind_general_learning_esol/CG_Communicator_Report_BOS.pdf (accessed 29 November 2009).

O'Sullivan, B. (2009b). *City & Guilds Achiever Level IESOL Examination (B1) CEFR Linking Project Case Study Report*. City & Guilds Research Report.

O'Sullivan, B. (2009c). *City & Guilds Expert Level IESOL Examination (C1) CEFR Linking Project Case Study Report*. City & Guilds Research Report.

O'Sullivan, B. (2011). The City & Guilds Communicator Examination linking project: a brief overview with reflections on the process. In W. Martyniuk (Ed.) *Relating Language Examinations to the Common European Framework of Reference for Languages: Case studies and reflections on the use of the Council of Europe's Draft Manual*. Cambridge: Cambridge University Press.

QALSPELL (2004). *Quality Assurance in Language for Specific Purposes, Estonia, Latvia, and Lithuania*. Leonardo da Vinci funded project. Available at http://www.qalspell.ttu.ee/index.html (accessed 18 July 2009).

Selvaruby, P. (2006). *Validating a National Test of Physics*. Unpublished PhD thesis. Roehampton University, School of Education.

Selvaruby, P., O'Sullivan, B. and Watts, M. (2008). School-based assessment in Sri Lanka: ensuring valid processes for assessment-for-learning in physics. In R. Coll and N. Taylor (Eds), *Education in Context: An International Perspective of the Influence of Context on Science Curriculum Development, Implementation and the Student-Experienced Curriculum*. Rotterdam: Sense Publishers, pp. 131–144.

Shaw, S. and Weir, C. J. (2007). *Examining Writing: Research and Practice in Assessing Second Language Writing, Studies in Language Testing 26*. Cambridge: Cambridge University Press and Cambridge ESOL.

Skehan, P. (1988). State-of-the-Art article: Language testing, Part 1. *Language Teaching, 21*(4): 211–221.

Spearman, C. (1904). The proof and measurement of association between two things. *American Journal of Psychology, 15*, 72–101.

SurveyLang (2008). *Inception Report for the European Survey on Language Competence*. Submitted to Directorate general Education and Culture of the European Commission.

Swain, M. (1985). Large-scale communicative language testing: A case study. In Y. P. Lee, A. C. Y. Y. Fok, R. Lord and G. Low (Eds.), *New Directions in Language Testing*. Oxford: Pergamon Press, pp. 35–46.

Taylor, L. (2000). Stakeholders in language testing. *Research Notes, 2*, 2–4.

Taylor, L. (ed.) (2011). *Examining Speaking: Research and Practice in Assessing Second Language Speaking, Studies in Language Testing 30*. Cambridge: UCLES/Cambridge University Press.

Taylor, L., Barker, F., Geranpayeh, A., Green, A., Khalifa, H. and Shaw, S. (2006). *Defining the Construct(s) Underpinning the Cambridge ESOL UMS Tests: A Socio-Cognitive Perspective on Overall Language Proficiency and the Four Language Skills*. Cambridge ESOL internal report.

Taylor, D., O'Sullivan, B and Quilter, N. (2009). *Advanced International Ophthalmology Examination Proposal*. London: International Council of Ophthalmology.

Thighe, D. (2006). Placing the international legal English certificate on The CEFR. *Research Notes, 24*, 5–7.

Torres Pereira de Eça, M. T. (2005). Using portfolios for external assessment: an experiment in Portugal. *International Journal of Art & Design Education, 24*(2), 209–218.

Weir, C. J. (1993). *Understanding and Developing Language Tests.* London: Prentice Hall.

Weir, C. J. (2005a). *Language Testing and Validation: An Evidence-Based Approach.* Oxford: Palgrave Macmillan.

Weir, C. J. (2005b). Limitations of the Common european framework for developing comparable examinations and tests. *Language Testing, 22*(3), 281–300.

Widdowson, H. G. (2003). *Defining Issues in English Language Teaching.* Oxford: Oxford University Press.

Wu, J. and Wu, R. (2010). Relating the GEPT reading comprehension tests to the CEFR. In W. Martyniuk (Ed.), *Relating Language Examinations to the Common European Framework of Reference for Languages: Case studies and Reflections on the Use of the Council of Europe's Draft Manual, Studies in Language Testing 33.* Cambridge: Cambridge University Press.

Young, R. F. (2000). Interactional competence: challenges for validity. Paper presented at the *Language Testing Research Colloqium,* Vancouver, Canada, 9 March 2000.

2
describing language levels

brian north

language proficiency descriptors

This chapter concerns descriptor scales of language proficiency, with reference to the illustrative descriptors in the Common European Framework of Reference (CEFR: Council of Europe, 2001). The chapter will not repeat information available elsewhere in CEFR overviews (e.g. North, 2008a, b), impact studies (e.g. Little, 2007; North, 2007, 2009) or validity studies (e.g. Jones, 2002; Kaftandjieva and Takala, 2002; North, 2002). Descriptors defined at different curriculum levels, such as those in the CEFR and the related European Language Portfolios (ELPs), have become increasingly popular because they help to relate learning objectives to real world needs in a framework for task-oriented learning. Descriptors can be used as "signposting" in curriculum aims, syllabuses, cross-referenced resources lists, weekly/monthly plans, classroom displays, lesson aims, evaluation checklists, report cards, personal profiles, certificates and so on. Within a class, such signposting helps to set priorities, explain syllabus choice and lesson relevance, select appropriate communicative tasks and assess progress. In a school, descriptors facilitate discussion between teachers, organisation of materials, articulation of programmes, communication with other departments or institutions, and reporting results to parents and other stakeholders. Descriptors can also be useful to determine what tasks could be used for performance assessments (spoken, written, integrated skills) and, of course, to formulate the assessment criteria used for grading performance in such assessments. With illustrative DVDs and scripts, teachers' understanding of the levels defined by the descriptors can be deepened and, to some extent, standardised. In such an exercise, the descriptors again fulfil a "signposting" function, pointing out what one should be looking out for at B2, and so helping to create consensus and providing a structure for the resolution of disagreement.

Various forms of such signposting are common in EAQUALS (European Association for Quality Language Services) – from a Greek primary school (aims box on the whiteboard each lesson, checklists for teachers, report cards for parents) through language schools providing intensive courses in a country and extensive courses at home (syllabus cross-referencing, checklists for teacher/self-assessment) to a Turkish university (defining exit levels and detailed objectives, communication within faculty and with parents, continuous teacher and self-assessment). For example, in Eurocentres intensive in-country courses, every classroom has a standardised display of (i) the scale of CEFR levels, with defined sub-levels, (ii) the detailed learning objectives for the CEFR level in question ("Our Aims") and (iii) the communicative and related linguistic objectives of the actual week's work ("Weekly Plan"). The weekly plan is introduced by the teacher on the Monday, and a review lesson at the end of the week combines a quiz on the main linguistic content with a small group discussion of achievement of the week's objectives, and the need for further class or individual work. The signposting provided by the descriptors allows learners to be treated as partners in the learning and teaching process.

levels

Our way of organising language learning into curriculum levels goes back at least to Comenius. He defined four language levels (1632, 1896/1967): "Vestibule" when one is waiting to get started; "Gate" as one enters into the language; "Palace" with all its corridors and pathways, and "Treasure" the ultimate goal.[1] It is typical of John Trim that at the start of the Council of Europe's work on describing language levels he changed the possibly negative image of Gate (gatekeeping) to that of the gate's threshold one crosses in "The Threshold Level" (van Ek, 1976; van Ek and Trim, 2001b). This invention of images to describe curriculum levels is not confined to Europe. A good example can be seen in the levels used in Eurocentres Kanasawa in teaching Japanese. First comes "Hana" (flower – with the image of petals opening up), then "Tori" (a bird – stretching wings to fly), then "Kaze" (the wind, blowing across the land), "Tsuki" (the moon, in orbit), "Niji" (rainbow – the bridge to the stars), and finally in the firmament: "Hoshi" (a star itself). Notice that all this imagery suggests stages of personal development.

British imagery tends to be somewhat more prosaic, as with the current "Language Ladder" for the Asset Language Project (Walker et al., 2007). A ladder can be a positive image representing a lot of little steps. The translation of "ladder" into French is "échelle", the word used for "scale". Is a ladder a scale? Strictly speaking it is a set of ascending steps, ordinal categories. Is the number of such steps arbitrary, each representing simply a section of the continuum on the ladder? The IRT-calibrated descriptor scale behind the CEFR actually had ten rather than six steps, with the steps in the middle subdivided (North, 2000: 273–281; Council of Europe, 2001: 31–36). Does this bulge in the middle of the CEFR empirical scale reflect the relative abundance of descriptors there, that is to say, is it just a reflection of our ability to describe distinctions between steps in words? Are the limits on the number of possible steps (i) a natural aspect of the second language acquisition process, (ii) a limitation imposed by our ability with language to describe such differences or (iii) a reflection of the number of categories we can mentally juggle at once? It is generally accepted that there is a link between the number of steps/categories and reliability – higher reliability allows more steps (Pollitt, 1991; Fisher, 1992) – but that only addresses the third issue above. In any case, if the decision being made is at elementary level, one could have five steps on the elementary rating scale, so that five levels each equipped with such a scale would give a total of 25 steps (or maybe 20 allowing for overlap). Arguments based on the reliability of judgements/cut-offs thus do not give an answer to the question of how many steps one can have in a framework of levels.

Should steps be considered equal, suggesting linear progress? Or does language learning happen in a series of shifts, with slow, less dramatic changes in between? Progress in the mastery of grammatical form does not appear to be linear (Klein, 1986: 108; Fulcher 1993, 1996). There are two ways of visualising the issue: on the one hand, scale steps can be seen as steps on a ladder (linear); on the other hand, they can be seen as steps leading to landings (or plateaux) part way up a long staircase. These two images reflect the tension present in criterion-referenced assessment (CR) since its origin. CR is usually interpreted in terms of mastery/non-mastery of a particular "level" of qualification. There may be grades rather than pass/fail, and over time several "levels" may be united into a framework of levels, as happened with Cambridge examinations for English. This is, however, only one interpretation of CR. Glaser, in the article that founded the concept of CR, talked of: "a continuum of knowledge ranging from no proficiency at all to perfect performance." His original definition goes on to say:

> Along such a continuum of attainment, a student's score on a criterion-referenced measure provides explicit information as to what the individual can and cannot do. (...) Criterion-referenced measures indicate the content of the behaviour repertory, and the correspondence between what an individual does and the underlying continuum of achievement. Measures which assess student achievement in terms of a criterion standard thus provide information as to the degree of competence attained by a particular student which is independent of reference to the performance of others. (Glaser, 1963: 519–520)

It is not necessary to cut a continuum into levels. One could imagine a scale of 1–1000 with descriptors pegged to particular scores as illustrations. This was, in fact, an approach popular in descriptor scales for work evaluation in the 1960s–1970s (Borman, 1986: 103), following the lead of Smith and Kendall (1963), who pioneered a data-based approach to descriptor scale development in order to encourage accurate observation and record-keeping in the continuous assessment of trainee nurses. Their aim was "to enhance future observation and to foster a *common frame of reference* in observers' ratings" in order to improve the effectiveness of training (Bernadin and Smith, 1981: 458). Such scales were called Behaviourally Anchored Rating Scales (BARS), with the behavioural descriptors pegged to certain scores perceived as "anchors". By the late 1970s it was increasingly common to associate descriptors directly with the scale steps in Behavioural Summary Scales (BSS) (Landy and Farr, 1983: 104–109). BSS were found more practical for giving feedback, with Landy et al. (1982: 21–23) estimating that the addition of transparent proficiency descriptors improved performance by between 10 and 30 per cent. BSS probably influenced the "Language for Specific Purposes" (LSP) scales that also began appearing in Europe in the mid-1970s (IBM, 1974; ELTDU, 1976). These consisted of a set of sub-scales concerned with different activities that employees needed to perform, such as writing letters, dealing with enquiries, attending meetings, and so on.

If one does cut the continuum into levels, can one cut it anywhere? Is the decision on cut-offs essentially arbitrary? To put it another way, if progress is by little steps or modules to the next landing, are the broader levels (= criterion, certificated levels) represented by each of those "flight of steps plus landing" in some way "natural"? Or could the landings occur anywhere? Hargreaves (1992) argued that the levels that became the six CEFR reference levels were in some sense "natural", in that they made sense as curriculum levels. The European adult education, publishing and examination industries had been slowly harmonising on them for decades. In the CEFR descriptor research project the process of cutting the continuum of descriptors into levels was partly a question of marking out equidistant spaces on the scale, but also, crucially, a matter of expert judgement with reference to the sources, and above all to recognition of the fact that descriptors describing a similar task or quality tended to bunch together on the scale, with the result that there was sometimes a sudden, radical change in what was being described. Clearly such points, where a radical shift in content was apparent, made sense as cut-offs, so the "equidistant ruler" was juggled up and down until all the cut-offs made sense. Does that tendency for the levels to almost suggest themselves on the logit scale suggest (i) an aspect of the nature of the second language acquisition process, that learning occurs in shifts (Hargreaves's "natural levels" argument) or (ii) a limitation imposed by our ability to describe differences in words with conventions? We do not have an answer to that question, just personal experience and anecdotes. In that regard, one reason for the separation into three broad levels – A, B and C – in the CEFR was personal experience that language learning could be a little like snakes and ladders. Until one reached a kind of "second threshold" (which became C1), characterised by spontaneous fluency, discourse competence and a mastery of syntax, it seemed all too easy to slide from a confident B2 plus (= Eurocentres level 7) back down to a bare B1 (= Eurocentres level 4) through lack of use.

levels or domains?

The discussion so far has assumed that growth in language proficiency is unidimensional, essentially going in the same direction, even if this might sometimes be in fits and starts. Unidimensionality is actually a purely technical concept: it just means that one can report one overall result from an assessment, even though one can also divide each result to give a more detailed profile. Language is more unidimensional than the majority of areas that are studied and assessed at school, because it is only partly a learnt subject as opposed to an acquired natural phenomenon. Although initially promising research on orders of acquisition (e.g. Meisel et al., 1981; Pienemann, 1985) has been relativised, it is generally accepted that at cognitive and syntactic levels there is an underlying progression. The results in the CEFR descriptor project for the amounts of differential item functioning shown by the CEFR descriptors across target languages, language regions and educational systems and sectors reflected this common perception of progression, being remarkably small and easily explained by context (e.g. adult/13 year old). One would not necessarily expect the same stability of values in descriptors for mathematics or geography across different contexts, because the structure of those subjects is more modular, meaning that sequencing decisions may differ radically between curricula.

However, even if language is conveniently unidimensional in the sense that one can have a set of levels like those of the CEFR, illustrated with descriptors that show a good degree of consistency in interpretation across different contexts, it is clear that no two people's profiles of proficiency will be identical. Language ability develops through a process of accumulating constructions ("form-meaning mapping, conventionalised in the speech community and entrenched as knowledge in the learner's mind") (Ellis, 2006: 101) that are formed into a semantic network through generalisation from thousands of examples to which one is exposed. Clearly, therefore, the expansion of one's repertoire is related to the contexts to which one is exposed and the experiences and encounters one has. Therefore everybody's profile of language ability must logically be unique, since no two people completely share a history; the experience of language learning and language use will determine the possible scope of the profile. In a company language training context, this fact has long been recognised. Figure 2.1 illustrates the result of a "language audit" conducted with the ELTDU scale. It originates from an early 1980s edition of a German journal for teachers of Business English.

The concentric rings represent the ELTDU levels A–H. The lighter shaded area is the perceived requirements of the subject's job; the darker shaded area is their current profile of abilities, self-assessed with the same descriptor scales. The process of comparing requirements to current abilities is the "audit" that defines the subject's needs and hence the specification for a tailor-made course. Notice that the current profile (darker shading) is not necessarily a profile of the subject's complete abilities; we don't know that they cannot follow a training course or take notes in a meeting – they just are not required to do that for this job.

The figure appeared in the internal versions of the CEFR and was referred to as "Antarctica" because of the image it offered of progress being a question of occupying territory over time – like the ice cap.

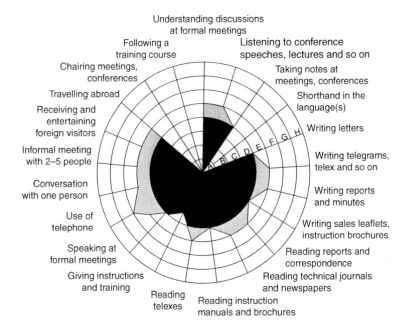

Figure 2.1 Product of a language audit = "Antarctica"

As a profiling model, however, Figure 2.1 has a flaw. In common with the then prevailing LSP school of thought, there is no generative core. It is about the job, not the person; training, not education. Yet everyone would agree that language does have a generative core. One can hypothesise that progress in that core, predominantly concerned with spoken interaction, will be similar for all learners in terms of communicative ability (= an appearance of unidimensionality). As Van Lier (1989: 500) says: "it is possible that a common core of general conversational proficiency underlies interaction in all specialised forms of spoken language use". That was the reason spoken interaction was taken as the core construct in the construction of the scale of CEFR descriptors. However, around this common core will be areas in which progress is dependent on a number of factors, among which will be exposure to context and the development of specialised cognitive abilities at least partly associated with that exposure. As a result, one may have a very developed ability in certain domains and a relatively rudimentary one in others.

This issue is related to the frequently heard claim that "not all native speakers are C2." The question is: C2 in what? Language originated as "chat" (Swales, 1990: 58–61), spoken interaction as casual conversation, "a type of speech in which ties of union are created by a mere exchange of words" (Malinowski, 1946: 315). Storytelling (oracy), the precursor of all production and literacy (Swales, 1990: 61), emerged from and is embedded in the turn-taking of casual talk (Jefferson, 1978: 220). Both oracy and literacy develop culturally specific discourse conventions that have to be learnt. In oracy and literacy a native speaker may, therefore, not necessarily be C2. Cummins (1980, 1983, 1984) developed this distinction into BICS (Basic Interpersonal Communication Skills)/ CALP (Cognitive Academic Language Proficiency). CALP is a culturally determined, learnt skill correlated to intelligence, whereas BICS can be picked up fairly easily. Everyone who has a mother tongue and who does not have a brain malfunction is *above* Level C2 in BICS in their idiolect. Compare a set of CEFR C2 descriptors closer to BICS (in Table 2.1) with those in Table 2.2 concerned with aspects of CALP. These distinctions between BICS and CALP, between chat and oracy/literacy, plus Canale's (1984) distinction between communicative competence and autonomous competence, influenced the distinction between interaction and production adopted in the CEFR (North, 2000: 104).

Hulstijn (2007) puts forward a not dissimilar argument in relation to "core language proficiency":

> I hypothesise that…the core makes up most of the language proficiency of adult NSs of lower educational backgrounds; the part of their proficiency beyond the core is relatively small. NSs with higher educational backgrounds are indistinguishable from NSs of lower educational backgrounds with respect to core language proficiency, but their profiles will differentiate beyond the core. The part of their proficiencies beyond the core is relatively large. (Hulstijn, 2007: 665)

Table 2.1 CEFR level "C" descriptors: closer to BICS

Listening to an interlocutor	I can understand any interlocutor, given an opportunity to adjust to a non-standard accent or dialect.
Conversation	I can converse comfortably, appropriately and without limitations in casual conversation, at social events and in more formal discussions and debates; I can employ irony and understatement in an appropriate manner.
Interaction	I can interact naturally, picking up and using non-verbal and intonational cues without effort, and interweaving my contribution into the joint discourse with fully natural turn-taking, referencing, allusion making and so on.
Fluency	I can express myself naturally and effortlessly; I only need to pause occasionally in order to select precisely the right words.

Table 2.2 CEFR level C2 descriptors concerned with aspects of CALP

Reading – info and argument	I can understand texts (e.g. newspaper columns and satirical glosses) in which much is said in an indirect and ambiguous way and which contain hidden value judgements.
Argue a case	I can argue a case on a complex issue, adapting the structure, content and emphasis in order to convince particular listeners of the validity of my argument.
Summarising	I can summarise orally information from different sources, reconstructing arguments and accounts accurately, coherently and concisely without including unnecessary detail.
Linking	I can make full and appropriate use of a variety of organisational patterns and a wide range of connectors in order to organise what I say and write.
Monitoring and repair	I can edit my written work to achieve the effect I want in a more differentiated and appropriate style.

Rather than a map of Antarctica, therefore, maybe ring planets offer a better image of the profile of the language proficiency of an individual. In the view of Saturn in Figure 2.2, one sees what could be a core language proficiency on the left. The rings on the right could represent levels of learnt competences in different domains and activities, which will be at least partly determined by exposure to and training for different contexts.

categories of description

Profiling abilities in the ring around the core requires categories that can become the subject of descriptor scales, like the ELTDU sub-scales shown in Figure 2.1. Selecting categories for sub-scales requires some care. On the one hand, teachers and learners should be able to relate to the categories, but, on the other hand, they should bear some relation to theoretical concepts. The CEFR's set of the sub-scales is an example of the kind of compromise that can result. This compromise appealed to Canadian reviewers (MacDonald and Vandergrift, 2007) for the following reasons: construct validity: the CEFR level descriptors are based on a theory of communicative competence and empirically validated; face validity: the level descriptors are congruent with teachers' perceptions and experiences with language learners (i.e. they are not ivory tower-applied linguistic constructs); contextual validity: the branching approach to both levels and categories is able to accommodate the different needs and pedagogic cultures of the Canadian provinces and territories.

Figure 2.2   View of Saturn

The CEFR descriptor scheme is a considerable advance on Lado's (1961) "four skills" scheme operationalised in very many second language course books and examinations. Table 2.3 contrasts the CEFR categories with those from that popular model.

This theory/practice compromise in the CEFR descriptor scale categories did not happen by itself. The first mock-up for a common European scale (North, 1992) was conceived as a "Can Do" ELP reporting scale, much influenced by the LSP scales referred to (IBM, 1974; ELTDU, 1976). It had a global scale, three summary scales (Reception, Interaction, Production) and nine sub-scales (Listening, Reading, Viewing; Conversation, Transactions, Discussion; Presentations, Reports/Essays, Letters). The full set of the 51 CEFR scale categories emerged through an interplay between the work of the Council of Europe authoring group and experimentation with categories in a series of workshops with teachers in Switzerland. In those workshops, teachers sorted descriptors into the categories they were supposed to describe, and commented on

Table 2.3 Four skills versus CEFR descriptor categories

	"Four Skills" (Lado, 1961)	CEFR 1996/2001	CEFR scales
Skills	Listening, speaking, reading, writing	Reception: Listening and reading	11
		Interaction: Spoken and written	12
		Production: Spoken and written	8
		Text processing	2
Linguistic	Grammatical accuracy, vocabulary range, pronunciation	General linguistic range	1
		Vocabulary range	1
		Grammatical accuracy	1
		Vocabulary control	1
		Phonological control	1
		Orthographic control	1
Pragmatic	(Spoken *Fluency*)	Propositional precision	1
		Flexibility	1
		Spoken fluency	1
		Discourse	3
Socio-cultural	Culture as subject	*Domain of use*	0
		Inter-cultural competences	0
		Sociolinguistic	1
Strategic		Reception	1
		Interaction	3
		Production	3

descriptor style. In addition, discussions between pairs of teachers concerning the relative proficiency of two learners in a video were recorded and analysed to see what categories teachers used in their argument (North, 2000: 185–188).

descriptor style

Having selected the categories, one needs to consider the style of description. Fundamentally, there are two approaches to formulating distinctions between levels in words. One approach takes salient features of the level and describes these in as concrete a way as possible. This style can be seen as a further development of the Behaviourally Anchored Rating Scales: what is it that sticks out at this level? This was the approach teachers preferred, and the CEFR descriptors are of this type.

In the CEFR descriptor research, the calibrated descriptors for particular areas were summarised in charts in order to check the concreteness and the coherence in the description. Table 2.4 gives the chart for the conversation scale (Council of Europe, 2001: 76). The CEFR descriptor style has been very influential, as can be seen by the bank of descriptors from European Language Portfolios available on www.coe.int/portfolio. Descriptors of this type can form a checklist

Table 2.4   CEFR conversation scale showing salient features

	Setting	Topic/register	Specific functions	Limitations
C2	Full personal and social life		Converse comfortably and appropriately	
C1	Flexible, effective language use for social purposes	Emotional, allusive, joking usage		
B2+				
B2	Sustain relationships with NSs – without unintended irritation/ amusement Engage in extended conversation Clearly participatory, naturally, fluently	Most general topics	Convey degrees of emotion Highlight personal significance	
B1+			Express thoughts about, for example, music, films	
B1	Enter conversation unprepared Maintain conversation and discussion Initiate, maintain and close simple face-to-face conversation	Familiar topics Topics that are familiar or of personal interest	Express feelings like surprise, happiness, sadness, interest, indifference	May sometimes be difficult to follow when trying to say exactly what he wants to
A2+	Participate in short conversation Initiate, maintain and close simple, restricted face-to-face conversation Establish social contact	In routine contexts on topics of interest	Greetings, farewells, thanks Ask for, give or refuse permission	May need to ask for repetition or reformulation from time to time
A2	Handle very short social exchanges	Personal news Likes and dislikes	Express how feels, Likes/dislikes Offers, invitations Apologies, thanks Greeting, farewells, intros	Rarely able to understand enough to keep it going
A1	Ask how people are	Personal news	Make an introduction and use basic greeting and leave-taking expressions	
Tourist			Some basic greetings, please, thank you and so on.	

of criterion statements to which one can answer "Yes" or "No", which Skehan (1984) proposed as the test for whether a scale is really criterion-referenced or not.

The alternative to this concrete, "salient feature" style is an abstract normative style that uses qualifiers to vary meaning. A good example is provided by the following scale for sociolinguistic ability (Cohen and Olshtain, 1993; Cohen, 1994: 283–287).

sociolinguistic ability

5 The speaker uses linguistic forms that are fully appropriate for expressing the intended speech act.

4 The speaker uses linguistic forms that are mostly appropriate for expressing the intended speech act.

3 There is some use of inappropriate linguistic forms for expressing the intended speech act.

2 There is much use of inappropriate linguistic forms for expressing the intended speech act.

1 There is continuous use of inappropriate linguistic forms for expressing the intended speech act.

There are two main problems with this type of scale. First, as Trim (1978) pointed out, the bottom half is negative, so the descriptors cannot be used as educational objectives. Second, it does no more than define the construct involved; differences between levels are restricted to alternating qualifiers, as shown in Table 2.5.

Yet, to be valid, a descriptor scale:

> must be more than mere words. It should describe behaviour with as much concrete vividness as is compatible with the breadth of the definition. The use of words like "rarely", "usually", "slightly", and "extremely", is only excusable if the scale value does not depend on them. (Champney, 1941: 144)

Table 2.5 An abstract scale as labels

	1	2	3	4	5
Sociolinguistic ability Appropriateness of linguistic forms for expressing the intended speech act.	*Fully*	*Mostly*	*Some negative*	*Much negative*	*Continuous negative*

Apart from style, there are decisions to make about descriptor length and complexity: short descriptors are clearer and easier to use; longer ones are more differentiated but more complex to use. In the CEFR authoring group there was considerable discussion over the reason the descriptor "Can make a complaint" (Council of Europe, 2001: 80) was calibrated at B1 and not at A2. How could that happen, when the linguistic means to articulate the complaint will be found at A2? The conclusion we came to was that the teachers assessing with that descriptor appear to have interpreted it to mean *successfully* make a complaint. Calibration at B1 then makes sense in relation to the B1 descriptors for conversation, range and fluency. To successfully make a complaint you need to be able to initiate and maintain a conversation on a familiar subject, keeping going comprehensibly, admittedly with hesitation and circumlocutions, until you get some kind of result. An A2 learner simply could not do that. Is it a good thing, however, to have unarticulated assumptions in descriptors? In retrospect, it might have been better to add such elements to make a more complex but more differentiated descriptor like: "Can make a complaint on a familiar subject, keeping going comprehensibly with some hesitation and circumlocutions until he/she gets an explanation or redress."

Fleming (2009) discusses this issue with the example of writing a letter:

> Trying to formulate language achievement and progression in simple statements is difficult because so much is necessarily left unsaid. For example, the claim that a learner can 'write a letter' does not say whether the intended language use is formal or informal, whether the subject matter is familiar or unfamiliar, whether the key focus is pragmatic communication or accuracy. A partial solution is to make the statements of learning outcomes more complex and nuanced (e.g. 'can write an informal letter to a friend on a familiar topic at a level of accuracy that does not inhibit communication') but this process, when extended to whole range of statements, can detract from their practical utility because they become too complex. There is a compromise to be found between brevity and simplicity on the one hand and expansion and complexity on the other.

descriptor development

Whatever decisions one makes about content and style, development should follow three steps: first, conceptualisation (defining the

construct); second, construction (finding, writing, editing and organising descriptors); and finally validation (checking that people interpret
the descriptors consistently).

conceptualisation

There is a real need to achieve clarity about the construct concerned
before one embarks on a descriptor project. What aspects of language are
to be described and why? Is there a consensus about what is involved in
language learning in the context? What standards are realistic? For the
CEFR this work took place between 1991 and 1995, based on the work
in the Modern Languages Project in the 1970s and 1980s. With regard
to the development of descriptors for the Language of Schooling, the
Council of Europe has so far had two major international conferences
(e.g. Martyniuk, 2007) plus several workshops to share perceptions and
definitions of the construct, with more conferences planned.

The chaos that can be caused by not achieving such a consensus on
the construct and on the meaning of key concepts before operationalising a language policy is demonstrated by the United States "No Child
Left Behind" project. One of the requirements of this project was for
states to ensure through standardised tests that children who spoke languages other than English had the opportunity to become "proficient"
in "academic English language". Chalhoub-Deville (2009) documents
the consequences of the failure to define "academic English language
proficiency" (meant in this context as the language abilities needed
to cope with English used as the medium of instruction), which some
states and testing agencies managed to confuse with "English Language
Arts" (basically creative writing for native speakers). Perie (2008) documents how the concept "proficient" was operationalised across the
states in at least 15 significantly different ways in the process, making
any comparison impossible.

construction

It is only sensible to build on what has already been developed in the
field. A rigorous conceptualisation phase will prevent the danger of mere
copying and enable creative efforts to be focused on writing descriptors
for those parts of the descriptive scheme not adequately covered in the
source documents available. It is a good idea to document the adoption
of existing descriptors, or elements of them, if only to avoid accusations
of plagiarism and to help map the relationship of the final descriptor
scale to existing scales.

For the CEFR, a classified pool of approximately 2000 descriptors was
created as a starting point. Some two-thirds came from a collation of

those scales existing at the time, while the other third were written to cover areas that were under-defined (North, 2000: 181–185). The steps involved in this construction phase are: collating and pulling apart all sources into individual descriptors; organising them into a classi-fied bank of descriptors sorted by category; eliminating repetition and redundancy; identifying gaps and authoring descriptors for them; con-firming style and harmonising formulation; and, finally, authoring missing categories based on relevant documents and reports of studies.

validation

There are essentially two approaches to validation. Descriptor sorting tasks offer a qualitative approach, the weakness of which is that there has been no analysis of the descriptors in their educational use. This may be appropriate for an institutional project in a low-stakes con-text. The second, quantitative, approach only makes sense after such a descriptor sorting phase has shown that the descriptors are appropri-ate and of good quality. Descriptors can be scaled to levels through an IRT analysis of assessment data from teachers (North and Schneider, 1998; North, 2000: 223–309) or from self-assessment (Jones, 2002; North, 2002). Ideally one would have assessment with descriptors from both teachers and learners, linked in both data collection and analysis to objective tests for the same areas. This was the original aim in the CEFR scale research project, but the tests had to be dropped due to the minimal resources available. The current European Survey of Language Competence project is adopting this approach. It not only validates descriptors, but also provides scale-based standard setting for the test items, which will be durable over time (North and Jones, 2009).

Descriptor sorting workshops with informants as a methodology to validate descriptors go back to Thurstone (1928), Champney (1941) and Smith and Kendall (1963). Pairs of informants sort 40–50 descriptors and should be encouraged to highlight the descriptors they like, iden-tify those they don't like and suggest reformulations where they feel it necessary. The sorting can be by category or level. Sorting by cat-egory validates that informants can identify a meaningful distinction between 3- and 5-related categories, putting descriptors into the correct envelopes. It also helps identify weakly formulated descriptors. Sorting by level is an essential final step. One can combine sorting by both category and level, with placement onto a grid, but this is cognitively challenging.

An IRT analysis of the way descriptors are used in assessment is a step to be recommended in a major undertaking. One can construct the scale from the descriptors for the core construct and then bolt onto this "core scale" sets of descriptors for categories that may be less core areas. In the CEFR project, the core construct was spoken interaction/ production, including listening in interaction. Listening outside interaction was then "bolted on" in a second analysis that was anchored to the scale from the first analysis. Reading descriptors were then analysed together with the listening descriptors to create a separate scale for reception. The listening items common to both the "core scale" and the "reception scale" were then used to equate the two scales.

In the process of creating the scale, one can discover which descriptors are interpreted in an inconsistent fashion (= "misfit"). Sub-analyses can also be contrasted in order to confirm communality of the interpretation of the descriptors across target languages, regions/countries and educational sectors. The process is described in detail in North (2000: 223–270). It is important to emphasise that this IRT approach will only work (i) if the construct is well defined, with a common understanding of what is being described and rated, (ii) if descriptors are well formulated, clear and relevant, (iii) if teachers/learners are capable of making judgements about the areas concerned, and (iv) if there is a solid anchor design in the data collection.

validity issues

Descriptor scales of language proficiency are educationally useful in bringing transparency and coherence to a second language programme, but are also inevitably a simplification of a very complex phenomenon. The essential problem is that descriptors reflect a *perception* of language levels rather than stages of second language acquisition in a scientific sense. Whereas in the natural sciences descriptions of even the human genome have achieved almost 100 per cent completeness, the process of describing language levels is still based on expert opinion and on conventions of description that are only partially informed by research. The best that one can do in describing language levels is to create a practical descriptive scheme informed by theory and research as a heuristic model, to validate the scheme and the descriptive style selected as being appropriate for the purpose and context at hand, to seek sources of independent data to verify that the descriptors make sense and are consistently interpreted, and to identify points for further development.

One should be careful not to confuse a valuable educational heuristic with scientific truth in that process.

From a research point of view that situation may be unsatisfactory, but the language teaching and testing professions cannot sit still and do nothing while waiting for researchers to provide the answer to the ultimate question. As Mislevy (1993: 28) put it:

> A learner's state of competence at a given point in time is a complex constellation of facts and concepts, and the networks that interconnect them; of automatized procedures and conscious heuristics, and their relationships to knowledge patterns that signal their relevance; of perspectives and strategies, and the management capabilities by which the learner focuses his efforts. There is no hope of providing a description of such a state. Neither is there any need to.

The aim of the CEFR descriptor project (North and Schneider, 1998; North, 2000) was not to provide the last word in describing language levels, but rather to scale objectively an intersubjective consensus and to investigate in the process how that consensus held up across languages (English, French, German) in translations and as target languages, across educational sectors (lower and upper secondary, vocational, adult) and in different language regions (French-speaking, German-speaking, Italian-speaking). One validation project (Kaftandjieva and Takala, 2002) involved the teaching of Swedish in Finland, another (Jones, 2002) took data from English examination candidates all round the world.

The validity of the CEFR descriptors can be further supported by qualitative and quantitative follow-up studies, such as those taking place in the Cambridge "Common Scale" and "English Profile" projects. However, the results from such projects do not significantly change the situation that Mislevy described. Even when performances are analysed by informants to agree salient features at each level, as in the Cambridge Common Scale project (Hawkey and Barker, 2004), the resulting formulations tend to paint a similar picture to that described in the CEFR descriptor scales (North, 2008: 62–66). Is that a validation of the content of the CEFR descriptors or a demonstration of how constrained by convention we are with respect to what we look for? It is interesting that the sole example of a contradiction between the Cambridge Common Scale content and the CEFR descriptors concerned an element of sociolinguistic ability, one of the three CEFR scales without an empirical basis. A recent analysis for the English Profile project of the consensus in terminology used to describe functions at different levels, particularly the advanced "C levels" (Green, 2008), shows the danger of circular argument involved in validating descriptors. Of course words like "coherent", "confidently", "conveys", "critically" and so on show a high frequency and even uniqueness at C levels across different ELT descriptions, scales, syllabuses and so on. The first thing anyone developing a level description does is to collect other people's descriptions, so these formulations are not independent. With the CEFR descriptor development, the circular subjectivity of such conventions was at least challenged by scaling descriptors individually on the basis of their interpretation when actually used for assessment (North, 2000). As Green suggests, his analysis of the consensus regarding the functional description could be a valuable step towards the formulation of richer C level descriptors. However, such descriptors would still, like the current CEFR descriptors, reflect a consensus of expert perception rather than a scientific fact. "English Profile" itself (Hawkins and Buttery, 2009) is actually only a cross-sectional study on a grander scale than usual. It will, no doubt, provide more detailed insights, but, informative though the results will no doubt be, they cannot by the nature of the data collected lead to any significant breakthrough concerning development stages, internal processes or variability of performance under different conditions. Thus the results will enrich the descriptive apparatus around the CEFR, but will be unlikely to radically alter our style and habits of description.

limits to validity

For a language policy instrument concerned with second language curriculum design, teacher training and assessment, the fact that description of language levels is based on a consensus perception of proficiency rather than a proven description of stages of second language acquisition is not a central problem. In such a context, what is important is that the conventions associated with describing levels are confined to the field in which they originate – in this case second language teaching to adults and teenagers. After all, in this field proficiency descriptors represent a collective expertise accumulated over half a century. They originated in foreign language teaching in the United States towards the end of the Second World War (Wilds, 1975; Spolsky, 1995: 175–179). They had been the subject of academic criticism as well as being objects in constant use for some 20 years before the CEFR descriptors were developed. The descriptive scheme of the CEFR – to which the descriptors are related – was itself the result of a process of debate over 20 years. Following the publication of "The Threshold Level" by the Council of Europe (van Ek, 1976), language-specific "Thresholds" were developed for over 30 languages. The CEFR itself took ten years of planning, consultation, feedback and revision before definitive publication (1991–2001). More recently, the series of language-specific "reference levels" have documented linguistic content at different levels in relation to each language concerned (e.g. van Ek and Trim, 2001a–c; Glaboniat et al., 2002/2005; Beacco et al., 2004, 2006, 2007; Instituto Cervantes, 2007; Beacco and Porquier, 2008), with "English Profile", the next in the series, taking a corpus approach rather than relying on documentation and reflection.

It is difficult to say to what extent the CEFR and the projects related to it have documented the current consensus with respect to objectives in European second language teaching and to what extent they have created that consensus. As Goullier (2007) has pointed out, with the CEFR there was an element of lucky timing. It might be truer to say that the CEFR's metalanguage and descriptors have facilitated convergence between pedagogic cultures and a description of divergence between contexts, for example through the context-specific descriptors elaborated from the CEFR originals in many of the 80-plus European Language Portfolios (ELPs). That convergence/divergence appears like a consensus, but perhaps it is actually a metalanguage to use in discussing and even disagreeing about what to teach in a specific context. The provision of such a metalanguage was in fact the primary aim of the CEFR: to stimulate reflection through facilitating communication beyond the traditional boundaries dividing countries, sectors and languages. There was no suggestion that people should apply the CEFR levels and descriptors in their original form, but rather a recommendation to adapt them to context, being careful to elaborate and complement the concepts in the originals. To guide this process, the Council of Europe's Language Policy Division set up an ELP validation committee.

However, one really must emphasise that the CEFR descriptors may not be appropriate to significantly different sectors (e.g. primary as opposed to secondary), pedagogic cultures (e.g. Chinese as opposed to French education system) or language domains (e.g. mother tongue education as opposed to modern languages). Spolsky pointed out nearly a quarter of a century ago (1986: 148) that lifting descriptors from the context for which they were developed and using them in another context is quite simply irresponsible. The ELP descriptor adaptations mentioned above take account of this warning. But the point that seems to be generally overlooked is that this caveat applies not just to descriptor content but to descriptor orientation and style as well. For a variety of reasons, descriptors of second language proficiency for adults/teenagers, such as the CEFR descriptors, focus on observable outcomes. In fact, in addition to the CEFR "Can Do" descriptors provided for different communicative language activities (Chapter 4), which tend to attract more notice, the CEFR does provide descriptors for qualitative aspects of language proficiency (Chapter 5) such as the following examples for B1:

> Has enough language to get by, with sufficient vocabulary to express him/herself with some hesitation and circumlocutions on topics such as family, hobbies and interests, work, travel, and current events, but lexical limitations cause repetition and even difficulty with formulation at times. (General Linguistic Range: B1. Council of Europe, 2001: 110)

> Can keep going comprehensibly, even though pausing for grammatical and lexical planning and repair is very evident, especially in longer stretches of free production. (Spoken Fluency: B1. Council of Europe, 2001: 129)

While still focused on outcome rather than process, at least these two descriptors give some picture of emerging competence. It is at least questionable whether descriptors for mainstream child education should confine themselves to describing "Can Do" outcomes, as seems to be the trend in current European school reform projects inspired by the CEFR (e.g. the Swiss project "HarmoS"). During the development of the primary language, surely there should be more educational interest in desirable features of emerging aspects of generative competence, and in the quality of performance achievable with different degrees of scaffolding (e.g. context, explanations, support, opportunities to practice, reference material), rather than just in defining "to-do lists" of tasks children should be able to perform?

Ironically, such approaches tend to be described as "competence-based approaches", with each individual item on the "Can Do" lists being considered to be a "competency". In CEFR terms, they are proficiency tasks, related to CEFR Chapter 4 (Language Use and the Language User/learner) and have nothing to do with CEFR Chapter 5 (The Competences of the User/Learner), where generative abilities such as socio-cultural and inter-cultural competence, linguistic, pragmatic and sociolinguistic competence are described. The reason for this confusion between proficiency and competence is partly the lack of an adequate term with which to translate "proficiency" into European languages and partly confusion of the ELP with the CEFR. However, it also goes back to use of the term "competence" in applied psychology to include skills, proficiency and even performance: "unlike the linguistic view of competence and performance, the communication view considers performance as part of competence – not as a separate concept" (Wiemann and Backlund, 1980: 188). Goffman (1981) summarises:

> A competency, then, can be defined as the capacity to routinely accomplish a given complicated end. An implication is that this end could not have been achieved were the actor unable to accomplish a whole set of slightly different ones, all in the same domain of expertise. (Goffman, 1981: 8, in Davies, 1989: 160)

With regard to children, the problem is that there is a danger that the superficial introduction of a competency approach (= outcomes approach) risks losing sight of the development of precisely the generative competences necessary for lifelong flexibility and learning, the need for which in a changing world is so frequently cited as the reason for such reform in the first place. When the competencies (= descriptors) are then operationalised in standardised test items, the school and teachers made accountable for results on those standardised tests and the curriculum narrowed as a consequence, the result is no longer language education at all.

It is worth pointing out that what is being described here has nothing whatsoever to do with the CEFR and very little to do with the ELP. In a European context it describes the educationally disastrous policies adopted under the English National Curriculum in the early 1990s, now unthinkingly being imported as a panacea to improve PISA results at precisely the point at which they look like finally being abandoned in England itself. This is rather a negative point to end on, but we seem to be in a situation in which, despite the best efforts of the Council of Europe's Language Policy Division to encourage debate and exchange of ideas at an international level, there is a danger that the very success of the CEFR in its domain (second language teaching and learning) is leading to copy-cat operational projects in other educational domains that are not grounded in research or the CEFR literature and that do not think through what they are doing.

note

1. I am grateful to Angeles Ortega Calvo of the Spanish Ministry of Education for this reference.

references

Beacco, J.-C. and Porquier, R. (2008) *Niveau A2 pour le français: Un référentiel.* Paris: Didier.

Beacco, J.-C., Porquier, R. and Bouquet, S. (2004) *Niveau B2 pour le français : Un référentiel.* 2 Vols. Paris: Didier.

Beacco, J.-C., De Ferrari, M., Lhote, G. and Tagliante, C. (2006) *Niveau A1.1 pour le français/référentiel DILF livre.* Paris: Didier.

Beacco, J.-C., Porquier, R. and Bouquet, S. (2007) *Niveau A1 pour le français: Un référentiel.* Paris: Didier.

Bernardin, H. J. and Smith, P. C. (1981). A clarification of some issues regarding the development and use of behaviourally anchored rating scales (BARS). *Journal of Applied Psychology, 66*(4), 458–463.

Borman, W. C. (1986) Behavior-based rating scales. In R. Berk (Ed.), *Performance Assessment: Methods and Applications.* Baltimore, MD: The Johns Hopkins University Press, pp. 100–120.

Canale, M. (1984) On some theoretical frameworks for language proficiency. In C. Rivera (Ed.), *Language Proficiency and Academic Achievement.* Clevedon: Multilingual Matters, pp. 28–40.

Chalhoub-Deville, M. (2009) Standards-based assessment in the U.S: social and educational impact. *Language Testing Matters: Investigating the Wider Social and Educational Impact of Assessment – Proceedings of the ALTE Cambridge Conference, April 2008.* Studies in Language Testing Series 31, Cambridge: Cambridge University Press, pp. 281–300.

Champney, H. (1941) The measurement of parent behavior. *Child Development, 12*(2), 131–166.

Cohen, A. (1994) *Assessing Language Ability in the Classroom* (2nd edition). Rowley, MA: Newbury House/Heinle and Heinle.

Cohen, A. and Olshtain, E. (1993) The production of speech acts by EFL learners. *TESOL Quarterly, 27*(1), 33–56.

Comenius, J. A. (1632) *Didáctica Magna*, Madrid: Akal 1986:222 (cap. XXII). Trad. Saturnino López Peces. English version: *The Great Didactic of John Amos Comenius (Translated into English and edited with biographical, historical, and critical introductions by M. W. Keatinge).* London: A & C. Black, 1896; New York: Russell & Russell, 1967.

Council of Europe (2001) *Common European Framework of Reference for Languages: Learning, Teaching, Assessment.* Cambridge: Cambridge University Press.

Cummins, J. (1980) The cross-lingual dimensions of language proficiency: implications for bilingual education and the optimal age issue. *TESOL Quarterly, 14,* 175–187.

Cummins, J. (1983) Language proficiency and academic achievement. In J. W. Oller (Ed.), *Issues in Language Testing Research.* Rowley, MA: Newbury House, pp. 108–130.

Cummins, J. (1984) Wanted: a theoretical framework for relating language proficiency to academic achievement among bilingual students. In C. Rivera (Ed.), *Language Proficiency and Academic Achievement.* Clevedon: Multilingual Matters, pp. 2–19.

Davies, A. (1989) Communicative competence as language use. *Applied Linguistics, 10*(2), 157–170.

van Ek, J. A. (1976) *The Threshold Level in a European Unit/credit System for Modern Language Learning by Adults*. Strasbourg: Council of Europe.

van Ek, J. A. and Trim, J. L. M. (2001a) *Waystage*. Cambridge: Cambridge University Press.

van Ek, J. A. and Trim, J. L. M. (2001b) *Threshold 1990*. Cambridge: Cambridge University Press.

van Ek, J. A. and Trim, J. L. M. (2001c) *Vantage*. Cambridge: Cambridge University Press.

Ellis, N. (2006) Cognitive perspectives on SLA: the associative-cognitive CREED. *AILA Review, 19*, 100–121.

ELTDU (1976) *Stages of Attainment Scale*. Oxford: English Language Development Unit, Oxford University Press.

Fisher, W. P. (1992) Reliability Statistics. *Rasch Measurement, Transactions of the Rasch Measurement Special Interest Group of the American Educational Research Association, 6*(3), 238.

Fleming, M. (2009) The use of descriptors in learning, teaching and assessment. Paper prepared for the conference *Languages in Education; Languages for Education: Languages of Schooling and the Right to Plurilingual and Intercultural Education*, Strasbourg, 8–10 June 2009, Council of Europe, Language Policy Division, http://www.coe.int/t/dg4/linguistic/LangEduc/ConfLE09-ProgrammePresent_bil.asp#TopOfPage (accessed 6 July 2009).

Fulcher, G. (1993) *The Construction and Validation of Rating Scales for Oral Tests in English as a Foreign Language*, PhD thesis, University of Lancaster.

Fulcher, G. (1996) Does thick description lead to smart tests? A data-based approach to rating scale construction. *Language Testing, 13*(2), 208–238.

Glaboniat, M., Müller, M., Schmitz, H., Rusch, P. and Wertenschlag, L. (2002/2005) *Profile Deutch*, Berlin: Langenscheidt.

Glaser, R. (1963) Instructional technology and the measurement of learning outcomes. *American Psychologist, 18*, 519–521.

Goffman, E. (1981) *Forms of Talk*. Oxford: Basil Blackwell.

Goullier, F. (2007) Impact of the common European framework of reference for languages and the Council of Europe's work on the new European educational area. *The Common European Framework of Reference for Languages (CEFR) and the Development of Language Policies: Challenges and Responsibilities*. Intergovernmental Language Policy Forum, Strasbourg, 6–8 February 2007, Council of Europe, 29–37.

Green, A. (2008) English profile: functional progression in materials for ELT. *Cambridge ESOL Research Notes, 33*, 19–25.

Hargreaves, P. (1992) Round table discussion on the European language portfolio. In B. North (Ed.), *Transparency and Coherence in Language Learning in Europe: Objectives, assessment and certification*. Symposium held in Rüschlikon, 10–16 November 1991. Strasbourg: Council for Cultural Co-operation, 150–158.

Hawkey, R. and Barker, F. (2004) Developing a common scale for the assessment of writing. *Assessing Writing, 9*, 122–159.

Hawkins, J. A. and Buttery, P. (2009) Using learner language from corpora to profile levels of proficiency (CEFR) – Insights from the English profile project. *Language Testing Matters: Investigating the wider social and educational impact of assessment – Proceedings of the ALTE Cambridge Conference, April 2008*. Studies in Language Testing Series 31, Cambridge: Cambridge University Press, 158–175.

Hulstijn, J. (2007) The shaky ground beneath the CEFR: quantitative and qualitative dimensions of language. *Modern Language Journal, 91*(4), 663–666.

IBM (1974) *IBM France Performance Charts.* (Appendix B in Trim, 1978).

Instituto Cervantes (2007) *Niveles de Referencia para el español, Plan Curricular del Instituto Cervantes.* Madrid: Biblioteca Nueva.

Jefferson, G. (1978) Sequential aspects of storytelling in conversation. In J. Schenkein (Ed.), *Studies in the Organization of Conversational Interaction.* New York/London: Academic Press, pp. 219–248.

Jones, N. (2002) Relating the ALTE framework to the common European framework of reference. In J. C. Alderson (Ed.), *Case Studies in the Use of the Common European Framework.* Strasbourg: Council of Europe, pp. 167–183.

Kaftandjieva, F. and Takala, S. (2002) Council of Europe scales of language proficiency: a validation study. In J. C. Alderson (Ed.), *Case Studies in the Use of the Common European Framework.* Strasbourg: Council of Europe, pp. 106–129.

Klein W. (1986) *Second Language Acquisition.* Cambridge: Cambridge University Press.

Lado, R. (1961) *Language Testing. The Construction and Use of Foreign Language Tests: A teacher's book.* London: Longman.

Landy, F. J. and Farr, J. L. (1983) *The Measurement of Work Performance.* New York: Academic Press.

Landy, F. J., Farr, J. L. and Jacobs, R. R. (1982) Utility concepts in performance measurement. *Organizational Behavior and Human Performance, 30,* 15–40.

Little, D. (2007) The common European framework of reference for languages: perspectives on the making of supranational language education policy. *Modern Language Journal, 91*(4), 645–655.

Macdonald, J. and Vandergrift, L. (2007) The CEFR in Canada. Paper given at the intergovernmental Language Policy Forum *The Common European Framework of Reference for Languages (CEFR) and the Development of Language Policies: Challenges and Responsibilities,* Strasbourg, 6–8 February 2007.

Malinowski, B. (1946) The problem of meaning in primitive languages (Supplement 1). In C. K. Ogden and I. A. Richards (Eds), *The Meaning of Meaning* (8th edition), New York: Harcourt, Brace and World, pp. 296–336

Martyniuk, W. (Ed.) (2007) *Towards a Common European Framework of Reference for Languages of School Education? Proceedings of a Conference.* Krakow: Describing and Testing Language Proficiency 12. Universitas.

Meisel, J. H., Clahsen, H. and Pienemann M. (1981) On determining developmental stages in second language acquisition. *Studies in Second Language Acquisition, 3*(2), 109–135.

Mislevy, R. J. (1993) Foundations of a new test theory. In N. Frederiksen, R. J. Mislevy and I. I. Bejar (Eds), *Test Theory for a New Generation of Tests.* Hillsdale, NJ: Lawrence Erlbaum Associates, pp. 19–40.

North, B. (1992) European language portfolio: some options for a working approach to design scales for proficiency. In Council of Europe (1992) *Transparency and Coherence in Language Learning in Europe: Objectives, assessment and certification.* Symposium held in Rüschlikon, 10–16 November 1991. Strasbourg: Council for Cultural Co-operation, 158–174 (Reprinted in Schärer, R. and North, B. (1992) *Towards a Common European Framework for Reporting Language Competency,* NFLC Occasional Paper, Washington D.C.: National Foreign Language Center).

North, B. (2000) *The Development of a Common Framework Scale of Language Proficiency*. New York: Peter Lang.

North, B. (2002) A CEF-based self-assessment tool for university entrance. In J. C. Alderson (Ed.), *Case Studies in the Use of the Common European Framework*. Strasbourg: Council of Europe, pp. 146–166.

North, B. (2007) The CEFR illustrative descriptor scales. *Modern Language Journal*, *91*, 655–658.

North, B. (2008a) The CEFR levels and descriptor scales. In L. Taylor and C. Weir (Eds), *Multilingualism and Assessment: Achieving Transparency, Assuring Quality, Sustaining Diversity– Proceedings of the ALTE Berlin Conference*, Studies in Language Testing Series 27, May 2005. Cambridge: Cambridge University Press, pp. 21–66.

North, B. (2008b) Levels and goals – Central frameworks and local strategies. In B. Spolsky and F. M. Hult (Ed.), *Blackwell Handbook of Educational Linguistics*. Malden, MA: Basil Blackwell, pp. 220–232.

North, B. (2009) The educational and social impact of the CEFR. In L. Taylor and C. Weir (Eds), *Language Testing Matters: Investigating the Wider Social and Educational Impact of Assessment – Proceedings of the ALTE Cambridge Conference*, Studies in Language Testing Series 31, April 2008, Cambridge: Cambridge University Press pp. 357–377.

North, B. and Jones, N. (2009) *Relating Language Examinations to the Common European Framework of Reference for Languages: Learning, Teaching, Assessment (CEFR): Further Material on Maintaining Standards across Languages, Contexts and Administrations by exploiting Teacher Judgment and IRT Scaling*, Strasbourg: Council of Europe, www.coe.int/lang (accessed 10 December 2010).

North, B. and Schneider, G. (1998) Scaling descriptors for language proficiency scales. *Language Testing*, *15*(2), 217–262.

Perie, M. (2008) A guide to understanding and developing performance-level descriptors. *Educational Measurement, Issues and Practice*, Winter 2008, 15–29.

Pienemann, M. (1985) Learnability and syllabus construction. In K. Hyltenstam and M. Pienemann M. (Ed.), *Modelling and Assessing Second Language Development*. Clevedon: Multilingual Matters, pp. 23–75.

Pollitt, A. (1991) Response to Alderson, bands and scores. In J. C. Alderson and B. North (Eds), *Language Testing in the 1990s*. London: Modern English Publications/British Council, Macmillan, pp. 87–94.

Skehan, P. (1984) Issues in the testing of English for specific purposes. *Language Testing*, *1*(2), 202–220.

Smith, P. C. and Kendall, J. M. (1963) Retranslation of expectations: an approach to the construction of unambiguous anchors for rating scales. *Journal of Applied Psychology*, *47*(2), pp. 149–155.

Spolsky, B. (1986) A multiple choice for language testers. *Language Testing, 3*, 147–158.

Spolsky, B. (1995) *Measured Words*. Oxford: Oxford University Press.

Thurstone, L. (1928) Attitudes can be measured. *American Journal of Sociology*, *33*, 529–554.

Trim, J. L. M. (1978) *Some Possible Lines of Development of an Overall Structure for a European Unit/Credit Scheme for Foreign Language Learning by Adults*. Strasbourg: Council of Europe.

Swales, J. M. (1990) *The Genre Analysis: English in Academic and Research Settings*. Cambridge: University Press.

Van Lier, L. (1989) Reeling, writhing, drawling, stretching, and fainting in coils: oral proficiency interviews as conversation. *TESOL Quarterly, 23*(3), 489–508.

Walker, T., Jones, N. and Ashton, K. (2007) Asset languages: a case study of piloting the CEFR Manual. Paper given at the seminar for a joint reflection on the use of the preliminary pilot version of the Manual for *"Relating Language Examinations to the CEFR" 2004–2007: Insights from Case Studies, Pilots and other Projects*. Cambridge, 6–7 December 2007.

Wiemann, J. M. and Backlund, P. (1980) Current theory and research in communicative competence. *Review of Educational Research, 50*(1), 185–199.

Wilds, C. P. (1975) The oral interview test. In B. Spolsky and R. Jones (Eds), *Testing Language Proficiency*. Washington, D.C.: Center for Applied Linguistics, pp. 29–44.

3
testing linguistic relativity
alan davies

introduction

Present doubts about cultural and linguistic universals and concern about the seductive power of relativism, reflecting widespread opposition to globalisation, invite us to recognise that in language testing the social and the cognitive are necessarily linked. What the history of language testing reveals is how the seemingly rival claims of the relative and the absolutist or universal regularly challenge one another, appearing and reappearing over time. To an extent, conflicting interests of the sociolinguistic and the psycholinguistic reflect the enduring philosophical debates between the universal/realist and the relativist/nominalist. In language testing these are the competing claims of the structural and the communicative, a particular example of which is the still current debate on Language for Special Purposes (see below). In each case we see a formal model, which may be regarded as general or canonical, as against a substantial model, which is embedded in local context and dependent on it for its meaning and relevance.

Given the saliency of the universalist/relativist debate in language testing, it is perhaps surprising that language testing has not taken (or has not had to take) account of the Linguistic Relativity Principle; surprising, given the importance accorded to this principle in modern linguistics and the move away in applied linguistics from a formal and formulaic structuralism.

In this chapter, we examine the Linguistic Relativity Principle (also known as the Sapir–Whorf Hypothesis) and seek to explain how, if at all, it relates to the wider concerns of applied linguistics and the narrower concerns of language testing.

linguistic relativity principle

The Linguistic Relativity Principle (LRP) concerns the relationship between language, culture and thought (Hoijer, 1953). The nature of that relationship has always exercised philosophers, surfacing from time to time in the Gog–Magog contests they engage in, which we see in the opposition of universalists/realists and nominalists/relativists. Language has always been a notable prime site for this struggle to take place; hardly surprising, since language is both the medium in which the struggle operates and the source in itself of the struggle.

Similar oppositions occur in language testing: we examine in this article three of these and consider how far the Sapir–Whorf Hypothesis caused these divisions and how it explains them. The three divisions for language testing are:

(1) Language use and language structure
(2) Proficiency: variety or unitary?
(3) The "old" and the "new" validity questions.

The original idea of the LRP was that the semantic structures of different languages are (or might be) incommensurable, and, if they are, then there are possible implications for speakers of particular languages in terms of their thinking and behaviour. In other words, language, thought and culture could be so intertwined that for each language there would or might be a distinctive world view. Given this orientation, it is not surprising that the proponents of this idea were the Germans Herder and Humboldt (1836/1988), who in the early nineteenth century, concerned with promoting the establishment of a united Germany, took a dramatically ideological view of the nation state, Humboldt formulating the doctrine of "one language one nation". Such a view has negative as well as positive links, the negative aligning the view with the fascism of ethnic cleansing in today's Latvia, the positive side (also very much alive today) linking with the movements to maintain minority languages such as the Celtic languages and the somewhat ideological condemnation of linguicide and linguistic imperialism (Phillipson, 1992).

Ideology aside, common sense indicates that there is a relationship of some kind between language and thought. Miscommunication across genders and in international affairs makes this all too obvious, a problem amusingly captured by the ethnomethodological tic-tac-toe studies of Garfinkel (1962). Besides, communication is always messy – you are never sure that your intended message has got through. And so we exaggerate our messages by repeating them in different ways in order to make clear our intention, taking advantage of the linguistic feature of redundancy. Or we limit the opportunity for variety (and therefore for miscommunication) by expanding the range of lingua francas such as today's English. Even between native speakers there are mismatches. Language, it seems, is an attempt to repair cultural mistakes, and, since these are enduring, it may be a vain attempt.

And yet, although miscommunication is pervasive, common sense would suggest that communication is real: however inadequately, individuals do interact with one another; messages do get exchanged; translation, even of poetry, that most difficult and context-bound of all media, does take place. We manage, many of us, to learn other languages to a reasonable degree of fluency. None of this would be possible if we were imprisoned in the language with which we grew up.

There is a sense in which anthropology is the natural academic home of those who take a linguistic relativity view, while psychology belongs to those who dispute it. Ethnography versus positivism: it is not, of course, the case that anthropologists and ethnographers are necessarily relativists, or that psychologists are always positivists. It is just that the psychologist is properly interested in human cognition, which is, as it were, universal, local and regional differences being at a rather more surface level. The ethnographer, on the other hand, is focused on context and how groups are socialised into distinctness and difference.

benjamin lee whorf

Benjamin Lee Whorf, leading advocate of the Linguistic Relativity Principle, graduated from MIT in Chemical Engineering in 1918 and, after a graduate traineeship in fire prevention engineering, became an officer of the Hartford Insurance Company in Connecticut, where he remained until his early death at the age of 44. Whorf was entranced by language and languages. He took a particular interest in the American Indian (now Native American) language Hopi, and when Edward Sapir moved to Yale University in 1931 Whorf enrolled part-time in Sapir's first course in American Indian linguistics. Nominally, Whorf was registered for the degree of PhD, but he never sought or obtained the degree. He was in linguistics for its intellectual interest. What interested him about Hopi was that its grammar seemed to indicate a way of perceiving and thinking that was very different from that of the English speaker. Whorf published articles in the late 1930s and early 1940s on the Hopi language and language situation and what this meant for the way in which the Hopi perceived and organised the world.

> The idea of Linguistic Relativity did not emerge in a full-fledged form until after Whorf had started studying with Sapir...he began to appreciate that the notion of linguistic relativity could be developed not only in 'lexation' but also in grammatical structure' (for example) in the tense and aspect systems of the Hopi verb. (Carroll, 1956: 26)

The following well-known quotation gives a sense of Whorf's view:

> We dissect nature along lines already laid down by our native languages. The categories and types that we isolate from the world of phenomena we do not find there because they stare every observer in the face; on the contrary, the world is presented in a kaleidoscopic flux of impressions which has to be organised by our minds – and this means largely by the linguistic systems in our minds. (Whorf, 1956: 213)

In this Whorf was echoing Sapir, who had famously written:

> Human beings do not live in the objective world alone...The fact of the matter is that the 'real world' is to a large extent unconsciously built up out of the language habits of the group. We see and hear and otherwise experience very largely as we do because the language habits of our community predispose certain choices of interpretation. (Sapir, 1929[1958]: 69)

Whorf was a scientist by training. To support his general philosophical view about the LRP, he needed evidence; hence his detailed analyses of Hopi grammar and hence the question he addressed in his 1930 paper:

> Are not our concepts of 'time' and 'space' or 'matter' given in substantially the same form by experience to all men, or are they in part conditioned by the structure of particular languages? (Sapir, 1929[1958]: 138)

It is this question that underlies the principle of linguistic relativity (the Sapir–Whorf Hypothesis), that these concepts are not substantially the same in different languages. Whorf took as evidence the grammatical systems of Hopi and Standard Average European (SAE, which seems to have been a euphemism for English). He concluded:

> Concepts of 'time' or 'matter' are not given in substantially the same form by experience to all men but depend upon the nature of the language or languages through the use of which they have been developed. They do not depend so much upon any one system (e.g. tense or nouns) within the grammar as upon the ways of analyzing and reporting experience which have become fixed in the language in integrated 'fashions of speaking'... Our own 'time' differs markedly from Hopi 'duration'... Certain ideas born of our own time-concept, such as that of absolute simultaneity, would be either very difficult to express or impossible and devoid of meaning under the Hopi conception and would be replaced by operational concepts. (Sapir, 1929[1958]: 158)

Whorf clearly meant more than the naïve observation that the grammars (and their uses) of both languages differ. So much we know; so much is obvious. What matters is whether these differences have impact on thought and on behaviour. Whorf appears to have decided that they did; I say "appears" because it has never been entirely clear what Whorf really meant. Gumperz and Levinson (1996: 22) maintain that "Whorf's own considered position seems to have been that language influences habitual thought, rather than limiting thought potential." If that indeed is what Whorf meant, he could not properly be accused of "linguistic determinism", the view that there exists a strong causal relationship between one's language and one's thought; that, indeed, what cannot be said cannot be thought. Indeed, it chimes with his admission (see above) that where SAE concepts of time had no Hopi equivalent, they "would be replaced by operational concepts" (ibid.: 158). In other words, languages can always accommodate to new ideas by using periphrasis and alternative lexical resources.

In French you cannot say: "the teacher is pregnant" because "the teacher" is masculine, therefore *Le professeur est enceinte* is ungrammatical. But of course teachers do become pregnant and so "operational concepts" have to be called into operation; thus: *Le professeur, (elle) est enceinte* perhaps.

The idea that there is a relationship, that language influences but not that it determines thought, has come to be regarded as the weak form of the Sapir–Whorf Hypothesis. The strong form of the LRP takes the linguistic determinism position, and, while this is attractive because it allows no compromise, it is not clear whether anyone has seriously taken this extreme position or indeed thought that Whorf himself did. Gumperz and Levinson comment: "many authors find the thesis of linguistic determinism wildly adventurous or even ridiculous" (1996: 23).

But, while discussion of the LRP assumes the "unconscious, repetitive coercive patterning on the grammatical level" (Carroll, 1956: 11), it is common now for scholars to extend the range of its claims into other than grammatical systems. Distinctive grammatical codings are not the only way in which "meanings" or interpretations can vary systematically across cultures. Meaning, in other words, is determined in context, within language in use. Whorf did indeed signal this, as we have seen: "They (different concepts of time etc) 'do not depend so much upon any one system…within a grammar as upon the ways of analysing and reporting experience which have become fixed in the language as integrated 'fashions of speaking'" (Carroll, 1956: 158).

In trying to reach a conclusion on the LRP, we meet a fundamental logical problem. There is no way in which we can know how far the thinking and the behaviour of, for example, the Hopi Indians (or any group) are influenced by their language. Even if we determined that "all" Hopi think and behave the same way, it does not necessarily follow that this is an effect of their Hopi language. It could be other influences, such as modes of upbringing. Whorf, of course, in his primary argument, went further, linking the linguistic patterning to ways of thinking. Perhaps we need (as Gumperz and Levinson suggest) to look beyond language at modes of thought:

> If new theories of language make possible new connections between meaning and context, there are also new, if still incipient, ideas about the nature of thinking and context…the idea of 'technologies of the intellect' by externalizing thoughts or representing them, we are able to manipulate them in quite different ways. (Gumperz and Levinson, 1996: 9)

LRP and language testing

We now explore the three contrasts, mentioned at the beginning of the chapter, that have affected (and still do affect) language testing construct formation. These are:

(1) The opposition between language use and language structure;

(2) The opposition between the approach to proficiency via varieties, as in LSP, and the approach via a unitary view of language. As will be obvious, this opposition has a close affinity to (1);

(3) The opposition between the inductive and the deductive approaches to questions of test validity, in particular to the so-called old and new validity questions.

We take these in turn.

language use and language structure

The idea that language is either use or structure is, of course, false and can be viewed as a heresy (Davies, 2003). The fact is that it is both. If it were only structure, there would be no messages, no meanings; if it were only use, there would be no learning and all exchanges would be by rote memorisation. What this must mean is that the Linguistic Relativity principle is quite neutral in this debate. Language can influence thought whether it is language structure or language "in operation", as Whorf put it. As we have seen, Whorf anticipated the need to range more widely than linguistic structure. But, as we have also seen, the accommodation to language in use for the LRP does surrender the strong view all too easily. After all, it must be the case that language in use (however we term it – discourse, communication) differs from one setting, speaker, and purpose to another.

Even the most certain positivist would have to admit that language use differs for men and women, for example, just as the use of English differs for Americans, British, Australians and so on. Context, in other words, does affect language structure in normal engaged activities. If it did not, there would be no modulation across contexts; again there is no implication for the influence of the LRP. In moving from a largely structural to a moderate communicative/performance view in language testing, there was no commitment on the part of language testing either to a relativist or to a universalist position. It is not that in this move language testing took on board the LRP; rather, it recognised that contexts differed and that within those contexts the "same" language (vocabulary, grammar and so on) would not always mean the same. That would move the onus of responsibility from the language on to its use and thereafter to cultural influences. However, it is never disputed that language has an influence. That influence can be minimal and momentary. But what the strong version of the LRP insists on is that it is in the structure of language that its primary influence on thought belongs. To that extent, then, it could paradoxically be said that the part-move from structural to communicative put on hold for language testing the argument about LRP; and, if language testing must take some account of the LRP, this must be in its weak formulation.

proficiency via varieties and proficiency as unitary

The debate in the language testing literature of the 1970s between the unitary and the multi-competence views was finally ended when John Oller accepted the weakness of his position and the strength of the multi-competence model (Oller, 1984). The argument was not confined to theoretical discussion. The general acceptance of the multiple view made credible the development of tests of LSP, tests that are still widely used in business and the professions and also in the academic context. There, academic language is recognised as a type of LSP. English for academic study is, after all, not the English of everyday life, especially not in its oral mode. And so we have English for chemists, English for medicine, Japanese for tour guides, Italian for hospitality and so on. We also have the International English Language Testing System (IELTS) test of English for academic purposes. However, it is too simple a judgement to say that the unitary–multiple debate is no more. The IELTS test itself is evidence of that ongoing debate; it may still present a kind of LSP-ness by its targeting of academic English. But in the last ten or so years it (and its predecessor the ELTS test) has retreated more than once from the embrace of a full LSP offering. After all, in its heyday the ELTS test made available 6 + 1 alternative Englishes to suit what were thought to be different academic needs. Furthermore, tests of language structure continue to be developed and continue to be used. And the argument, which is basically an argument about the nature of language and the construct of language learning, continues. It is ironically a non-argument, in that it opposes two views that are not commensurable. Language is, as we have argued, both structure and variety, just as music is both rhythm and harmony. On the face of it the *strong* LRP would be very much in favour of the LSP approach, on the grounds that it is only (necessarily) in the language of its domain (medicine, business, tourism, law, teaching) that the meaning can be appreciated, because the domain (content, subject matter, conceptualisation) is indissolubly linked to the language. Indeed, the experience of the ELTS project review (Criper and Davies, 1988) made this very clear; the subject specialists who participated were mostly in favour of the modular approach in the test (one module for one subject specialism), precisely on these grounds. To the investigators, the subject specialists were being naïve; what they believed to be subject-specific was not so at all, except cosmetically (or in terms of Face Validity). Since no module (e.g. medical English) could be specific to a particular discipline (e.g. Anatomy, Psychiatry) itself containing multiple sub-disciplines, it was inevitable that the language of the module was quite general and paid lip service to the notion of specificity by, for example, certain lexical references. The evidence presented by Alderson and Urquhart (1988) demonstrated that students specialising in one or other of the module-specific areas were not advantaged by tests in their area, and others invited to take a test that was not specific to their academic interests were not disadvantaged. What remains is, of course, the dimension of difficulty: the development from basic to advanced literacy is coterminous with gaining access to and understanding of academic discourse. Whether that really should be regarded as an LSP is moot, as is the assumed isomorphism that the strong LRP imputes between the conceptualisation of a domain and the language in which it is expressed. The use of the IELTS test for migration control in Australia does seem to assume that academic discourse, which IELTS is said to exemplify, is not an LSP.

the "old" and the "new" validity questions

The "old" validity question asks: "to what extent does this test measure what it purports to measure?" while the new validity question asks: "just what is it that this test does measure?" (Tyler, 1971). The "old" approach is at bottom a deductive approach; there is an agreed criterion, and what the test at issue aims to do is to represent or simulate that criterion. The new approach is inductive; there is no predetermined criterion. While the old approach thinks it knows, the new approach does not. It looks for a range of types of evidence, all of which are criterial, since there may be different criteria, for example, seeking different predictive information and providing feedback on learner behaviour.

Which approach favours the LRP? Given its strong theoretical orientation (reminiscent of the Contrastive Analysis contentions that language learning problems derive from the lack of fit between the first and the target languages), it must surely be the case that the LRP belongs to the deductive approach. However, while the deductive/inductive and the structural/communicative are not isomorphic, any more than either matches the positivist or the interpretivist, nevertheless there is a likely relation such that deductive, structural, positivist load on one axis while inductive, communicative, interpretivist load on the other. And the attention to context necessarily links the inductive/communicative/interpretivist to the LRP, which insists on the centrality of context.

But it also insists on the centrality of structure. That being so, it seems, once again, that there is no necessary influence either way of the LRP on either the old or the new validity question.

One current issue is whether a local variety of English, say Indian English or Singaporean English, should replace Standard English in national and international tests. It seems clear that such local varieties are not "the same" as Standard English, whether British, American or whatever. How far should this influence the construction of an international test such as IELTS or TOEFL? Since Standard English – in whichever version – has more provenance than a local variety, it is difficult to argue for the inclusion of local variation in an international test if that test is intended for international use. But what of a test intended for national use, for use in the school system of Singapore, for example? This is more problematic. On the basis of the LRP, strong or weak version, a convincing case can be made for using the local standard as the model of a national test of English. That is, of course, if there is agreement on what that local standard is and also if that local standard is acceptable to the local stakeholders, the education authorities, the teachers, parents and students. So far it seems that there is little appetite among local stakeholders – in any polity – to abandon an internationally acceptable standard for a local norm as criterion. Performance on English tests by educated NNS is rated no differently by local and international judges, suggesting that an international standard is as much international as local. Of course, it might be argued that this is only so because NNS are compelled to reach for an international standard and that what they should be allowed to do is to make their own local criterion or norm, to which the only response must be that of course they should be allowed to do so and to point out that it is they themselves who wish to achieve an international standard. In other words, while they could, of course, perform acceptably on a locally normed test, based on what must be a weak LRP, they can also perform satisfactorily on an international test not based on such norms. That suggests either that they can do both – thus discrediting the strong LRP – or that there are no significant differences between the local and the international norm. In either case there is no support here for the strong LRP. Cultures do indeed differ, but they are accessible to outsiders, as anthropologists demonstrate by their research. The problem with English at this point of time is which culture it reflects, given its worldwide spread. But that is just the large-scale version of what is the case for all varieties of English, including the Englishes spoken by mother tongue speakers. All are different, and yet all find their reflection in some version of standard English. Language does indeed reflect thought, but you can express that thought in any language. Thought is indeed prior: the LRP cannot be supported.

references

Alderson, J. C. and Urquhart, A. H. (1988). The effect of students' academic discipline on their performance on ESP reading tests. *Language Testing*, 2(2), 192–204.

Carroll, J. B. (Ed.) (1956). *Language Thought and Reality, Selected Writings of Benjamin Lee Whorf*. Cambridge, MA: The MIT Press.

Criper, C. and Davies, A. (1988). *ELTS Validation Project Report*. London: British Council.

Davies, A. (2003). Three heresies of language testing research. *Language Testing*, 20(4), 355–368.

Garfinkel, H. (1962). Studies in the routine grounds of everyday activities. In J. M. Scher (Ed.), *Theories of the Mind*. New York: The Free Press of Glencoe, pp. 689–712 (Also in H. Garfinkel (1967/1984). *Studies in Ethnomethodology*. Cambridge: Polity Press, pp. 35–75).

Gumperz, J. J. and Levinson, S. C. (Eds) (1996). *Rethinking Linguistic Relativity*. Cambridge: Cambridge University Press.

Hoijer, H. (1953). The relation of language to culture. In A. L. Kroeber (Ed.), *Anthropology Today*. Chicago, IL: Chicago University Press, pp. 554–573.

Humboldt, W. von (1988). *On Language: The Diversity of Human Language-Structure and Its Influence on the Development of Mankind* (Peter Heath, trans). Cambridge: Cambridge University Press (Original work published in 1836).

Oller, J. W. Jr (1984). "g" what is it? In A. Hughes and D. Porter (Eds), *Current Developments in Language Testing*. London: Academic Press.

Phillipson, R. (1992). *Linguistic Imperialism*. Oxford: Oxford University Press.

Sapir, E. (1929). The status of linguistics as a science. In D. G. Mandelbaum (1958). *Edward Sapir Culture, Language and Personality*. Berkeley, CA: University of California Press.

Tyler, L. E. (1971). *Tests and Measurements* (2nd edition). Englewood Cliffs, NJ: Prentice-Hall.

Whorf, B. L. (1956). Science and linguistics. In J. B. Carroll (Ed.), *Language Thought and Reality, Selected Writings of Benjamin Lee Whorf*. Cambridge, MA: The MIT Press (First published in *Technology Review*, MIT, 43, 229–231, 247–248).

4
componentiality in L2 listening

paul joyce

introduction

A theoretically sound understanding of a language skill is an invaluable aid to learning, teaching and testing that discipline. In the case of L2 listening, despite its growing recognition as the "primary channel for language input and acquisition"(Peterson, 2001: 87), aural processing has remained comparatively neglected in both research and pedagogy. As a consequence, there remains a lack of agreement on practically every aspect of the listening process (Powers, 1985; Joiner, 1986). This deficiency is apparent in the dearth of empirical validation for the myriad of sub-skills postulated to influence second language (L2) listening comprehension. These sub-skills have hitherto largely been selected through "logico-deductive speculation, fuelled by professional intuition"(Dunkel, 1991: 444). Such educated assumptions have had far-reaching consequences, forming the basis for theories and taxonomies that shape aural cognitive learning models, classroom pedagogy and language testing constructs.

research procedure

This chapter reports on an experimental study, conducted at a university in Japan, which was designed to shed light on the L2 listening construct. For the purposes of this study, a multi-componential research methodology was employed. The component skills approach involves analysing a unitary concept as a set of interrelated parts. This widely adopted approach is germane, as it can enable the modelling of a complex cognitive process, such as listening, through its constituent components. Indeed, in reference to the closely related skill of read-ing, Carr and Levy (1990: xi) declare that: "Many investigators believe that the kind of full characterization that results from component skills analysis is the only way to get an accurate picture of reading ability, how it changes developmentally, and what creates individual differ-ences among readers". This chapter explains why the particular lin-guistic and psycholinguistic components that were considered to be important for L2 listening were selected and how the sub-skills and the general listening construct were operationalised, and explores the relationship between the various components and listening proficiency through statistical analyses.

literature review and methodology

In this section, there is a brief overview of a number of component skills that are considered predictive of aural comprehension ability and a description of how these sub-skills were operationalised in the study.

L2 syntactic knowledge

A variable that is widely regarded as important to L2 listening profi-ciency is grammar (Brindley and Nunan, 1992; Hansen and Jensen, 1994; Chaudron, 1995). Nevertheless, given that the processing of syn-tax has long been an active research topic, there has been relatively little componential research examining the importance of L2 aural grammatical knowledge to L2 listening. Kertoy and Goertz (1995) corre-lated students' scores on an L1 listening task with their performance on an established L1 grammar sub-test (Stevens and Montgomery, 1985). There was found to be a correlation between the grammar and listen-ing tests of 0.51 ($p < 0.05$). In a second componential study, Alderson (1993) reported on the statistical relationship between a grammar test and an aural proficiency measure. The correlation between the two sets of scores was found to be an impressive 0.78.

The operationalisation of the L2 Syntactic Knowledge construct was based on an adaptation of the Listening Comprehension Test (LCT), a commercially produced aural grammar test (*ELI LCT Manual*, 1986). The content of the LCT was drawn from two commonly used student textbooks of the time, *English Pattern Practices* (Lado and Fries, 1958) and *English Sentence Structure* (Krohn, 1971). To maintain the purity of the construct, the grammatical forms were presented in short decontex-tualised questions or statements. The learners were tasked with select-ing a multiple-choice option that either answered the question or was similar in meaning to the statement. When reviewing the LCT, Kuehn (1993) noted that: "inferences made from [LCT] scores should be limited only to recognition of basic structures in English." To improve the trait purity of the LCT, it was ensured that all vocabulary items in the test were contained in either the 1000 most frequent English words or the vocabulary syllabus followed by all Japanese Junior High School students. Also, when the listening texts were re-recorded, the material was uttered in a relatively slow and formal manner to minimise the influence of reduced forms.

L2 vocabulary breadth

There is also widely believed to be a causal relationship between L2 Vocabulary Breadth and L2 listening proficiency (e.g. Boyle, 1984; Nissan et al., 1996; Goh, 1999, 2000). Nevertheless, Joyce (2003) found there to be a moderate correlation ($r = 0.22$, $p < 0.001$) between the performance of 383 Japanese students on the Vocabulary Levels Test (VLT) (Nation, 1983) and the listening section of a university in-house test. However, since the VLT is delivered through the visual modality, the test may not have provided an accurate reflection of the learners' aural vocabulary breadth. In studies where L2 vocabulary knowledge has been measured aurally, dictation tasks have often been used (e.g. Kelly, 1991; Bonk, 2000; Pemberton, 2003). The results from these studies suggest that vocabulary is important in the understanding of L2 listening. Nevertheless, in all three cases, since participants were required to transcribe connected speech, the construct measured was a conflation of the learners' vocabulary breadth and their ability to recognise words. For the purposes of this research, it was essential that the L2 vocabulary breadth component of the construct remained distinct from the dissociable skill of recognising words within the speech stream.

The assessed material for the L2 Vocabulary Breadth test was sampled from a lemmatised version of the ten-million-word spoken component of the British National Corpus (BNC). To ensure that the meaning of the assessed vocabulary items could not be inferred from context, lexical items were each aurally presented in isolation. However, given the lack of contextual support for the vocabulary, and the consequential potential for misperception, the target items were each presented twice. As the criterion for knowing a word, the participants were required to select the meaning of the presented words from five multiple-choice options. Since all of the participants shared a common first language, the available answer choices consisted of lexical items in the test takers' first language. This approach is recognised to safeguard the trait purity of a vocabulary instrument (Nation, 2001).

L2 phonological modification knowledge

The understanding of fluent spoken input is contingent upon the listener's recognition of words in the speech stream. Since spoken language is phonologically modified through a variety of processes, which "reduce[s] the overt markedness or perceptual saliency, of morphemes"(Henrichsen, 1984: 103), the ability to compensate for the reduced perceptual saliency of the input is regarded as an important factor in L2 listening (Ahn, 1987). Henrichsen (1984) and Ito (2001) employed dictation tasks to investigate the importance of phonological modification knowledge to L2 listening. However, contrary to the researchers' expectations, in the presence of reduced forms there was not found to be a significant interaction between L2 proficiency level and dictation test performance. In an alternative approach, Brown and Hilferty (1986) investigated the effectiveness of teaching reduced forms. The post-test performance of the treatment group was found to be greater than the control group on a reduced forms dictation, the Integrative Grammar Test (IGT) (Bowen, 1976), and a norm-referenced multiple-choice test. However, a statistically significant difference was only recorded between the IGT and dictation scores. On the basis of the results from the above studies, the importance of reduced forms to L2 listening remained inconclusive. Nevertheless, since "a lack of [phonological modification] knowledge is likely to be reflected in reduced comprehension"(Buck, 2001: 33), it was determined that a phonological modification knowledge component would be included in this study.

As was the case with previous phonological modification studies (e.g. Henrichsen, 1984; Brown and Hilferty, 1986; Ito, 2001), the reduced forms construct was operationalised through a dictation test. Since there is currently a lack of quantitative data on the frequency of common reduced forms, the test content was based on the reduced forms that researchers (Weinstein, 1982; Ur, 1984; Brown and Hilferty, 1989; Bond, 2006) considered to be the most important. To ensure the trait purity of the test, three steps were undertaken. Firstly, aural material contained in the test was presented in decontextualised sentences to reduce the influence of semantic processing. Through decontextualising the aural material, it could be ensured that there was sufficient bottom-up focus that: "students can perform very well on a dictation test, and yet have very little understanding of the gist of what they have written down"(Dirven and Oakeshott-Taylor, 1985: 14). Secondly, to ensure that the participants did not have to parse the chunks of language and thereby call upon their linguistic knowledge of the L2, the transcribed sentences were very short. Thirdly, the linguistic difficulty of the assessed material was carefully controlled. This was achieved by ensuring that the structural forms within the sentences were contained in a foundation level textbook (Murphy, 2003) and that all of the vocabulary was on the list of core vocabulary items that are taught at all Japanese Junior High Schools. When marking the tests, one point was awarded for each correctly identified assessed word.

working memory (english) and (japanese)

Working memory (WM) refers to the limited capacity cognitive mechanism involved in the simultaneous storage and processing of information in real time (Harrington and Sawyer, 1992). WM is considered to play a crucial role in a range of cognitive activities, including L1 and L2 comprehension (Ellis and Sinclair, 1996; Miyake and Friedman, 1998; Waters and Caplan, 2004) and warrants inclusion in the study. A highly influential conceptualisation of WM has proven to be the multi-componential model (Baddeley, 1983; Baddeley and Hitch, 1994). According to this paradigm, the WM system is divided into two parts: firstly, the short-term store (STS), which is only capable of storing phonological information for a few seconds; secondly, the central executive (CE), which performs a large number of functions including liaising with aspects of long-term memory to facilitate language processing, as well as interpreting, verifying, and analysing information. While it has been found that learners' L1 and L2 STS capacities are closely related (Glicksberg, 1963; Cook, 1977), the performance of the CE has been found to be heavily dependent on whether the target language is in the participants' L1 or L2 (Loe, 1964; Cook, 1977). As suggested by Buck (1990), this is likely to be due to the tasks measuring the CE being dependent to some degree on language proficiency. Therefore, to avoid conflating WM scores with L2 listening ability, it was determined that the focus would be on the role of the STS in L2 listening.

Working memory was operationalised through English and Japanese random digit tasks. In both cases, after hearing each string of digits, the participants attempted to reproduce the sequence of numbers on a word card. Both measures contained 16 items.

L2 phonological awareness

For successful listening, it is widely acknowledged that word recognition must occur with tremendous accuracy (Buck, 2001; Rost, 2002). It has been found that when there are structural mismatches between the listener's L1 and L2, such that there are meaningful phonetic distinctions in the L2 that are absent from the L1, learners are subject to strong L1 interference (Byrnes, 1984; Yamada et al., 1997; Mora, 2005). For instance, in a study examining the influence of L1 phonological interference on L2 comprehension, Mack (1988) reported that over 70 per cent of the L2 learners' transcription errors were phonemic in nature. Also, Pemberton (2003) found that, when there was a phonological mismatch between Cantonese and English word structures, participants were much less likely to recognise the items.

L2 Phonological Awareness was operationalised through a minimal pair (AX) phonemic discrimination test format. This task involved the participants listening to 80 different word pairs. After hearing each word pair, the test takers were required to indicate whether they had heard the same word repeated or heard two different items. While there were 20 identical distracter pairs, there were 60 items that contained one of six non-native phonemic contrasts that are deemed particularly difficult for Japanese learners to differentiate (Kenworthy, 1987).

L2 sentence stress awareness

As an important aspect of prosody (e.g. Underhill, 1994; Pennington, 1996), sentence stress is used to draw attention to certain information within an utterance. Within the sentence, the syllable receiving primary stress is differentiated from other word sounds through its loudness, length and higher pitch (Roach, 2001). In one of the few studies on the role of sentence stress in L2 listening (Vanderplank, 1985), learners were found to vary widely in where they located the primary stress in a sentence. However, the most proficient students were significantly ($p < 0.05$) more accurate than the remaining learners at locating sentence stress.

The L2 Sentence Stress Awareness task involved the participants listening to a series of 30 decontextualised sentences, which were also printed in the test booklet. After listening to each of the sentences, the learners indicated which of the lexical items carried the main stress. To simplify the task, for each sentence, there were only five possible answer choices. To ensure that reading ability did not become a contaminating factor, the test sentences were drawn from a foundation level L2 English grammar book (Murphy, 2003). Furthermore, it was ensured that all of the lexical items contained in the sentences were either within the 1000 most frequent word families or encompassed by the list of core vocabulary items that are taught at all Japanese Junior High Schools. The word that was selected to receive the primary stress was chosen at random. To ensure that the test was fair, the items were independently validated by a group of native English speakers.

L2 metacognitive listening strategies usage

To this point, there has been a focus on the lower-level processes involved in aural perception. However, there is evidence to suggest that higher-level factors are also of importance (e.g. Bacon, 1992; Goh, 1998, 2000; Vandergrift, 1998). In particular, metacognitive strategies, which enable learners to plan, manage and regulate their learning, have been widely posited to be of value for L2 listening (e.g. Vandergrift, 1996, 1998, 2003; Goh, 1998).

Metacognitive Listening Strategy Usage was measured through an established instrument, the Metacognitive Awareness Listening Questionnaire (MALQ) (Vandergrift, 2005). The questionnaire consists of a series of statements. Each of these statements corresponded to a strategy required for successful L2 listening comprehension. The participants provide information on the frequency of their strategy usage through a five-point scale. To ensure that the questionnaire could be easily understood by the participants, the instrument was translated into the learners' L1. After piloting, it was decided that a revised 17-item version of the MALQ would be used in the main study.

operationalising the criterion variable

As the focus of this study concerns the relationship between the sub-skill components and general listening proficiency, the criterion variable measure needed to focus on a general listening construct. However, the general listening proficiency domain covers a wide range of communicative contexts, and methodological approaches to test construction differ. Therefore, to ensure a robust operationalisation of the criterion variable, two different listening proficiency tests were employed.

The first communicative proficiency instrument was the listening section of the Kanda English Proficiency Test (KEPT). The KEPT listening test is a norm-referenced, video-mediated, general proficiency test of English as a foreign language. The version of the KEPT test that was employed in this study contained 39 MCQ items. Of these, 35 were based on six extended passages. These extended passages encompassed a wide range of genres, functions and difficulty levels. The remaining four questions were based on four short single item texts. The second operationalisation of the criterion variable was the listening section of the TOEFL. The paper-based version of the TOEFL was used, which assesses a very broad construct of "the ability to understand English as it is spoken in North America" (ETS, 2009).

There are important similarities and differences between the listening sections of the KEPT and TOEFL. In terms of their similarities, both tests have a shared emphasis on assessing the learners' ability to infer beyond literal meanings. This is important, as inferencing is considered to be at the core of language processing (Weir, 1993; Thompson, 1995; Buck, 2001). Furthermore, the inclusion of inferential items clearly differentiated the general proficiency tests from the sub-skill instruments that required a more mechanistic understanding of localised linguistic information. On the other hand, there is a significant difference in the length of the assessed material that is used in the two tests, and the number of questions associated with each dialogue. The bulk of the KEPT listening section is based upon extended texts with around six items per passage. In contrast, for the most part, the assessed material for the TOEFL consists of short texts that are associated with a single item. Furthermore, since the KEPT test questions are printed in the test booklet, the candidates have a clear purpose for listening. Yet, in the case of the TOEFL, the questions are presented aurally, after the listening passage has been heard. Also, while the listening section of the KEPT was video-mediated, the TOEFL was not accompanied by visual images. Therefore, although the two communicative language tests share a number of similarities, the instruments also vary significantly in their format and delivery.

participants

The research population was drawn from a Japanese university specialising in foreign languages. After the removal of two outliers, 443 students undertook all nine of the different research instruments. In terms of proficiency, the participants could broadly be described as being from a false beginner to an upper intermediate level (TOEFL scores of approximately 357–513).

data processing

To enable a comparison of the participants across different tests, the Rasch model was used to convert the raw scores into IRT ability estimates. However, since IRT values are often negative, which are both unintuitive and unsuited to some statistical techniques, the logit figures were transformed into positive scores that were centred on a mean of 50.

The KEPT and TOEFL tests are separately able to provide important perspectives on listening proficiency. However, by combining the results from the two research instruments, a less method-dependent estimate of the participants' ability could be derived. To obtain a composite score, the IRT person ability estimates for each learner on the KEPT and TOEFL tests were first separately calculated, transformed, and then averaged. An established procedure for deriving the reliability estimate for the combined test was used (see Evans, 1996).

To ensure that the data met the assumptions necessary for the later statistical analyses, the data were screened. Firstly, the univariate outliers were identified. The six cases with z-scores in excess of 3.29 ($p < 0.001$, two-tailed) were considered potential outliers (see Tabachnick and Fidell, 2001). These outlying scores were assigned a value one unit greater than the next most extreme non-outlying value in the distribution (see ibid.; Field, 2005). Secondly, the data were screened for multivariate outliers through the use of Mahalanobis distances. With the criterion set at $p < 0.001$, there were found to be two such outliers. These discrepant cases were removed from the study, leaving 443 in the final population sample. After the removal of the outlying cases, it was ensured that the score distribution was normal. Since larger data-sets that scarcely deviate from normality are often found to be non-normally distributed, Bachman (2004) recommends that absolute skewness and kurtosis figures of between –2 and +2 are indicative of a reasonably normal distribution.

results

background data

The transformed IRT scores for the various tests can be found in Table 4.1. The Cronbach alpha values for the test scores were found to range between 0.74 and 0.87, while the Rasch person reliability estimates fell between 0.75 and 0.84. Furthermore, since the various sets of scores were considered to be normally distributed, it was considered that the results formed a robust basis upon which to explore the individual and collective relationship between the sub-skill components and listening proficiency.

measured variables accounting for L2 listening performance

As a first step in investigating the relationship between the measured variables, the Pearson correlations between the sub-skill test scores were examined (see Table 4.2).

All of the raw correlations between the criterion variable and the eight aural sub-skills were found to be statistically significant. The largest

Table 4.1   Summary of the test results ($n = 443$)

Test	k	Mean	SD	Min.	Max.	Skew.	Kurt.	Rel. (α)
KEPT–TOEFL	N/A	51.67	6.26	33.95	71.05	0.43	0.23	0.85
KEPT	39	53.43	7.40	31.90	75.40	0.24	−0.10	0.74
TOEFL	50	49.91	6.47	31.80	71.00	0.45	0.22	0.76
Syntactic knowledge	60	53.83	7.27	35.00	77.80	0.35	0.31	0.82
Vocab. Breadth	40	60.63	11.03	29.90	90.50	0.33	0.08	0.86
PMK	69	55.80	9.43	29.40	87.70	0.49	0.75	0.87
WM (English)	16	52.98	13.94	15.40	84.70	0.04	−0.14	0.77
WM (Japanese)	16	40.58	15.03	14.30	84.70	0.26	−0.27	0.79
Phon. awareness	60	58.53	8.89	42.00	80.10	0.67	0.57	0.80
Sentence stress	30	59.22	11.48	31.30	87.40	0.12	−0.22	0.84
Metacognitive usage	17	56.13	5.35	40.00	72.10	0.11	0.64	0.74

Table 4.2   Simple bivariate correlations among the variables ($n = 443$)

	1	2	3	4	5	6	7	8	9
1. KEPT–TOEFL	–	0.72***	0.23***	0.64***	0.10*	0.19***	0.23***	0.36***	0.26***
2. Syntactic know.		–	0.31***	0.60***	0.14**	0.24***	0.23***	0.34***	0.20***
3. Vocabulary Br.			–	0.19***	0.10*	0.12**	0.11*	0.09*	0.04
4. Phon. mod. know.				–	0.15**	0.17***	0.30***	0.34***	0.22***
5. WM (English)					–	0.51***	0.07	0.19***	−0.01
6. WM (Japanese)						–	0.09*	0.18***	0.04
7. Phon. awareness							–	0.23***	0.16***
8. Sent. Stress aw.								–	0.11**
9. Metacog. strats.									–

Note: ***$p < 0.001$, **$p < 0.01$, *$p < 0.05$ (one-tailed)

disattenuated correlation was found to be between KEPT–TOEFL and Syntactic Knowledge at 0.72 ($p < 0.001$). This correlation was slightly higher than that of the Phonological Modification Knowledge sub-skill, which was 0.64 ($p < 0.001$). The greatest correlation between the various explanatory variables was found to be between Syntactic Knowledge and Phonological Modification Knowledge at 0.60 ($p < 0.001$). The two

WM measures were found to have weak correlational relationships with L2 listening proficiency. In the case of WM (Japanese), a corrected correlation of 0.19 ($p < 0.001$) was recorded, which compared favourably with the 0.10 ($p < 0.05$) correlation for the WM (English) scores. Unsurprisingly, there was a 0.51 ($p < 0.001$) intercorrelation between the two sets of scores.

The multiple regression procedure was performed with the composite KEPT–TOEFL scores as the dependent variable (DV) and the eight skill and knowledge variables as the independent variables (IVs). Since the order in which the variables are entered into the regression model should be taken on a principled theoretical basis (Wright, 1997; Tabachnick and Fidell, 2001; Field, 2005), the hierarchical approach to the order of variable entry was adopted. When determining the entry order, it was important to recognise the hierarchical nature of the skill and knowledge variables, and to prioritise the lower-level sub-skills over the more complex ones. The WM (Japanese) scores were the first to be entered, followed by those for WM (English). The WM scores were succeeded by the Phonological Awareness and the Sentence Stress Awareness scores, as these tasks were designed purely to tap perception. Following the lexical breadth test, the scores on the L2 Phonological Modification Knowledge measure were submitted. The penultimate scores to be employed were those from the Syntactic Knowledge test. The results from the L2 Metacognitive Listening Strategy Usage questionnaire were entered last. After each variable was entered into the model, there was an assessment of whether the remaining predictors significantly contributed to the statistical model (F at $p < 0.05$).

A statistically significant regression model comprising four explanatory variables emerged (F 4, 438 = 158.58, $p < 0.001$). As can be seen in Table 4.3, the standardised partial regression coefficients indicate that Syntactic Knowledge ($\beta = 0.50$, $p \leq 0.001$) made the greatest independent contribution to L2 listening performance. This was followed by L2

Table 4.3 Summary of multiple regression for variables predicting KEPT–TOEFL performance ($n = 443$)

Variable	B	S.E. (B)	β	p
Sentence stress awareness	0.04	0.02	0.08	0.012
Phonological mod. know.	0.19	0.03	0.29	0.000
Syntactic knowledge	0.43	0.03	0.50	0.000
Metacognitive strategies	0.11	0.04	0.09	0.004

Table 4.4   Two factor pattern matrix after a direct oblimin rotation (*n* = 443)

	Component	
	1	2
KEPT	0.820	−0.003
TOEFL	0.827	−0.086
Syntactic knowledge	0.828	0.059
Vocabulary breadth	0.323	0.138
Phon. mod. know.	0.791	0.017
WM (English)	−0.014	0.865
WM (Japanese)	0.093	0.816
Phonological awareness	0.412	0.017
Sentence stress awareness	0.473	0.220
Metacognitive strategies	0.424	−0.210

Phonological Modification Knowledge (β = 0.29, $p \leq 0.001$). Although reaching statistical significance, L2 Sentence Stress Awareness (β = 0.08, $p \leq 0.05$) and L2 Listening Metacognitive Strategy Usage (β = 0.09, $p \leq 0.01$) were much weaker predictors. Collectively, the four variables accounted for 59 per cent of the variance (adjusted R^2 = 0.59).

identifying latent variables: exploratory factor analysis

In order to explain the relationships between the observed variables through a smaller number of latent variables, the results were first submitted to principal components analysis (PCA). As a prerequisite to analysing the PCA results, through the Kaiser–Meyer–Olkin measure of sampling adequacy (0.82) and Bartlett's Test of Sphericity (approx. Chi-Square =1190.06, df = 45, $p < 0.001$), it was found that the variables would yield sufficiently distinct and reliable factors.

Through both the Kaiser Criterion method of component identification and an examination of the scree plot, the data was found to contain two explanatory factors. The first component received a 3.51 eigenvalue loading, while the loading value for the second component was 1.42. After extracting the two factors, since EFL-related factors are likely to correlate, an oblique factor rotation (direct oblimin) was used. The analysis yielded the two factor pattern matrix contained in Table 4.4.

Although the model was found to explain 49 per cent of the variance in the scores, the first factor accounted for the vast majority of the explained variance (35 per cent). When interpreting the strength of a factor loading, a figure of below 0.40 is considered unworthy of interpretation (Stevens, 1992). Of the ten variables, seven were found to have an interpretable loading of more than 0.40 on this first factor. Notably, the two aural proficiency measures of KEPT (0.820) and TOEFL (0.827) yielded particularly high loadings. Furthermore, the two best predictors of L2 aural proficiency, Syntactic Knowledge (0.828) and Phonological Modification Knowledge (0.791), also generated excellent values. Given the pattern of loadings, there is a clear suggestion that the common underlying trait is closely associated with a global listening skill. Therefore, this unobserved variable was labelled "L2 Aural Processing". It is noteworthy that, in accordance with the results from the measured variables, Vocabulary Breadth was not found to make an interpretable contribution to this global dimension. The second factor accounted for 14 per cent of the score variance and was constituted of WM (English) (0.865) and WM (Japanese) (0.816). Owing to the composition of this latent variable, it will henceforth be termed "Working Memory". The correlation between the two components (0.17) suggests that, while Working Memory is somewhat correlated with Aural Processing Proficiency, the two are distinctly different skills.

testing the principal components analysis model using structural equation modelling

To further investigate the preliminary model derived from the PCA, the data were submitted to SEM. To ensure that the model was not mis-specified, only those skill variables that were shown by the PCA to meaningfully overlap with the two components were entered. As can be seen in Figure 4.1, conventional SEM symbols were employed. That is, circles or ellipses represent unobserved latent variables, and rectangles denote observed variables. The single-headed arrows symbolise regression paths, and the double-headed arrow portrays a covariance with no implied direction of effect. For each of the measured variables, there is an associated measurement error (e1–e9).

For the purposes of model estimation, the maximum likelihood estimation technique was used. To ensure that this statistical approach could be applied, the data were examined using Mardia's (1970)

Table 4.5 Model fit statistics

χ^2	p	χ^2/df	RMSEA	GFI	CFI	NFI	PGFI	PCFI	PNFI
48.331	0.005	1.859	0.044	0.976	0.980	0.958	0.564	0.708	0.692

normalised estimate of multivariate normality, and three outlying cases were removed. To evaluate how well the data fitted the theoretical model, a wide range of fit indices were used. As can be seen in Table 4.5, the CMIN test yielded a value of 48.331 ($p = 0.005$), which denotes that the difference between the model and the data was not small enough to be statistically non-significant. However, since the χ^2 statistic is sensitive to sample size, there is a tendency for there to be a false negative result for population sizes exceeding 200 (Arbuckle and Wothke, 1999; Schumacker and Lomax, 2004). The other fit indices suggested that there was a good fit between the specified model and the data. The χ^2/df was within 2.0 (see Byrne, 2001), the comparative indices of the GFI, CFI and NFI were all greater than 0.95 (see Schumacker and Lomax, 2004), the parsimony adjusted indices (the PGFI, the PCFI, and the PNFI) exceeded 0.5 (see Mulaik et al., 1989), and the RMSEA value was less than 0.05 (see Hu and Bentler, 1999; Byrne, 2001; Kline, 2005).

The structural equation model consisting of two latent variables that has been found to satisfactorily account for the observed covariance matrix is depicted in Figure 4.1. The unobserved L2 Aural Processing factor was found to have a significant, direct, positive relationship with seven of the observed variables.

The standardised regression values for these seven variables ranged between 0.30 and 0.81. The best predictor of L2 Aural Processing was found to be Syntactic Knowledge (0.81). This result further suggests that grammatical knowledge is closely related to L2 Aural Processing. However, the strength of the association between grammar and the latent variable was matched by the proficiency scores for KEPT (0.81), and closely followed by TOEFL (0.77). Therefore, the findings confirm that the main unobserved factor is also closely tied to a global L2 listening ability. An additional strong predictor of L2 Aural Processing was Phonological Modification Knowledge (0.73). Although the strength of the regression coefficient for this sub-skill was marginally less than that for the preceding sets of scores, the ability to segment connected speech is confirmed as central to L2 listening. The remaining predictors of Sentence Stress Awareness (0.43), Phonological Awareness (0.31) and Metacognitive Strategies (0.30) formed a weaker relationship with L2 Aural Processing. However, the substantial standardised regression weights for these variables suggest that the awareness of prosody and phonemic contrasts, as well as the use of Metacognitive Strategies, are significant dimensions to L2 Aural Processing.

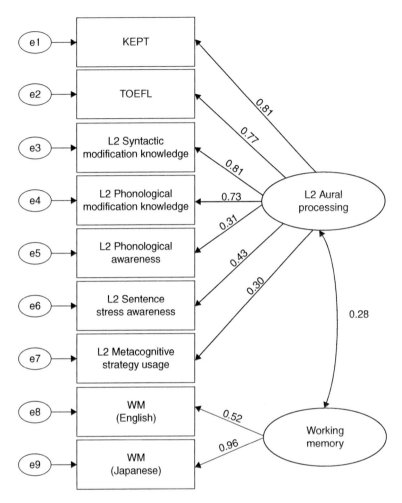

Figure 4.1 SEM standardised parameter estimates

The second unobserved factor was Working Memory. While both of the indicators of Working Memory were statistically significant, WM (Japanese) (0.96) formed a greater association with the latent variable than WM (English) (0.52). As was envisaged, L2 Aural Processing and Working Memory were found to covary (0.28). However, since the correlation between the two factors was fairly weak, it is clear that the two unobserved variances are distinct components.

discussion

As previously discussed, this study sought to explore the individual and collective relationship between the various linguistic and psycholinguistic sub-skills and L2 listening proficiency. In summary, the selected linguistic knowledge and psycholinguistic processing sub-skills were found to collectively account for 59 per cent of the variance in the Japanese learners' L2 listening comprehension ability. In terms of the individual sub-skills, the sub-skills most closely related to the latent L2 Aural Processing factor were L2 Syntactic Knowledge (r = 0.81) and Phonological Modification Knowledge (r = 0.73). The correlation and regression findings do not necessarily indicate that the relationship between the two primary predictors and L2 aural proficiency is causative. Nevertheless, since listening involves the complex interaction of syntactic and phonological modification skills, it seems reasonable to surmise that knowledge of these sub-skills has an important role in rendering the input comprehensible. In this section, the relationship between the grammatical and lexical results from this study and previous research in the field is considered.

The findings from this study have supported the value of Syntactic Knowledge to L2 listening performance. The results bear the greatest similarity to studies that have also attempted to systematically isolate the effects of Syntactic Knowledge on listening comprehension. As was previously discussed, after correlating their participants' L1 grammar and L1 listening task scores, Kertoy and Goertz (1995) found the relationship between the scores to be 0.51 ($p < 0.05$). Similarly, Alderson (1993) reported a covariance of 0.78 between a written L2 grammar test and a L2 listening aural proficiency measure. The findings from this study are also consistent with much of the previous qualitative work. For instance, in a study involving Chinese L2 learners (Goh, 2000), a commonly reported problem was the inability of learners to form a mental representation of the input by connecting the language. For instance, one L2 learner remarked: "I can understand most of the words, but I can't join them together and understand whole sentences meaning"(p. 62), while another lamented that: "I could not put all of the words into a full sentence to get a full idea"(p. 64).

When considering the importance of vocabulary to L2 listening, it is worth recalling the multidimensional nature of lexical knowledge (McCarthy, 1990; Nation, 2001; Qian, 2002). For the purposes of aural comprehension, the listener is essentially faced with two particular tasks: Firstly, the segmentation of the speech stream into individual lexical items; secondly, the activation of word meanings. The ability to accurately segment phonologically modified speech was found to be a strong predictor of the latent L2 Aural Processing variable ($r = 0.73$). However, perhaps more strikingly, although the lexical items in the test were among the most common in the language, the learners were only capable of transcribing 59 per cent of them from connected speech. Indeed, although this figure is considered low, it compares favourably with the results from other phonological modification studies. For instance, the control group in Brown and Hilferty's (1986) study recognised a mere 35 per cent of the highly frequent words that they heard. And, at the first attempt, Pemberton (2003) found that his participants were only capable of transcribing 50 per cent of words from the most frequent 1000 words of the language.

In deciphering connected speech, the participants were found to partly rely on their knowledge of grammar, as there was a 0.60 ($p < 0.001$) correlation between Phonological Modification Knowledge and Syntactic Knowledge. Therefore, as suspected by Henrichsen (1984) and Ito (2001), grammatical knowledge can compensate for a loss of saliency in the acoustic signal. Nevertheless, since the recognition of reduced forms made a substantial unique contribution to the prediction of L2 listening performance ($\beta = 0.29$, $p \leq 0.001$), it is considered that Phonological Modification Knowledge and Syntactic Knowledge tap overlapping but distinct capabilities.

The L2 Vocabulary Breadth results stand in contrast to much of the lexical research that was reviewed (i.e. Kelly, 1991; Bonk, 2000; Pemberton, 2003). However, as was discussed, although many of the previous studies primarily ascribe poor performance to insufficient lexical breadth, the researchers made little attempt to differentiate between whether the vocabulary was unknown to the learners or simply not recognised. In contrast, in the reviewed study that utilised a trait definition of vocabulary (Joyce, 2003), there was found to be a similarly moderate relationship between L2 listening proficiency and L2 Vocabulary Breadth ($r = 0.22$, $p < 0.001$).

The reason for the relatively unimportant role of L2 Vocabulary Breadth in L2 listening proficiency is less clear. However, it is likely that the results are due to a combination of factors. Firstly, since studies of spoken language suggest that a vocabulary of 2000 word families can provide over 95 per cent coverage of aural texts (e.g. Schonell et al.,

1956), it is possible that most of the participants may have acquired a sufficiently broad vocabulary to understand the vast majority of the lexis within the assessed material. Secondly, provided that the test takers understand enough of the aural texts, there is evidence to suggest that they can infer the meaning of unknown vocabulary from context (Hu and Nation, 2000). Thus, when undertaking the listening proficiency measures, L2 listeners may simply be able to compensate for any lexical gaps in their understanding. Thirdly, rather than evaluating the learners' vocabulary breadth, there is evidence to suggest that many test questions inadvertently assess the listeners' ability to match the lexical items from the text with the correct multiple-choice option (Freedle and Kostin, 1996). Therefore, rather than rewarding those with a broad vocabulary, many items could favour those with developed test-taking strategies.

summary and implications for language testing

This study has sought to provide a clearer understanding of the character of L2 listening by adopting a multivariate approach. The findings have affirmed L2 listening to be a complex active skill that is comprised of multiple processes. More specifically, the findings have not only provided a guide to the collective importance of the selected aural components, but have also enabled a comparison between the various linguistic and psycholinguistic sub-skills. There are a number of implications from the findings for the testing of L2 listening. Firstly, since the results shed light on the nature of the L2 listening construct, the study provides test developers with a new perspective on the sub-skills underpinning L2 aural proficiency. This guide contrasts with the benchmark descriptors, such as the CEFR, which are not based on a theoretical perspective of language. Secondly, more specifically, the results suggest that, when developing an L2 listening comprehension test, it is essential that test designers include the ability to accurately process syntax and reduced forms. Thirdly, due to the importance of grammar and connected speech to L2 listening, when seeking to adjust the difficulty of a text, these sub-skills could be used as constraints on comprehension. Indeed, there is an argument for calibrating the difficulty of listening tests through the selection of grammatical forms. This could be done by embedding selected syntactic forms into the necessary information required to correctly answer particular test questions. Nevertheless, in the interests of face and content validity, L2 listening tests need to retain a broad focus on the application of understanding to the wider communicative context.

references

Ahn, S. (1987). *Sandhi-Variation and Affective Factors as Input Filters to Comprehension of Spoken English Among Korean Learners*. Austin, TX: University of Texas at Austin.

Alderson, J. C. (1993). The relationship between grammar and reading in an English for academic purposes test battery. In D. Douglas and C. Chapelle (Eds.), *A New Decade of Language Testing Research: Selected Papers From the 1990 Language Testing Research Colloquium*. Alexandria, VA: TESOL.

Arbuckle, J. and Wothke, W. (1999). *AMOS 4.0 User's Guide*. Chicago, IL: Smallwaters.

Bachman, L. F. (2004). *Statistical Analyses for Language Assessment*. Cambridge: Cambridge University Press.

Bacon, S. M. (1992). The relationship between gender, comprehension, processing strategies, and cognitive and affective response in foreign language listening. *Modern Language Journal, 76*, 160–178.

Baddeley, A. D. (1983). Working memory. *Philosophical Transactions of the Royal Society of London, B, 302*, 311–324.

Baddeley, A. D. and Hitch, G. J. (1994). Developments in the concept of working memory. *Neuropsychology, 8*, 485–493.

Bond, K. (2006). Reduced forms. *The Literacy Builder, 6*, 3. Available at http://ww2.copiaguelibrary.org/literacy/LitBuilderMar06.pdf (accessed 18 November 2006).

Bonk, W. J. (2000). Second language lexical knowledge and listening comprehension. *International Journal of Listening, 14*, 14–31.

Bowen, J. D. (1976). Current research on an integrative test of English grammar. *RELC Journal, 7*, 30–37.

Boyle, J. (1984). Factors affecting listening comprehension. *ELT Journal, 38*(1), 34–38.

Brindley, G. and Nunan, D. (1992). Draft bandscales for listening. *IELTS Research Projects 1992*. National Centre for English Language Teaching and Research. Macquarie University, Sydney, Australia.

Brown, J. and Hilferty, A. (1986). Listening for reduced forms. *TESOL Quarterly, 20*(4), 759–763.

Brown, J. and Hilferty, A. (1989). Teaching reduced forms. *Gendai Eigo Kyoiku*, January, 26–28.

Buck, G. (1990). *The Testing of Second Language Listening Comprehension*. Unpublished PhD thesis. Lancaster University.

Buck, G. (2001). *Assessing Listening*. Cambridge: Cambridge University Press.

Byrne, B. N. (2001). *Structural Equation Modeling with AMOS*. Rahwah, NJ: Erlbaum.

Byrnes, H. (1984). The role of listening comprehension: A theoretical base. *Foreign Language Annals, 17*, 317–329.

Carr, T. H. and Levy, B. A. (1990). Preface. In T. H. Carr and B. A. Levy (Eds), *Reading and its Development: Component Skills Approaches*. San Diego, CA: Academic Press.

Chaudron, C. (1995). Academic listening. In D. Mendelsohn and J. Rubin (Eds.), *A Guide for the Teaching of Second Language Listening*. San Diego, CA: Dominic Press, pp. 74–96.

Cook, V. J. (1977). Cognitive processes in second language research. *IRAL*, *15*(1), 1–20.

Dirven, R. and Oakeshott-Taylor, J. (1985). Listening comprehension (Part 2). *Language Teaching*, *18*, 2–20.

Dunkel, P. (1991). Listening in the native and second/foreign language: towards an integration of research and practice. *TESOL Quarterly*, *25*(3), 431–457.

ELI LCT Manual. (1986). English Language Institute: The University of Michigan.

Ellis, N. C. and Sinclair, S. G. (1996). Working memory in the acquisition of vocabulary and syntax: putting language in good order. *The Quarterly Journal of Experimental Psychology*, *49*(A)(1), 234–250.

ETS. (2009). *TOEFL PBT Test Content*. Available at http://www.ets.org/portal/site/ets/menuitem.1488512ecfd5b8849a77b13bc3921509/?vgnextoid=ed872d363 1df4010VgnVCM10000022f95190RCRD&vgnextchannel=555ad898c84f4010 VgnVCM10000022f95190RCRD (accessed 5 August 2009).

Evans, L. D. (1996). Calculating achievement composite scores for regression discrepancy models. *Learning Disability Quarterly*, *19*(4), 242–249.

Field, A. (2005). *Discovering Statistics Using SPSS* (2nd edition). London: Sage.

Freedle, R. and Kostin, I. (1996). *The Prediction of TOEFL Listening Comprehension Item Difficulty for Minitalk Passages: Implications for Construct Validity*. Princeton, NJ: ETS Research Report RR 96-29.

Glicksberg, D. H. (1963). *A Study of the Span of Immediate Memory among Adult Students of English as a Foreign Language*. PhD dissertation. University of Michigan.

Goh, C. C. M. (1998). How ESL learners with different listening abilities use comprehension strategies and tactics. *Language Teaching Research*, *2*, 124–147.

Goh, C. C. M. (1999). How much do learners know about the factors that influence their listening comprehension? *Hong Kong Journal of Applied Linguistics*, *4*(1), 17–39.

Goh, C. C. M. (2000). A cognitive perspective on language learners' listening comprehension problems. *System*, *28*, 55–75.

Hansen, C. and Jensen, C. (1994) Evaluating lecture comprehension. In J. Flowerdew (Ed.) *Academic Listening: Research Perspectives*. Cambridge: Cambridge University Press.

Harrington, M. and Sawyer, M. (1992). L2 working memory capacity and the L2 reading skill. *Studies in Second Language Acquisition*, *14*, 25–38.

Henrichsen, L. E. (1984). Sandhi-variation: A filter of input for learners of ESL. *Language Learning*, *34*(3), 103–126.

Hu, L. T. and Bentler, P. M. (1999). Cut-off criteria for fit indices in covariance structure analysis: Conventional criteria versus new alternatives. *Structural Equation Modeling*, *6*, 1–55.

Hu, M. and Nation, I. S. P. (2000). Vocabulary density and reading comprehension, *Reading in a Foreign Language*, *13*, 403–430.

Ito, Y. (2001). Effect of reduced forms on ESL learners' input-intake process. *Second Language Studies, 20*(1), 99–124.

Joiner, E. (1986). Listening in the foreign language. In B. H. Wing (Ed.), *Listening, Reading, Writing: Analysis and Application*. Middlebury, VT: Northeast Conference on the Teaching of Foreign Languages, pp. 43–70.

Joyce, P. D. (2003). The breadth of vocabulary learning at a Japanese university. *KOTESOL Conference Proceedings 2003*. Seoul, 18–20 October, 2003, 171–182.

Kelly, P. (1991). Lexical ignorance: The main obstacle to listening comprehension with advanced foreign language learners. *IRAL, 29*(2), 135–149.

Kenworthy, J. (1987). *Teaching English Pronunciation*. London: Longman.

Kertoy, M. K. and Goertz, K. M. (1995). The relationship between listening comprehension performance on the sentence verification technique and other measures of listening comprehension. *Contemporary Educational Psychology, 20*, 320–339.

Kline, R. B. (2005). *Principles and Practice of Structural Equation Modelling* (2nd edition). New York: Guilford.

Krohn, R. (1971). *English Sentence Structure*. Ann Arbor, MI: University of Michigan Press.

Kuehn, P. (1993). *Review of the Listening Comprehension Test*. Buros Institute of Mental Measurements Test Reviews Online.

Lado, R. and Fries, C. C. (1958). *English Patterns Practices*. Ann Arbor, MI: University of Michigan Press.

Loe, B. M. (1964). *Immediate Memory Span in English and Chinese Sentences of Increasing Length*. Unpublished Master's thesis. Georgetown University, Washington, DC.

McCarthy, M. (1990). *Vocabulary*. Oxford: Oxford University Press.

Mack, M. (1988). Sentence processing by non-native speakers of English: Evidence from the perception of natural and computer-generated anomalous L2 sentences. *Journal of Neurolinguistics, 3*, 293–316.

Mardia, K. V. (1970). Measures of multivariate skewness and kurtosis with applications. *Biometrika, 57*, 519–530.

Miyake, A. and Friedman, N. (1998). Individual differences in second language proficiency: Working memory as language aptitude. In A. F. Healy and L. E. Bourne (Eds), *Foreign Language Learning: Psycholinguistic Studies on Training and Retention*. Mahwah, NJ: Erlbaum, pp. 339–364.

Mora, J. C. (2005). Lexical knowledge effects on the discrimination of non-native phonemic contrasts in words and non-words by Spanish/Catalan bilingual learners of English. *Proceedings of the ISCA Workshop in Speech Perception*. London, June 15–17, 2005.

Mulaik, S. A., James, L. R, Van Altine, J., Bennett, N., Lind, S. and Stilwell, C. D. (1989). Evaluation of goodness-of-fit indices for structural equation models. *Psychological Bulletin, 105*, 430–445.

Murphy, R. (2003). *Essential Grammar in Use with Answers: A Self-Study Reference and Practice Book for Elementary Students of English*. Cambridge: Cambridge University Press.

Nation, I. S. P. (1983). Testing and teaching vocabulary. *Guidelines, 5*(1), 12–25.

Nation, I. S. P. (2001). *Learning Vocabulary in Another Language*. Cambridge: Cambridge University Press.

Nissan, S., DeVincenzi, F. and Tang, L. (1996). *An Analysis of Factors Affecting the Difficulty of Dialogue Items in TOEFL Listening Comprehension [TOEFL Research Report 51]*. Princeton, NJ: Educational Testing Service.

Pemberton, R. (2003). *Spoken Word Recognition and L2 Listening Performance; An Investigation of the Ability of Hong Kong Learners to Recognise the Most Frequent Words of English when Listening to News Broadcasts.* Unpublished PhD thesis. University of Wales, Swansea.

Pennington, M. C. (1996). *Phonology in English Language Teaching.* London: Longman.

Peterson, P. (2001). Skills and strategies for proficient listening. In M. Celce-Murcia (Ed.), *Teaching English as a Second or Foreign Language.* Boston: Heinle and Heinle. pp. 87–100.

Powers, D. E. (1985). *A Survey of Academic Demands Related to Listening Skills. TOEFL Res. Rep. No. 20.* Princeton, NJ: Educational Testing Service.

Qian, D. D. (2002). Investigating the relationship between vocabulary knowledge and academic reading performance: An assessment perspective. *Language Learning, 52*(3), 513–536.

Roach, P. (2001). *English Phonetics and Phonology* (3rd edition). Cambridge: Cambridge University Press.

Rost, M. (2002). *Teaching and Researching Listening.* Applied Linguistics in Action Series. Harlow: Pearson Education Press.

Schonell, F. J., Meddleton, I. G. and Shaw, B. A. (1956). *A Study of the Oral Vocabulary of Adults.* Brisbane: University of Queensland Press.

Schumacker, R. E. and Lomax, R. (2004). *A Beginner's Guide to Structural Equation Modelling* (2nd edition). Mahwah, NJ: Erlbaum.

Stevens, J. P. (1992). *Applied Multivariate Statistics for the Social Sciences* (2nd edition). Hillsdale, NJ: Erlbaum.

Stevens, M. I. and Montgomery, A. A. (1985). A critique of recent relevant standardised tests. *Topics in Language Disorders, 5*(3), 21–45.

Tabachnick, B. G. and Fidell, L. S. (2001). *Using Multivariate Statistics* (4th edition). Boston: Allyn and Bacon.

Thompson, I. (1995). Assessment of second/foreign language listening comprehension. In D. J. Mendelsohn and J. Rubin (Eds) *A Guide for the Teaching of Second Language Listening.* San Diego, CA: Dominie Press.

Underhill, A. (1994). *Sound Foundations: Living Phonology.* Oxford: Heinemann.

Ur, P. (1984). *Teaching Listening Comprehension.* Cambridge: Cambridge University Press.

Vandergrift, L. (1996). The listening comprehension strategies of core French high school students. *The Canadian Modern Language Review, 52*(2), 200–223.

Vandergrift, L. (1998). Successful and less successful listeners in French: what are the strategy differences? *The French Review, 71*, 370–395.

Vandergrift, L. (2003). Orchestrating strategy use: towards a model of the skilled L2 listener. *Language Learning, 53*, 461–494.

Vandergrift, L. (2005). Relationships among motivation orientations, metacognitive awareness and proficiency in L2 listening. *Applied Linguistics, 26*(1), 70–89.

Vanderplank, R. (1985). Isochrony and intelligibility. In J. Tommola and K. Battarbee (Eds), CDEF 84. *Papers from the Conference of Departments of English in Finland.* Turku, Finland: Publications of the Department of English, pp. 301–328.

Waters, G. S. and Caplan, D. (2004). Verbal working memory and on-line syntactic processing: evidence from self-paced listening. *The Quarterly Journal of Experimental Psychology, 57A*(1), 129–163.

Weinstein, N. (1982). *Whaddaya Say?* Culver City, CA: ESL Publications.

Weir, C. (1993). *Understanding and Developing Language Tests.* New York: Prentice Hall.

Wright, D. B. (1997). *Understanding Statistics: An Introduction for the Social Sciences.* London: Sage.

Yamada, R. A., Tohkura, Y. and Kobayashi, N. (1997). Effect of word familiarity on non-native phoneme perception: Identification of English /r/, /l/ and /w/ by native speakers of Japanese. In A. James and J. Leather (Eds), *Second Language Speech: Structure and Process.* Berlin: Mouton de Gruyter, pp. 103–117.

5
benchmarking and standards in language tests

elif kantarcioğlu and spiros papageorgiou

introduction

In the field of language testing, the word "standards" refers to different but interlinked concepts. It may refer to a set of guidelines on which tests are constructed and evaluated (Alderson et al., 1995: 236) or a pre-specified description of learning outcomes used as a basis for assessing and reporting learners' progress and achievement in the form of behavioural scales of language proficiency (Brindley, 1998). "Benchmarks" is another term used for standards even though language testers also use this term to refer to samples of performance of speaking and writing to train raters or familiarise test takers with the test content.

Every exam provider – be it a small school or an international examining board – is expected to be fully accountable for the accreditation or licensing decisions resulting from its tests and be able to provide high-quality data for such decisions. This requires standard setting, a process designed to make these decisions fairer, more valid and defendable. Standard setting will also offer explicit performance criteria on which the cut scores are based. When specific criteria to be met are made explicit to test users, that is, test takers or those who guide test takers, success in the test increases as a consequence (Weir, 2005; Cizek and Bunch, 2007: 8).

Recently, language testing bodies have turned to currently prevalent behavioural scales of language proficiency, primarily those in the Common European Framework of Reference (CEFR; Council of Europe, 2001), as well as earlier ones in Northern America, such as ACTFL (1986),

ILR (Lowe, 1986) and the Canadian Language Benchmarks (CCLB, 2000). These scales describe what a learner is able to do when using the language; thus they help language testers establish levels of performance for their exams and explain to test users what scores mean (see the detailed description of the CEFR in Chapter 2 of this book). The aim of this chapter is to explore issues regarding standard setting for language tests. Because the CEFR has come to be used as a benchmark by numerous national and international providers of language examinations (see Chapters 1 and 2), the chapter focuses on the CEFR standard setting context.

The CEFR scales and their constituent descriptors, developed during a large research project (North, 2000), describe what learners can do with language at six main levels (A1, the lowest, to C2, the highest). When setting cut scores, these descriptors can function as "Performance Level Descriptions" (PLDs) and the level names (A1, A2, etc.) are the summarising labels of these descriptions, called "Performance Level Labels" (PLLs; see Cizek and Bunch, 2007: 44–47). To assist test developers in relating their examinations to the CEFR, the Council of Europe has published a preliminary and recently a revised version of a Manual (Council of Europe, 2003, 2009; Figueras et al., 2005), which includes suggested standard setting procedures. A Reference Supplement (Takala, 2004) was also issued, with one section focusing on standard setting (Kaftandjieva, 2004).

standard setting

Standard setting is the term commonly used for "the proper following of a prescribed, rational system of rules or procedures resulting in the assignment of a number to differentiate between two or more states or degrees of performance" (Cizek, 1993: 100).

In order to determine whether examinees have passed or failed an exam, a point on the score scale needs to be defined, to function as the boundary between the pass and fail categories. This point on the score scale is called a "cut score", "a point on a test's score scale used to determine whether a particular score is sufficient for some purpose" (Zieky et al., 2008: 1).

Cut scores have to be defined for every boundary between levels. In the United States, where K-12 tests are reported with reference to the four levels of the National Assessment of Educational Progress (NAEP; Hambleton, 2001: 99), three cut scores are set to distinguish between the pairs of levels, as shown in Figure 5.1.

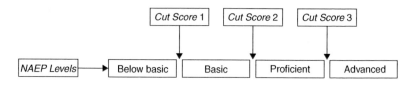

Figure 5.1   NAEP levels and cut scores

Thus the number of cut scores is always the number of levels or categories minus one. Outside K-12 education and language testing, for example licensing exams for doctors and pilots, there is typically one cut score, classifying examinees into either pass or fail levels.

Cizek and Bunch (2007: 14–17) discuss the difference between the *cut score*, which they see as the operational version of a desired level of performance, and the *performance standard*, which they see as the conceptualisation of the desired level of performance. Standard setting is thought of as a systematic process in which an abstraction (i.e. the performance standard) is translated into an operationalised location on the score scale (i.e. the cut score). Performance standards should not be confused with the term "content standards" found in the CRESST Assessment Glossary (National Center for Research on Evaluation Standards and Student Testing, 1999). While performance standards focus on examinees' performances in order to classify them into levels, content standards focus on what should be taught and prescribe what students should know and what skills they should have at different levels (see also AERA, APA and NCME, 1999: 179). Put differently, performance standards deal with examinees' performance, whereas content standards deal with the curriculum and prescribe expected skills and knowledge (Hambleton, 2001: 91).

the process of standard setting

During standard setting, a panel of expert judges (sometimes called "panellists") is required under the guidance of one or more meeting facilitators to make judgements on which examination providers will base their final cut score decisions. Statistical information about test items and the distribution of scores is also used to help panellists with their judgement task. A fairly common practice in standard setting meetings is that more than one round of judgements is allowed (cf. Hambleton, 2001). Between rounds, the panel discusses individual judgements, receives the statistical information about items and scores and repeats the judgements. Even though the panel will offer a recommended cut score, the decision on whether to accept this score rests with the examination provider. In this sense, standard setting is in fact a procedure for recommending cut scores for implementation by the provider of the test (Cizek and Bunch, 2007: 13).

The process of standard setting can be analysed under three main stages:

(1) Prior to the meeting
(2) During the meeting
(3) After the meeting.

prior to the meeting

A number of actions need to be taken prior to a standard setting meeting. First of all, the purpose for setting standards needs to be clarified. Reckase (2000: 5) calls this "policy development" and states that a policy for undertaking such a study must be defined by the agency or people who call for the standards. In language testing, it is usually the exam provider who calls for the standards.

Second, the standard setting method must be selected based on a set of considerations. Traditionally, standard setting methods are divided into "examinee-centred" and "test-centred" (Jaeger, 1991), depending on the focus of the judgement task. Other categorisations have also been proposed (Cizek and Bunch, 2007: 9). The method must be selected in relation to the purpose of the test, the format of the test and the type of knowledge or competencies measured by the test, the number of cut scores required and resources available. Those involved in organising standard setting meetings can consult a number of publications to review a variety of methods (e.g. Cizek, 2001; Kaftandjieva, 2004; Cizek & Bunch, 2007). For example, the Angoff method, probably the most frequently used method, requires judges to look at each item and state the probability that a "minimally acceptable person" would answer this item correctly (Angoff, 1971: 515). The mean of the judgements is then used to arrive at a cut score. Such a method is more appropriate for selected-response items such as multiple-choice, whereas for constructed-response items (i.e. speaking and writing prompts) the Extended Angoff method (Hambleton and Plake, 1995) would be more appropriate. Newer methods such as the Bookmark method (Mitzel et al., 2001), which can be used for both selected-response and constructed-response items, will most likely require more resources, for example, the use of computer software to run Item

Response Theory (IRT) analysis. Those embarking on a standard setting study should also consider using multiple methods. Comparing the cut scores derived by different methods can offer an additional validity argument with regard to how meaningful the cut score is, given the generally accepted principle that different methods will give different results (Zieky, 2001: 35).

Third, the judges need to be carefully selected because cut scores might differ not only across methods and occasions (i.e. different time points when meetings are held) but also across judges. For this reason, the selection and training of judges have been discussed in detail in the literature (Jaeger, 1991; Raymond and Reid, 2001). Panellists are expected to be familiar with the PLDs and the test-taking population and to be representative of groups involved in the interpretation and use of scores, for example teachers and admissions officers.

Finally, the scheduling of the standard setting meeting and the compilation of materials to be used during it require careful design and might be particularly time-consuming. Judges need to be notified well in advance, to ensure that they will be available during the days the meeting will take place. Item rating forms for the judges, statistical information about the items and other material (see Cizek and Bunch, 2007: 232) have to be prepared. No matter how careful the selection of participants and material may be, the schedule of the meeting has to offer the opportunity for the judges to perform their tasks without feeling rushed, but at the same time the meeting has to be of reasonable duration to avoid the issues of judge fatigue.

during the meeting

This stage comprises two parts: training the participants and implementing the standard setting process. Training the participants involves introducing them to the standard setting method(s) chosen and giving them guidance on working with the PLDs to be used. Implementing the process, on the other hand, requires working with actual test items or performance samples, providing feedback to the participants regarding the overall results and how they performed as judges, and aiding them in readjusting their judgements where necessary. Item facility values and the distribution of test scores, as well as ratings of performance samples, will need to be made available to the judges during the meeting, to help them review their judgements. Many standard setting methods require multiple rounds for this, and sometimes as many rounds as needed are carried out until the participants or the leaders of the standard setting meeting are confident in the cut scores they have selected.

after the meeting

As discussed in detail in the *Council of Europe Manual* (2009: chapter 7), the standard setting event must be evaluated and the results analysed in terms of three main categories:

- Procedural validity, examining whether the procedures followed were practical and implemented properly, whether feedback given to the judges was effective and whether documentation has been sufficiently compiled.
- Internal validity, addressing issues of accuracy and consistency of the standard setting results.
- External validation, by collecting evidence from independent sources which support the outcome of the standard setting meeting.

The outcome of the standard setting meeting needs to be reported to the exam provider, who then reviews the recommended cut score and comes to a decision over whether to accept, reject or modify the proposed cut scores (Reckase, 2000: 5).

issues regarding standard setting

the judgemental nature of standard setting

A central issue in standard setting is that "all procedures for setting cut scores require the application of judgement" (Zieky and Perie, 2006: 7). Judgements in standard setting are involved not only in choosing a cut score or an appropriate method, but in every step of the decision-making process, from the classification of examinees into levels, selection and training of judges, and the sequence of activities in the standard setting meeting to the selection of the standard setting method. This judgemental element has triggered debates in the early days of standard setting (Glass, 1978; Hambleton, 1978; Popham, 1978), even regarding the need to set cut scores.

Despite the inherent dependence of standard setting on human judgement, it seems very unlikely to us that the need to set cut scores will ever become extinct. Especially following the publication of the CEFR, standard setting has nowadays become a widely discussed topic in the language testing field. As noted in the Manual (Council of

Europe, 2009: 58), the judges involved in CEFR standard setting have to address an additional point: not only do they have to determine a cut score between a pass and a fail category, but they also need to examine whether examinees who are classified as "pass" demonstrate the performance and competencies described in the performance descriptors of the intended CEFR level. Thus, evaluating standard setting in terms of the categories described in the previous section is essential, in particular when it comes to addressing the judgemental nature of standard setting, for which implementing procedures efficiently and training judges, as well as exploring the accuracy and consistency of judgements, are of paramount importance.

tackling differences in judges' perceptions of proficiency levels and the notion of the borderline examinee

Papageorgiou (2009) shows that, even though trained judges were quite accurate in predicting the level of the CEFR descriptors during familiarisation activities, they still experienced difficulties distinguishing between adjacent levels (e.g. B2/C1 and C1/C2), despite the training they had received. In addition, Papageorgiou shows how some judges initially found the notion of the borderline examinee (a person who is just barely above the pass/fail border) difficult to comprehend, a point illustrated by the following extract.

Between the two rounds of cut score judgements, the judges discussed the importance of considering the notion of the borderline examinee when deciding on the cut scores. One of the judges, Rita (a pseudonym), explains to the others that when making initial cut score judgements she was not thinking of a borderline examinee but one who would obtain a secure pass. This examinee would still be in the same band as the borderline examinee (pass) but would perform higher than the borderline one.

> Rita:...*when we were saying there. distinction. merit. pass. I was thinking of a secure pass rather than someone who is a borderline. yeah. you're right. it is different.*

The two issues discussed here once again stress the need to properly train the judges to understand the different proficiency levels depicted by the PLDs, as well to ensure they have received enough training in performing their cut score judgements. For instance, Kantarcıoğlu and Thomas (2009: 122) report that in the context of the Bilkent University School of English Language (BUSEL) CEFR project, aimed at linking its proficiency examination (the Certificate of Proficiency in English – COPE) to the CEFR, the reading standard setting had to be repeated three times until the judges were confident in the use of the borderline examinee profile. Skorupski and Hambleton (2005) found that one of the judges expressed confusion with the judgement task even close to the end of the two-day meeting.

Nevertheless, there might be additional concerns for standard setting researchers, such as the validity of the PLDs in the contexts in which they are used. Related to this, Kaftandjieva (2004: 17) notes that the validity evidence of CEFR descriptors offered in the literature (e.g. Kaftandjieva and Takala, 2002; North, 2002) does not guarantee that they are valid for any context; see also the criticism of the CEFR in Chapter 1 of this book. In the context of assessing young learners, for example, Hasselgreen (2005) shows how the CEFR descriptors were not always appropriate. In addition, Kantarcıoğlu and Thomas (2009: 123) report that the EAP context was under-represented in the CEFR and had to clarify the terms in the descriptors for the academic context. For instance, what is meant by "a long text" in an academic context as opposed to a general English context might differ considerably. Similarly, the concept of "field of interest" might cover a wider range of topics when comparing a general English with a young learners' context. It is therefore important for those running standard setting meetings to carefully consider which PLDs should be used.

the use of multiple standard setting methods

Another concern for standard setting researchers relates to the selected standard setting method. If participants have problems understanding what their judgement task is (like, for example, Rita above, who was confused with the notion of the borderline examinee), apart from offering additional training, using an additional standard setting method is probably the best solution. This way results from the two methods can be compared, offering some additional validity evidence for the recommended cut score. With this in mind, in the Bilkent project two standard setting methods, the Angoff (Angoff, 1971: 515) and the Yes/No method, an Angoff-based method modified by Impara and Plake (1997), were employed for the standard setting of the receptive components. As demonstrated in Table 5.1 , the use of two methods contributed to the confirmation of the proposed cut score. The many-facet Rasch computer program FACETs (Linacre, 2007) was used to explore judges' agreement through a reliability index, indicating differences in rater severity.

Table 5.1   Agreement and consistency among judges – Bilkent project

	N	Mean	Rasch Reliability
Reading – Yes/No	10	20,5	0.32
Reading – Angoff	10	19,09	0.87
Listening – Yes/No	11	15.82	0.31
Listening – Angoff	11	14,65	0.81

In this analysis, a low reliability index is desired as it shows lack of differences in the way judgements are made (ibid.: 200), and, as the judgements using the Angoff method demonstrated a high reliability index, the decision to drop this method was made. The judgements based on the Yes/No method (Impara and Plake, 1997) together with those based on the Basket method (Council of Europe, 2009: 75), were used to arrive at a recommended cut score (Kantarcıoğlu and Thomas, 2009: 120–122; Kantarcıoğlu et al., 2010).

institutional implications

Perhaps one of the most significant outcomes of a standard setting event is its implications for institutions. The implications of standard setting may differ depending on the type of organisation, that is, whether it is an examining board or a school.

At the beginning of this chapter standard setting was defined as assigning a number to differentiate between degrees of performance by strictly following a system of procedures (Cizek, 1993). Standard setting is a judgemental process, and the challenge increases when some items in a test do not reflect the level they were intended to be at, in other words, the desired degree of performance. It should be acknowledged in advance that standard setting may result in modifications to the exam and then lead to another standard setting session. Kantarcıoğlu et al. (2010) report that, for the reading and listening components, the detailed analysis of the relationship between text and questions has provided a deeper insight into item writing, which has now been incorporated into the test specifications for item writers. As for the writing component, the task had to be slightly modified to better reflect the intended level. Similarly, the outcome of the standard setting project conducted by Trinity College London (2007) resulted in modifications in the examination syllabus to match the tasks that learners are expected to be able to perform at different CEFR levels.

The standards set for an exam will inevitably have an effect on other institutional exams in a school or on other exams delivered by an examining board as well. For instance, in BUSEL the first exam to be linked to the CEFR has been the exit level proficiency exam (COPE), which is now being used to calibrate and confirm the cut scores for other achievement tests administered at the end of courses that precede the exit level. Therefore, particularly in such scenarios as a multi-level preparatory language school, standard setting gains more importance and requires rigorous scrutiny.

Setting cut scores primarily requires judgements about the performance of the borderline examinee with the ultimate aim of making pass/fail decisions. However, users of a test might also be interested in setting cut scores to separate performances into higher levels, not just the pass/fail ones. This is because, apart from simply defining the minimum acceptable level for a given purpose at a given time point, institutions, as in the case of BUSEL, may also want to set future objectives for their students in the courses they offer and use these objectives in textbook writing. In other words, institutions may use standard setting as an opportunity to define content standards as well.

validation of the standard setting process

There are many approaches to validating cut scores (Hambleton, 2001: 91–108; Council of Europe, 2009), primarily relating to the three areas mentioned earlier: procedural validity, internal validity and external validation. Nevertheless, cut score validation shares some aspects with validation in language testing. To illustrate this, we consider the socio-cognitive approach to language testing validation (O'Sullivan and Weir, this book) and we examine how aspects of it can be used for cut score validation. Weir's validation framework is socio-cognitive in that "the abilities to be tested are demonstrated by the mental processing of the candidate (the cognitive dimension); equally, the use of language in performing tasks is viewed as a social rather than purely linguistic phenomenon" (Shaw and Weir, 2007: 3).

Weir (2005) argues that test developers or users are obliged to gather evidence regarding the test taker, context validity, theory-based validity, scoring validity, consequential validity and criterion-related validity. Among these main areas of Weir's validation framework, those that are pertinent to this chapter are the following, with the relevant questions as posed by Weir (2005: 48),

- Are the cognitive processes required to complete the tasks appropriate? (*Theory-based validity*)
- How far can we depend on the scores on the test? (*Scoring validity*)
- What effects does the test have on its various stakeholders? (*Consequential validity*)
- What external evidence is there outside of the test scores themselves that it is doing a good job? (*Criterion-related validity*)

We see another area of Weir's framework, context validity, as integrated into consequential validity as far as standard setting is concerned. Similarly, issues pertinent to the test taker are also considered when discussing consequential validity.

theory-based validity of performance level descriptors (PLDs)

The language testing literature on proficiency scales (see Brindley, 1998; Luoma, 2004: 67), whose descriptors are used in standard setting meetings, distinguishes between scales that are behavioural and theory-based. Among the scales used by examination providers to explain scores, the ACTFL scale (1986) is frequently mentioned as an example of a behavioural scale, as it describes features of learner language in specific, "real-life" language use contexts. A theory-based scale is based on a model of communicative language competence and describes degrees of language ability without reference to a specific situation (Bachman, 1990: 347). The CEFR scales have frequently attracted criticism (e.g. Fulcher, 2004a, b) for being behavioural and lacking theory. While the models of communicative language competence (inter alia Canale and Swain, 1980; Bachman, 1990) influenced the initial stages of the development of the CEFR scales (North, 2000: 3, 74), its scales are primarily a taxonomy that makes sense to practitioners, rather than empirically validated descriptors of the language learning process (North and Schneider, 1998: 242–243; O'Sullivan and Weir, this book). Even though the above might raise concerns among testers using the CEFR descriptors as the PLDs to set standards, it should be remembered that research mentioned in earlier sections provides some validity evidence of the CEFR descriptors in a variety of contexts, though clearly there is some cause for concern here.

scoring validity – analysing judge performance: consistency/reliability

Weir (2005: 44) argues that scoring validity is pertinent to "the validity considerations that arise at the point in time of the testing process where performances on test tasks are translated into scores". The process of translating performances into scores is at the core of any standard setting procedure. Judgements have to be made about examinee performance and test items; thus it is crucial for the validity of the cut score to investigate inter and intra-judge consistency, as well as decision consistency and accuracy (which, as discussed earlier, form part of internal validation). With respect to CEFR cut score setting studies, Kaftandjieva (2004: 21) emphasises that "lack of consistency can seriously jeopardize the cut off score credibility." Therefore, investigating consistency, which is a vital element of scoring validity, becomes an integral part of cut score validation.

criterion-related validity

Criterion-related validity involves exhibiting the relationship between test scores and an external criterion that measures the same ability (Weir, 2005: 207). With respect to CEFR studies, criterion-related validity involves the verification of the cut score recommended as a result of standard setting in relation to the CEFR (Council of Europe, 2003: 108). The cut score can be verified in two ways: linking through an anchor test or linking through teacher judgements. These two ways can offer external validity evidence (mentioned earlier in this chapter along with procedural and internal validity evidence).

As part of the Bilkent CEFR project (Kantarcıoğlu and Thomas, 2009), a preliminary study was carried out to collect criterion-related evidence to support the cut scores established as a result of standard setting. Starting from the beginning of the 2008–2009 academic year, a group of teachers (18 people) were trained in using the CEFR scales initially for about three months until the January 2009 administration. Before this administration, these teachers were asked to assess only three to four students in their classes using the CEFR scales. The teacher judgements were compared with the COPE results separately for reading (Table 5.2) and listening (Table 5.3) skills. This sample might be too small to make solid statistical statements about the cut score, but it does allow moderate approximations. The results were promising, as shown in Table 5.2. High levels of agreement were observed between the classifications based on the COPE performance and the teacher assessment of student ability for CEFR level B2: 76.19 per cent agreement (32 students out of 42) for reading and 80.95 per cent agreement (34 students out of 42) for listening.

Table 5.2   COPE reading paper

COPE reading paper (item bank)				
		Below B2	**B2**	**Above B2**	**Total**
Criterion (teachers)	Below B2	10	10		20
	B2		22		22
	Above B2			0	0
	Total	10	32	0	42

Table 5.3   COPE listening paper

Cope listening paper (item bank)				
		Below B2	**B2**	**Above B2**	**Total**
Criterion (teachers)	Below B2	5	8		13
	B2		29		29
	Above B2			0	0
	Total	5	37	0	42

consequential validity

Earlier in this chapter we talked about the effects of standard setting on institutions. Examinees are also likely to experience the consequences of standard setting. If a cut score is set too high, many examinees may fail an exam even though they should pass (false negative error classifications); if the cut score is set too low, many examinees, who should not pass, will actually pass (false positive error classifications). In both cases, unintended consequences might be observed. Examinees who failed, even though they deserved to pass, are likely to feel demotivated, and those who passed, even though they should not have, are likely to receive instruction in classes that are not appropriate for their proficiency level. Unfortunately, no test is perfectly reliable, and moving "the cut score up or down to reduce one type of error will necessarily increase the chances of making the other type of error" (Zieky and Perie, 2006: 8). Therefore, test developers involved in standard setting should carefully consider the consequences of the recommended cut scores within their education and broader social context, as in some contexts one type of classification error should be avoided more than the other. Large classification errors for CEFR-linked examinations will also threaten the primary aim set by the Council of Europe, that is, comparability of scores by different examinations. This is because examinees with similar proficiency levels will be receiving test scores that indicate different CEFR levels, or because examinees with different proficiency levels will be receiving scores that correspond to the same CEFR level, thus making interpretation and comparison of such scores quite difficult.

conclusion

The publication in 2001 of the CEFR has turned standard setting into a widely discussed topic among language testers. We feel it is crucial to conclude this chapter by pointing to two issues, namely the need to provide validity evidence of the recommended cut score to test users and the importance of validating the Performance Level Descriptors.

With regard to validity evidence of the cut score, examination providers should always fully document and provide score users with validity evidence for the adopted cut scores. It is almost always the case that language examinations nowadays refer to the CEFR levels to explain their scores, but unfortunately it is less common to find easily accessible information on how standard setting was conducted to arrive at such a decision. Especially with high-stakes examinations, for example those whose scores are used for university admission or job applications and/or promotion, the consequences of setting the cut score too high or too low are very important; therefore score users should have access to information on the relevant standard setting procedures.

With regard to the second issue, Performance Level Descriptors should be validated as well. We mentioned in this chapter studies that provide some validity evidence for the CEFR descriptors. However, in the very high-stakes context of aviation English, Alderson (2009) reports concerns about the development and validation of the descriptors introduced by the International Civil Aviation Organisation (ICAO) to set English language requirements for air traffic controllers and pilots. In such a context this is worrisome, especially because of potential false positive classification errors occurring when aviation English examinations are used to certify pilots and air traffic controllers. Nevertheless, this particular context clearly shows the importance of incorporating standard setting into the procedures for developing language tests and its crucial role in drawing valid interpretations of test scores.

references

ACTFL – American Council on the Teaching of Foreign Languages. (1986). ACTFL proficiency guidelines. Hastings-on Hudson, NY: ACTFL.
AERA, APA, NCME – American Educational Research Association, American Psychological Association, & National Council on Measurement in Education.

(1999). *Standards for Educational and Psychological Testing*. Washington, DC: American Educational Research Association.

Alderson, J. C. (2009). Air safety, language assessment policy, and policy implementation: The case of aviation English. *Annual Review of Applied Linguistics, 29*, 168–187.

Alderson, J. C., Clapham, C. and Wall, D. (1995). *Language Test Construction and Evaluation*. Cambridge: Cambridge University Press.

Angoff, W. H. (1971). Scales, norms and equivalent scores. In R. L. Thorndike (Ed.) *Educational Measurement* (2nd edition). Washington, DC: American Council on Education, pp. 508–600.

Bachman, L. F. (1990). *Fundamental Considerations in Language Testing*. Oxford: Oxford University Press.

Brindley, G. (1998). Describing language development? Rating scales and second language acquisition. In L. F. Bachman and A. D. Cohen (Eds), *Interfaces between Second Language Acquisition and Language Testing Research*. Cambridge: Cambridge University Press, pp. 112–140.

Canale, M. and Swain, M. (1980). Theoretical bases of communicative approaches to second language teaching and testing. *Applied Linguistics, 1*(1), 1–47.

CCLB – Centre for Canadian Language Benchmarks. (2000). *Canadian Language Benchmarks 2000*. Available at http://www.language.ca/pdfs/clb_adults.pdf (accessed 22 June 2009).

Cizek, G. J. (1993). Reconsidering standards and criteria. *Journal of Educational Measurement, 30*(2), 93–106.

Cizek, G. J. (ed.) (2001). *Setting Performance Standards: Concepts, Methods, and Perspectives*. Mahwah, NJ: Lawrence Erlbaum Associates.

Cizek, G. J. and Bunch, M. (2007). *Standard setting: A Guide to Establishing and Evaluating Performance Standards on Tests*. London: Sage Publications.

Council of Europe (2001). *Common European Framework of Reference for Languages: Learning, Teaching, Assessment*. Cambridge: Cambridge University Press.

Council of Europe (2003). *Relating Language Examinations to the Common European Framework of Reference for Languages: Learning, Teaching, Assessment: Manual, Preliminary Pilot Version*. Strasbourg: Council of Europe.

Council of Europe (2009). *Relating Language Examinations to the Common European Framework of Reference for Languages: Learning, Teaching, Assessment*. Strasbourg: Council of Europe.

Figueras, N., North, B., Takala, S., Verhelst, N. and Van Avermaet, P. (2005). Relating examinations to the Common European Framework: a manual. *Language Testing, 22*(3), 261–279.

Fulcher, G. (2004a). *Are Europe's Tests being Built on an 'Unsafe' Framework?* Available at http://education.guardian.co.uk/tefl/story/0,5500,1170569,00.html (accessed 20 September 2006).

Fulcher, G. (2004b). Deluded by artifices? The common European framework and harmonization. *Language Assessment Quarterly, 1*(4), 253–266.

Glass, G. V. (1978). Standards and criteria. *Journal of Educational Measurement, 15*(4), 237–261.

Hambleton, R. K. (1978). Use of cut-off scores. *Journal of Educational Measurement, 15*(4), 277–294.

Hambleton, R. K. (2001). Setting performance standards on educational assessments and criteria for evaluating the process. In G. J. Cizek (Ed.), *Setting*

Performance Standards: Concepts, Methods, and Perspectives. Mahwah, NJ: Lawrence Erlbaum Associates, pp. 89–116.

Hambleton, R. K. and Plake, B. S. (1995). Using an extended Angoff procedure to set standards on complex performance assessments. *Applied Measurement in Education, 8*(1), 41–55.

Hasselgreen, A. (2005). Assessing the language of young learners. *Language Testing, 22*(3), 337–354.

Impara, J. C. and Plake, B. S. (1997). Standard setting: an alternative approach. *Journal of Educational Measurement, 34,* 353–366.

Jaeger, R. (1991). Selection of judges for standard-setting. *Educational Measurement: Issues and Practice, 10*(2), 3–14.

Kaftandjieva, F. (2004). *Standard setting. Section B of the Reference Supplement to the Preliminary Version of the Manual for Relating Language Examinations to the Common European Framework of Reference for Languages: Learning, Teaching, Assessment.* Strasbourg: Council of Europe.

Kaftandjieva, F. and Takala, S. (2002). Council of Europe scales of language proficiency: a validation study. In J. C. Alderson (Ed.), *Common European Framework of Reference for Languages: Learning, Teaching, Assessment. Case studies.* Strasbourg: Council of Europe, pp. 106–129.

Kantarcıoğlu, E. and Thomas, C. (2009). Bilkent University School of English Language COPE CEFR linking project. In N. Figueras and J. Noijons (Eds), *Linking to the CEFR levels: Research Perspectives.* Arnhem: CITO.

Kantarcıoğlu, E., Thomas, C., O'Dwyer, J. and O'Sullivan, B. (2010). Benchmarking a high stakes proficiency exam: the COPE Linking Project. In M. Waldemar (Ed.), *Linking Tests to the CEFR: Case Studies and Reflections on Using the Council of Europe's Draft Manual for Relating Language Examinations to the CEFR.* Cambridge: Cambridge University Press, pp. 102–118.

Linacre, J. M. (2007). *Facets Rasch Measurement Computer Program.* Chicago, IL: Winsteps.

Lowe, P. (1986). Proficiency: Panacea, framework, process? A reply to Kramsch, Schulz and particularly to Bachman and Savignon. *Modern Languages Journal, 70*(4), 391–397.

Luoma, S. (2004). *Assessing Speaking.* Cambridge: Cambridge University Press.

Mitzel, H. C., Lewis, D. M., Patz, R. J. and Green, D. R. (2001). The bookmark procedure: psychological perspectives. In G. J. Cizek (Ed.), *Setting Performance Standards: Concepts, Methods, and Perspectives.* Mahwah, NJ: Lawrence Erlbaum Associates, pp. 249–281.

National Center for Research on Evaluation Standards and Student Testing (1999). *CREST Assessment Glossary.* Available at www.cse.ucla.edu/products/glossary.html (accessed 22 October 2004).

North, B. (2000). *The Development of a Common Framework Scale of Language Proficiency.* New York: Peter Lang.

North, B. (2002). A CEF-based self-assessment tool for university entrance. In J. C. Alderson (Ed.), *Common European Framework of Reference for Languages: Learning, Teaching, Assessment. Case studies.* Strasbourg: Council of Europe, pp. 146–166.

North, B. and Schneider, G. (1998). Scaling descriptors for language proficiency scales. *Language Testing, 15*(2), 217–262.

Papageorgiou, S. (2009). *Setting Performance Standards in Europe: The Judges' Contribution to Relating Language Examinations to the Common European Framework of Reference*. Frankfurt: Peter Lang.

Popham, W. J. (1978). As always, provocative. *Journal of Educational Measurement, 15*(4), 297–300.

Raymond, M. R. and Reid, J. B. (2001). Who made thee a judge? Selecting and training participants for standard setting. In G. J. Cizek (Ed.), *Setting Performance Standards: Concepts, Methods, and Perspectives*. Mahwah, NJ: Lawrence Erlbaum Associates, pp. 119–158.

Reckase, M. D. (2000). *The Evolution of the NAEP Achievement Levels Setting Process: A Summary of the Research and Development Efforts Conducted by ACT*. Iowa City, IA: ACT Inc.

Shaw, S. D. and Weir, C. J. (2007). *Examining Writing: Research and Practice in Assessing Second Language Writing*. Cambridge: Cambridge University Press.

Skorupski, W. P. and Hambleton, R. K. (2005). What are panelists thinking when they participate in standard setting studies? *Applied Measurement in Education, 18*(3), 233–256.

Takala, S. (Ed.) (2004). *Reference Supplement to the Preliminary Version of the Manual for Relating Language Examinations to the Common European Framework of Reference for Languages: Learning, Teaching and Assessment*. Strasbourg: Council of Europe.

Trinity College London (2007). *Relating the Trinity College London GESE and ISE exams to the Common European Framework of Reference: Piloting of the Council of Europe draft Manual* (Final project report). London: Trinity College London. Available at http://www.trinitycollege.co.uk/resource/?id=2261 (accessed 20 May 2009).

Weir, C. J. (2005). *Language Testing and Validation*. New York: Palgrave Macmillan.

Zieky, M. J. (2001). So much has changed: how the setting of cutscores has evolved since the 1980s. In G. J. Cizek (Ed.), *Setting Performance Standards: Concepts, Methods, and Perspectives*. Mahwah, NJ: Lawrence Erlbaum Associates, pp. 19–52.

Zieky, M. J. and Perie, M. (2006). A primer on setting cutscores on tests of educational achievement. Available at http://www.ets.org/Media/Research/pdf/Cut_Scores_Primer.pdf (accessed 25 January 2007).

Zieky, M. J., Perie, M. and Livingston, S. A. (2008). *Cutscores: A Manual for Setting Standards of Performance on Educational and Occupational Tests*. Princeton, NJ: Educational Testing Service.

6
producing an index of word difficulty through learner self-assessment data: an application of rasch modelling

toshihiko shiotsu

introduction

Improving lexical competence is one of the central aspects of second language (L2) development, and an increased awareness of this notion is reflected in the surge of published volumes during the past few decades on the lexical aspect of L2 learning, teaching and assessment (e.g. Nation, 1990, 2001; Arnaud and Béjoint, 1992; Huckin et al., 1993; Harley, 1995; Hatch and Brown, 1995; Coady and Huckin, 1997; Schmitt and McCarthy, 1997; Read, 2000; Bogaards and Laufer-Dvorkin, 2004; Lengyel and Navracsics, 2007; Fitzpatrick and Barfield, 2009).

Lexical competence is considered to be multidimensional (Richards, 1976; Meara, 1996; Nation, 2001). For a fully functional command of a language, one must acquire not only knowledge of each word's phonological/orthographic forms and semantic range but also of its syntactic behaviour, its association with other words, its derivations and the expected frequencies of its occurrence or co-occurrence with other words. However, some knowledge of a word's form–meaning correspondence needs to be acquired before our knowledge of that word becomes more complete (cf. Wesche and Paribakht, 1996).

There are individual differences in the number of words for which such form–meaning correspondence is known, and this dimension of lexical competence is often referred to as the vocabulary "size" (or "breadth"), with specific measurement instruments designed for the construct (e.g. Meara and Jones, 1990; Nation, 1990). In this chapter, the expression "knowing a word" refers to knowing the correspondence between at least one form and one sense of the word.

relative difficulties of words

The probability that a word is more or less likely to be known to a learner is typically associated with the frequency with which that word occurs in common usage, the not unreasonable assumption being that high-frequency words are generally more likely to be known than low-frequency words.

Word frequency lists are utilised for language pedagogy, testing and research (e.g. Nation, 2001), but the relationship between corpus-based word frequencies and the relative likelihoods of particular words being known by a specific group of individuals is not clear.

In addition, languages like English contain a number of lexical sets or multi-word phrases that have different semantic representations from those of their individual constituent words. Such phenomena as phrasal verbs are quite common, and objective data on their relative standings in importance or difficulty would be beneficial for language learners, teachers and researchers. However, common occurrences of object noun phrases within such phrasal verbs complicate the task of corpus-based frequency counts of phrasal verbs, while assigning values to single-word verbs and phrasal verbs on a common scale of importance or difficulty also poses a considerable challenge for corpus-based analysis.

One possible source of data to complement the corpus-based word frequencies is the responses of a target population to test questions based on specific lexical items. These responses may help generate a reliable database if they are systematically collected on a sufficiently large set of words from a sufficiently large group of individuals. The estimations of the relative difficulty of the target lexical items obtained from such an exercise could be used to support the modification or organisation of word lists for the context in which the responses were collected (see Gilhooly and Logie, 1980; Stadthagen-Gonzalez and Davis, 2006; and Yokokawa, 2006 for indices of some word attributes based on human ratings) and would have significant implications for research, testing and pedagogy.

IRT/rasch modelling of human responses

One research tool frequently adopted in language and other assessments that appears useful in constructing lexical difficulty measures from human responses is Item Response Theory (IRT) and Rasch modelling. The literature often treats Rasch modelling as a variant of IRT models (e.g. Bachman, 2004), and, although differences between IRT and Rasch have been noted (Shizuka, 2007), the present chapter focuses on those common features that are most relevant to the proposed research.

Henning (1987) defines IRT as "a systematic procedure for considering and quantifying the probability or improbability of individual item and person response patterns given the overall pattern of responses in a set of test data" (p. 108). Rasch modelling similarly considers such probabilities or improbabilities. Use of these procedures seems promising in the context of the present research, since we are essentially interested in quantifying the probability or improbability that a particular lexical item is known by an individual, given the pattern of his/her responses to the rest of the items tested and given the overall pattern of responses made on all the items by the rest of the respondents. Such probabilities may be calibrated to successfully assign difficulty ratings to the lexical items targeted in a test.

A feature of Rasch modelling of importance to the current research is that different sets of items administered to different groups of people can, with planning, be placed on a single scale, making them directly comparable. It thus becomes unnecessary to have the same people respond to all of the target lexical items; rather, each person is asked to provide his/her responses on a manageable set of unique and shared items.

response formats for assessing vocabulary breadth/size

There are a number of response formats available for assessing one's lexical knowledge (Read, 2000). For the purpose of the present study, however, a format that minimises the effects of contexts and clues is required in order that the target lexical items themselves become the sources of variability in the item difficulty estimates.

One of the most popular formats for testing one's vocabulary size is found in the so-called "Yes/No checklist test" (Meara and Jones, 1990), which simply presents a mixed list of words and non-words as the input to the examinees, who are asked to indicate their knowledge of the items with the dichotomous Yes/No responses. The lack of contexts and distractors makes this format more suitable for the present research than test formats such as those based on multiple choice questions.

Since the Yes/No checklist test is primarily aimed at estimating the candidate's vocabulary size, as opposed to obtaining difficulty statistics for the lexical items, the test developer often includes non-words as part of the input to discourage and adjust for random guessing and over-confident responses (e.g. Meara and Jones, 1990; Alderson and Huhta, 2005). However, it is not at all clear how responses on non-words should be treated (Mochida and Harrington, 2006; Read and Shiotsu, 2010), while Shillaw (1996) concluded that a Yes/No test without the non-words would function at least as well as those containing non-words. Since Rasch modelling allows us to code unexpected or non-functioning responses as unanswered or to simply delete specific items or people for reanalysis, we can avoid introducing noise into the calibration of the measures (Linacre, 2006). This means that the Yes/No checklist format without the non-words is worth considering as a method of collecting reliable data for the construction of a lexical difficulty index.

Analogous to the way corpora are differentiated on the basis of the speaker population from which language samples are extracted (cf. Brown Corpus vs. LOB; learner corpora), there can be separate estimates of lexical difficulty generated from separate populations. Native speakers (NS) and non-native speakers (NNS) have different kinds of knowledge about the relative difficulty of words, but quite likely so do two NNS groups from distinct L1 backgrounds or language learning contexts. Rasch difficulty estimates should thus be constructed for separate populations, and they can be compared for similarities and differences across the respondent populations. For instance, specific lexical items may be judged easy and basic by one group but more difficult by another.

the study

While there is substantial literature on testing one's vocabulary size and other dimensions of lexical competence (Read, 2000; Nation, 2001), no published research applying Rasch or IRT models to generate an index of lexical difficulty is available. The study reported here attempts to use a Rasch modelling-based approach to assigning difficulty values to a large set of words, on a single dimension.

methodology

participants

The study makes use of data collection opportunities in Japan, where the author is in close contact with groups of tertiary level EFL learners involved in the development of their English vocabulary. The data were drawn from two cohorts of first-year medical students and three cohorts of second-year humanities and social sciences majors in an intensive English programme. The total number of participants was 116.

task and materials

The class work took the form of a set of computer-assisted vocabulary learning tasks. Following an information session on the coverage of many English texts by high-frequency word families and on their significance (Nation, 2001), the participants were given a set of three spreadsheets. These consisted of the headwords from:

(1) The 1000 most frequently occurring word families (1K file), based on West's General Service List (GSL) (1953; see also Nation, 1990);
(2) The second 1000 most frequently occurring word families (2K file), also based on the GSL; and
(3) all of the 570 word families on the Academic Word List (AWL file) (Coxhead, 2000).

Nation (ibid.) explains that a word family consists of a headword, its inflected forms, and its closely related derived forms, such as those having affixes such as -ly, -ness, and un-. The exact number of words in each file was 941 for 1K, 1021 for 2K and 570 for AWL; hence their total was 2532. The participants were expected to learn as many of the words on these lists as possible in two semesters (30 weeks).

One of the first tasks for the participants at the beginning of the initial term was to identify the words they did not know the meaning of and thus needed further work on. One column of the spreadsheets contained the list of English words in random order, and the column beside it was used to mark those words requiring work, typically by entering a specific numeral like "1". The task was completed individually, mostly outside the class hours with assistance from the course instructor, and the responses on the three files were collected in approximately three weeks. While there were many other subsequent steps for the participants' vocabulary expansion, which have been detailed elsewhere (Shiotsu, 2008), this initial step provided the author with the opportunities for collecting their "Yes/No" responses on the 2532 headwords.

Of the 116 participants from the five cohorts, 70 responded to all three of the word lists (2532 words) but the remaining 46 only responded to the 1K and 2K lists (1962 words). Therefore, the collected responses yielded a total of 267,853 data points (sum of 2532 × 70 and 1962 × 46).

analysis procedure

The participants' Yes/No responses were submitted to a Rasch analysis on WINSTEPS version 3.6 (Linacre, 2006). Data from those participants who provided their responses to all three word lists (1K, 2K and AWL) and from the others who did 1K and 2K only were not separated but were submitted together for concurrent equating.

Before analysing the reliabilities of the person ability and item difficulty measures, the fit of each item and each person to the overall model of response patterns was evaluated in terms of infit and outfit mean square statistics. Linacre (2006) offers a guideline, according to which mean square values greater than 2.0 would degrade the measurement system while those between 0.5 and 1.5 would be productive of measurement. Outfit is more sensitive to outliers and is thus consulted and addressed before infit.

It is also possible to identify the most unexpected responses from their standard residuals and deal with such individual data points before deleting the full string of data points for a person or for an item as misfitting. Since the participants in this study gave their Yes/No responses on spreadsheets to a very large number of items (at least 1962 each), it would not be surprising if there were instances of simple input errors. A low-ability person reporting knowing a word that even most of the highest-ability people report not knowing, or vice versa, might result in large standard residuals. Such data points are likely to represent input errors and may be recoded as missing values.

After an iterative process of such corrections of unexpected responses and reanalyses, any people or items still having infit and/or outfit statistics higher than 1.5 need to be examined and, if necessary, removed from further analyses.

As a test of dimensionality, Principal Component Analysis of Rasch residuals (Linacre, 2006) was employed to investigate whether any other dimensions than those extracted by the Rasch measure should be considered to account for substantial portions of the residual variance. Following these processes, reliability statistics for the person ability and item difficulty measures were consulted to assess the overall validity of the approach. The Rasch word difficulty measure obtained for this study was then correlated against external indices on the same words to examine how similarly (or differently) the new measure ranks the words compared with such existing indices.

One such index is the word frequency based on the British National Corpus (Leech et al., 2001). Since the head word lists adopted for the present study do not distinguish the same word forms used as different parts of speech (e.g. the verb and noun usage of the word *test*) whereas the BNC does, frequency counts are combined for such cases to produce an ad hoc index for comparison with the Rasch measure. Another index that deserves comparison with the Rasch measure is JACET 8000 (JACET, 2003), which was developed for Japanese EFL learners. Since JACET 8000 is a ranked list of important words to study, a rank order correlation (Spearman's rho) was employed for all pairs of variables.

results

model fit, dimensionality and reliability

Initial observations of the outfit mean square values show that a few people and a large number of items exceeded the critical level of 2.0 (with people as high as 2.54; items as high as 9.90). Since many of the items with the highest outfit values were indicated as known by most and unknown by a very few respondents, it was suspected that the high outfit values could be caused by high-ability people misreporting on this limited number of easy words. Therefore, rather than deleting the individual respondents or items with high outfit statistics from the analysis list-wise, individual data points with large response residuals were recoded as missing values (cf. Linacre, 2006). This continued until the outfit and infit mean squares were lowered to around 2.0, by which time a total of 1200 data points had been recoded, which accounted for 0.004 per cent of the entire set of data points. This translates to an average of 10.3 out of 2309 words per person.

Following this initial treatment of data points with large residuals, any respondents or items with mean square values higher than 1.5 in either infit or outfit were tentatively considered under-fitting. An iterative process of deleting such items from the analyses continued until no person or item exceeded 1.5 in infit or outfit mean square. This process resulted in removing one person and 119 items from the Rasch modelling. No person or item had mean squares lower than 0.5 in infit, but 374 items and 23 respondents were below that threshold in outfit, which might indicate over-fit, but they were kept in the analysis since such items and cases are less of a threat to constructing valid measures (Linacre, 2006).

At this point, a decision had to be made on how to deal with the 119 words that were tentatively removed from the analysis for having mean square values higher than 1.5. It seemed desirable to include them in the analysis, in so far as they do not degrade the measurement system, because removing them would mean being unable to model their relative difficulties. Linacre (2006) states that items or respondents exceeding 2.0 in mean square can degrade the measurement system, but the 119 items in question had infit values only as high as 1.75 and outfit as high as 2.09. To assess the impact of including these items in accurately modelling the other, better-fitting items, a Pearson correlation coefficient was calculated between the Rasch difficulty estimates on the better-fitting items obtained after removing those 119 words and the difficulty estimates on the same words obtained before the removals (k = 1792, after additional deletions of words known to all respondents). The coefficient obtained was 0.99 ($p < 0.001$). This suggests that the impact of including those 119 items in modelling the relative difficulties of the better-fitting items is minimal. Therefore, instead of removing the items, the analyses included them, and thus the final analyses are based on the data with all of the original 2532 words and 116 respondents. Nevertheless, those words with mean squares greater than 1.5, especially in infit, may benefit from further examination.

From the Principal Component Analysis (PCA) of Rasch residuals, the Rasch dimension was found to explain 51.3 per cent of the total variance. Additionally, only 2.5 per cent of the variance unexplained by the Rasch dimension was accounted for by the first contrast or residual component, the impact of which is examined in Rasch PCA to determine whether it constitutes an additional dimension in the data. Both these percentages lend support to the assumption that there were no other substantive dimensions than the one extracted by the Rasch measures (Linacre, 2006).

The Rasch reliability coefficients obtained were 1.00 for respondents (labelled "persons" in the analysis output) and 0.97 for items, neither of which causes immediate concerns over the overall validity of the measurement model constructed.

item and person statistics

Table 6.1 presents a summary of the Rasch item estimates on the 2532 words. Of the 2532 words, 559 words were reported by all respondents to be known. WINSTEPS produces difficulty and other estimates for such items, but the standard error (S.E.) associated with such items tends to be large. The large S.E. mean and the maximum in Table 6.1 may be partially due to the large number of these easy words invariantly known to the university students in this study.

Table 6.2 lists the same categories of statistics but based on the 1974 items after excluding those 559 words reported as known by all

Table 6.1   Item statistics summary: all items (k = 2,532)

	Item difficulty in logits	S.E.	Infit mean sq.	Outfit mean sq.
Mean	−1.25	0.70	1.00	0.79
SD	3.15	0.63	0.15	0.33
Max	6.96	1.85	1.75	2.09
Min	−5.70	0.00	0.54	0.07

Table 6.2   Item statistics summary: 559 easiest items removed (k = 1,974)

	Item difficulty in logits	S.E.	Infit mean sq.	Outfit mean sq.
Mean	0.00	0.38	1.00	0.73
SD	2.36	0.20	0.17	0.35
Max	6.96	1.04	1.75	2.09
Min	−4.46	0.00	0.54	0.07

respondents. As expected, this process improved the S.E. mean to 0.38 and the maximum to 1.04.

Rasch person statistics based on a total of 116 respondents answering 1962 to 2532 items are found in Table 6.3. There was one person with an infit mean square of 1.51, but the others had values clearly lower than the 1.5 threshold.

comparisons with external measures

To investigate the extent to which the Rasch word difficulty measure ranks the given set of words similarly or differently as compared with the two external measures (BNC word frequency and JACET 8000), rank order correlations (Spearman's rho) were computed. The total number of word-pairs used in the analysis was 2432 due to a lack of overlap between the word lists. Spelling variations across the lists were unified where appropriate (e.g. *centre* for *center*).

As summarised in Table 6.4, all inter-measure correlations were significant. The Rasch-based word difficulty index correlated with the BNC word frequency at −0.69. The negative coefficient is due to the opposite directions in ranking the words: frequency counts lead to the most common words receiving the largest values, while Rasch analysis assigns the smallest logit values to the best-known words. The Rasch measure had an even stronger correlation with JACET 8000 at 0.83. The positive correlation here also makes sense, since JACET 8000 assigns smaller values to the more basic words for the learners. Therefore, it can

Table 6.3   Person statistics summary: all persons (*n* = 116)

	Person ability in logits	S.E.	Infit mean sq.	Outfit mean sq.
Mean	1.63	0.08	1.02	0.73
SD	1.89	0.03	0.13	0.27
Max	6.14	0.20	1.51	1.36
Min	−2.52	0.06	0.80	0.17

Table 6.4   Inter-measure rank order correlations (Spearman's rho)

	BNC frequency	JACET 8000 ranking
Rasch difficulty estimate	−0.69	0.83
JACET 8000 ranking	−0.92	

Note: All correlations significant at $p < 0.001$ level (two-tailed). List-wise $N = 2432$ items

be argued that the Rasch index ranks the 2432 words in a similar way to both the BNC frequency list and JACET 8000.

discussion

The goal of the study described in this chapter has been to explore whether Rasch modelling could be applied to learners' Yes/No responses to a large set of L2 lexical items in order to quantify the relative difficulties of these items.

In the context of tertiary level EFL learning in Japan, over 2500 high-frequency words were judged by more than 100 learners as being either known or unknown (Yes/No). The resultant self-report data were submitted to Rasch modelling, and, following an initial process of replacing the most unexpected responses, the fit statistics were consulted for all respondents and items, some of which gave indications of misfit. Though these "misfitting" words deserve a careful examination and will be listed below, they were kept in the Rasch model for the construction of the item difficulty and person ability measures, instead of being removed as a threat to reliable measurement. The reliability statistics and the test of dimensionality produced no indication of serious problems. Rather, they suggested that the words were placed on a single continuous scale with a good promise of replicability in other L2 learning contexts.

comparing rasch difficulty, BNC frequency and JACET 8000 ranking of ten example words

It is not possible to speak of the entire list of words analysed (see Appendix 6.1 for the full list of words and their difficulty estimates in logits), but, to illustrate how the actual words are placed on such a scale, ten words were randomly selected from the pool of all words (minus the 559 words that were invariantly known by the participants) and the relative difficulty of these words is represented graphically in

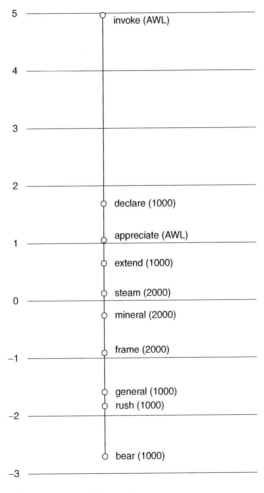

Figure 6.1   Ten example words on the Rasch difficulty scale

Figure 6.1. The values on the left margin are the item difficulty in logits (the common measurement scale), and the bracketed notation attached to each word shows in which list it was originally found: GSL-1000 (1K), GSL-2000 (2K) or Academic Word List (AWL).

In this small example, one can observe a general tendency for 1K words to be easiest, 2K words to be more difficult, and AWL words to be most difficult. However, there are also such cases as *declare* (1K) and *extend* (1K), which are found to be more difficult than all the 2K words and one of the two AWL words sampled here.

As reported earlier, the Rasch word difficulty measure correlated in rank order with the BNC frequency at –0.69 and with the JACET 8000 rankings at 0.83. Again, to illustrate how the ten sample words are positioned in terms of Rasch difficulty, BNC frequency and JACET ranking, two figures are produced here.

Figure 6.2 plots the same 10 words in terms of their Rasch difficulty and BNC frequency. The horizontal axis represents the word frequency in a sample of one million words in BNC. The word *general* has the highest frequency (348/million) among the ten words and stands out in frequency, but this is only the third easiest word in terms of logits. The most difficult word in logits, *invoke*, has the lowest occurrence at only ten per million, but the rest of the eight words show no explicable pattern. We obviously cannot expect a strongly linear relationship from two variables correlating at – 0.69, but the illustrated cases here might help us more clearly understand that the relative probability of a word meaning being known is unlikely to be highly predictable based on the word's frequency, at least as far as the given sample of language learners is concerned.

How the same ten words were ranked in the JACET 8000 word list is also graphically displayed in Figure 6.3. The horizontal axis in Figure 6.3 represents the ranking in the JACET 8000. The words nearer to No. 1 are considered the most important to learn for the Japanese EFL population, so they are more likely than the other words to be known by the Japanese learners. It is observed that the positions of the words with the highest and lowest rankings, *bear* (626th) and *invoke* (5051st) respectively, match their Rasch difficulty rankings. The second and third easiest words, *rush* (1143rd) and *general* (835th), are higher in ranking than the others and roughly in line with the overall expectations, but the remaining six words in the middle section defy any attempts at pattern interpretation. Despite the high rank order correlation between the Rasch word difficulty and the JACET ranking, many of the ten examples here speak to the unpredictability of the

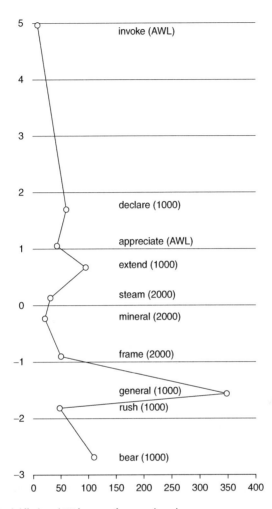

Figure 6.2 Rasch difficulty and BNC frequency of ten example words

relative difficulties of words even from a well-established word list like JACET 8000.

match and mismatch between difficulties and frequencies

Of all the 2532 head words analysed, 88 had word frequencies of more than 1000 per million. These 88 most frequently occurring words ranged in logit value from –5.70 to –3.73, meaning, as expected, that the students found them very easy.

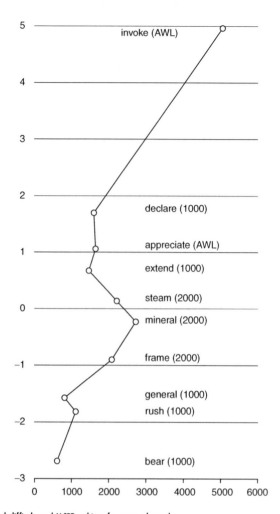

Figure 6.3 Rasch difficulty and JACET ranking of ten example words

There were an additional 88 words with 1000 to 501 occurrences per million, and they ranged in logit value from −5.70 to −0.31. With the exception of one word, *provide* (505 per million; −0.31 in logit), they were also quite easy, as anticipated.

In the frequency band of 500 to 251 per million, there were 211 words, for which the logit range was −5.70 to +2.31. The top end of this logit range seemed surprisingly high for this frequency band, and a follow-up search identified three cases with logit values higher than

1.0: *council* (348 per million; 2.31 in logit), *authority* (313 per million; 1.26 in logit) and *labour* (277 per million; 1.74 in logit). These appear to represent some rare cases of fairly high-frequency words found to be relatively unknown among the participants.

There were 508 words in the frequency band of 250 to 101 occurrences per million, and their spread in logits was from −5.70 to +3.32. The two words in this frequency band found to be relatively unknown were *scheme* (173 per million; 3.32 logits) and *commission* (128 per million; and 3.32 logits).

An additional 492 words belonged to the frequency band of 100 to 51 per million, with their logit score range being −5.70 to +3.80. A further 473 words were within the frequency range of 50 to 26 occurrences per million, and here the logit range was between −5.70 and +4.79.

Finally, some 674 words had frequencies with 25 per million or below, and their difficulties were from −5.70 to +6.96 logits. Negative logit values are unexpected in this category, and some of the less frequently occurring but easy words were as follows: *umbrella* (10 per million; −5.70 in logit), *congratulate* (9 per million; −3.27 in logit), *noon* (7 per million; −3.26 in logit).

Though not particularly principled, the analysis presented in this section may help attest to the unique role that Rasch modelling of word difficulty could play, since the kind of analysis reported here would not have been possible without it. The discrepancy between the relative difficulty of words (in logits) and the frequency with which they occur suggests that the former could be an additional source of information for predicting test item difficulty, for example, as the test developer is likely to have depended on frequency data only to infer the difficulties of words included in test tasks. Similar benefits might apply in the development of curricula or pedagogical materials.

misfitting words

As briefly explained earlier, the Rasch modelling of the 2532 words produced fit statistics suggesting that a number of them were slightly outside the recommended range of 0.5 to 1.5 (Linacre, 2006). As large infit values are often regarded as the more serious sources of concern than outfit (McNamara, 1996; Bond and Fox, 2007), they deserve the closest attention here. There were a total of 20 words exceeding 1.5 in infit mean square (these are listed in Table 6.5). Almost all the items exceeding 1.5 in infit also had outfit values larger than 1.5 (see Appendix 6.2 for a list of items with outfit mean squares larger than 1.5).

Table 6.5   Items exceeding 1.5 in infit mean square

Word	Infit mean sq.	Outfit mean sq.	Logit	Error
Noun	1.75	2.00	2.77	0.26
Spit	1.70	2.01	3.12	0.27
Coordinate	1.64	1.70	2.76	0.33
Weave	1.63	2.09	1.18	0.24
Landlady	1.62	1.65	3.12	0.27
Dip	1.59	1.98	3.04	0.27
Tray	1.57	1.79	1.88	0.25
Weed	1.57	1.73	2.50	0.26
Seize	1.56	2.01	0.26	0.24
Brass	1.56	1.82	1.88	0.25
Cushion	1.56	1.72	2.38	0.25
Tin	1.56	1.94	2.50	0.26
Expense	1.55	1.67	0.61	0.24
Veil	1.54	1.64	2.91	0.26
Pad	1.53	1.73	1.94	0.25
Millilitre	1.53	1.81	2.12	0.25
Norm	1.52	1.25	4.06	0.37
Clay	1.52	1.51	2.98	0.26
Penny	1.51	1.77	1.82	0.24
Onto	1.51	1.83	2.00	0.25

The word with the largest infit value was *noun* (1.75), followed by *spit* (1.70), *coordinate* (1.64), *weave* (1.63) and *landlady* (1.62). It is difficult to pinpoint any characteristics that make these words misfitting in the Japanese EFL context. Similarly, none of the items in Table 6.5 with lower infit values has any obvious features that might trigger a more varied pattern of responses by the learners in this study compared with other more fitting items. Some words here, such as *tray* and *cushion*, are so-called loanwords and well assimilated in the Japanese language, but so are many other words that were found to have good fit statistics. The grammar term *noun* is flagged here, but *verb* is not (1.23 in both infit and outfit mean squares). It remains to be seen whether these words with high infit values continue to have high values when judged by similar groups of other Japanese EFL learners.

Despite the high infit values of the words listed here, such words make up a very small fraction of the analysed words (0.8 per cent). Combined with the positive reliability and dimensionality data, the very small ratio of items having high infit values seems to add support for the general validity of the approach employed for the present research.

possible future directions

The approach introduced in this chapter can be advanced in several ways. It can be systematically expanded in terms of both respondent sample size and item sample size. An advantage of the Rasch and IRT procedure is its capacity for use in developing item banks. The initial bank of data based on the responses to the 2532 words obtained for the present study can be usefully joined with new sets of data on the same words from learners in similar language learning contexts to examine the stabilities of item characteristics outside the present sample of learners. This would offer a natural opportunity to review those words that had high infit values in the present study.

It may not be so easy to find individuals willing to give responses on over 2500 items, even if the task is a simple Yes/No type. With Rasch, however, various compromise solutions may be adopted instead. Depending on the needs and/or levels of the learners, parts of the three word lists given to the participants in this study could be chosen, and the data could still be incorporated with the existing set through the statistical linking of the items. Since many of the words in the most basic list (1K) in the present study were already known by all the participants, it benefited neither the participants nor the modelling of word difficulty very much. Response data on this same list from a lower-level learner group in Japan, for instance, might be more informative for both and they will still be compatible with the existing data. Similarly, learners at a more advanced level can be targeted for finer calibrations of the items in the most difficult of the three lists (AWL). It would also be an equally viable solution to sample words widely from all three lists and to prepare instruments of different length to adjust the tasks for specific data collection conditions.

There are many other words in the English language outside the three lists used in this study. The function in Rasch modelling which facilitates item linking could be used to compare the difficulty of a large number of lexical items with those already in the measurement model presented here. Multi-word expressions, including phrasal verbs (e.g. *sign up*), do not usually find their way into word frequency lists or rankings such as JACET 8000, but Rasch modelling of the sort described here could also be used to include such expressions for direct comparison with single-word expressions in terms of difficulty.

Different L1 and language learning contexts can shape the vocabulary development of one's target language to a large extent. In fact, the fairly strong correlation found between the Rasch-based index and JACET 8000 rankings may be partly attributable to the Japanese EFL context and the popularity of English loan words in the Japanese language, which could have shaped both the participants' response pattern on the Yes/No judgement and the word rankings in the JACET list. Such conjectures on the Japanese situation aside, it would be worthwhile to pursue comparisons across different L1 groups and identify words that function differently depending on the population.

A note of caution in this regard is that the relatively successful use of Yes/No type vocabulary knowledge measures with neither distractors nor non-words has only been reported from the Japanese EFL context (Shillaw, 1996; see also Mochida and Harrington, 2006). English language learners whose L1 is more closely related to English (e.g. Spanish or French) are likely to base their responses to cognates as much on their L1 knowledge as on their knowledge of English. Depending on the respondents' L1, some sort of mechanism, such as carefully controlled non-words, may need to be set in place to determine whether a person is reporting his/her knowledge at a useful level of accuracy. Self-reports of respondents lacking a sufficient level of accuracy may then need to be excluded from the analysis.

An alternative to the dichotomous Yes/No format is to introduce more graded responses, though the word sample size would need to be compromised. Our knowledge of a word is unlikely to be dichotomous, and attempts have been made to capture the so-called depth dimension of vocabulary knowledge (e.g. Wesche and Paribakht, 1996). A study conducted on self-reports of such graded reports by a smaller group of learners, but otherwise based on the same methodology as described in this chapter (Shiotsu, 2009), indicated that the Rasch word difficulty estimates from graded responses are very similar to those based on other learners' dichotomous Yes/No responses ($r=0.92$). Research in this area is still in its infancy, though it does appear to merit further work.

My discussion so far has considered only language learners or non-native speakers as respondents. However, native speaker (NS) responses would also be a valuable source of information. Alderson (2007) reported that there was a lack of a strong relationship between English words' corpus-based frequencies and an expert panel's impressions of their frequencies. His results may suggest difficulties in relying on expert judgments of word frequencies, but they could also be a warning against blindly accepting purely empirical frequency counts from corpora without human judgement. The degree to which language experts can consistently assign difficulty or importance ratings to many of the words in a language can be explored using the framework introduced in this chapter. The Yes/No format would be limiting when researching NS responses, so this is when the graded response format becomes useful. The respondents might, for instance, be asked to rate on a scale a list of words on the basis of importance for L2 learners. Also, since there seem to be languages that still lack reliable frequency counts (cf. ibid.), a Rasch-based index of word importance or difficulty based on the judgements of experts on these languages may be particularly useful as an alternative or a complement to underdeveloped corpus-based indices.

Finally, it has to be mentioned that a single-word form often represents multiple senses, and the kind of item organisation and format described above is unable to address a person's knowledge or lack of knowledge of such multiple senses of one word form. In fact, many of the high-frequency words included in the present study are polysemous (they can have many meanings), as are high-frequency words in general. Again, this will require compromise in the word sample size, but a possible approach might be to have expert judges respond to a word rating task in which each polysemous target word is presented together with its unique definition.

Overall, the applications of the approach introduced in this chapter seem quite wide, and careful programmes of research should be able to expand on the existing findings.

acknowledgements

Aspects of the present chapter were presented in the JALT 2006, LTF 2007 and AAAL 2009 conferences, and the author is grateful for the constructive feedback received from the participants at these conferences.

references

Alderson, J. C. (2007). Judging the frequency of English words. *Applied Linguistics*, 28(3), 383–409.

Alderson, J. C. and Huhta, A. (2005). The development of a suite of computer-based diagnostic tests based on the Common European Framework. *Language Testing*, 22(3), 301–320.

Arnaud, P. J. L. and Béjoint, H. (Eds) (1992). *Vocabulary and Applied Linguistics*. Houndmills: Macmillan.

Bachman, L. F. (2004). *Statistical Analyses for Language Assessment*. Cambridge: Cambridge University Press.

Bogaards, P. and Laufer-Dvorkin, B. (2004). *Vocabulary in a Second Language: Selection, Acquisition, and Testing*. Amsterdam: John Benjamins.

Bond, T. G. and Fox, C. M. (2007). *Applying the Rasch Model: Fundamental Measurement in the Human Sciences* (2nd edition). Mahwah, NJ: Lawrence Erlbaum.

Coady, J. and Huckin, T. N. (Eds) (1997). *Second Language Vocabulary Acquisition: A Rationale for Pedagogy*. New York: Cambridge University Press.

Coxhead, A. (2000). A new academic word list. *TESOL Quarterly*, *34*(2), 213–238.

Fitzpatrick, T. and Barfield, A. (Eds) (2009). *Lexical Processing in Second Language Learners*. Clevedon: Multilingual Matters.

Gilhooly, K. L. and Logie, R. H. (1980). Age of acquisition, imagery, concreteness, familiarity and ambiguity measures for 1944 words. *Behavior Research Methods and Instrumentation*, *12*, 395–427.

Harley, B. (Ed.) (1995). *Lexical Issues in Language Learning*. Ann Arbor, MI: Language Learning/John Benjamins.

Hatch, E. M. and Brown, C. (1995). *Vocabulary, Semantics, and Language Education*. Cambridge: Cambridge University Press.

Henning, G. (1987). *A Guide to Language Testing: Development, Evaluation, Research*. Cambridge, MA: Newbury House.

Huckin, T. N., Haynes, M. and Coady, J. (Eds) (1993). *Second Language Reading and Vocabulary Learning*. Norwood, NJ: Ablex.

JACET (2003). *JACET List of 8000 Basic Words*. Tokyo: JACET.

Leech, G., Rayson, P. and Wilson, A. (2001). *Word Frequencies in Written and Spoken English: Based on the British National Corpus*. London: Longman.

Lengyel, Z. and Navracsics, J. (Eds) (2007). *Second Language Lexical Processes: Applied Linguistic and Psycholinguistic Perspectives*. Clevedon: Multilingual Matters.

Linacre, J. M. (2006). *WINSTEPS Rasch Measurement Program*. Chicago, IL: Winsteps.com.

McNamara, T. F. (1996). *Measuring Second Language Performance*. London: Longman.

Meara, P. (1996). The dimensions of lexical competence. In G. Brown, K. Malmkjaer and J. Williams (Eds), *Performance and Competence in Second Language Acquisition*. Cambridge: Cambridge University Press, pp. 35–53.

Meara, P. and Jones, G. (1990). *The Eurocentres' 10K Vocabulary Size Test*. Zurich: Eurocentres.

Mochida, A. and Harrington, M. (2006). The Yes/No test as a measure of receptive vocabulary knowledge. *Language Testing*, *23*(1): 73–98.

Nation, I. S. P. (1990). *Teaching and Learning Vocabulary*. New York: Newbury House.

Nation, I. S. P. (2001). *Learning Vocabulary in Another Language*. Cambridge: Cambridge University Press.

Read, J. (2000). *Assessing Vocabulary*. Cambridge: Cambridge University Press.

Read, J. and Shiotsu, T. (2010). *Investigating the Yes/No Vocabulary Test: Input Modality, Context and Response Time*. Work-in-progress presented at the Language Testing Research Colloquium, Cambridge.

Richards, J. (1976). The role of vocabulary teaching. *TESOL Quarterly*, *10*(1), 77–89.

Schmitt, N. and McCarthy, M. (Eds) (1997). *Vocabulary: Description, Acquisition and Pedagogy*. Cambridge: Cambridge University Press.

Shillaw, J. (1996). *The Application of Rasch Modelling to Yes/No Vocabulary Tests*. Available at http://www.lognostics.co.uk/vlibrary/ (accessed May 2010).

Shiotsu, T. (2008). *Lexical Development Using Spreadsheets*. Paper presented at WorldCALL, Fukuoka, Japan, 5–8 August 2008.

Shiotsu, T. (2009). *Quantifying Word Difficulties from Learner Self-Assessment Data: An Application of Rasch Modelling and Vocabulary Knowledge Scale*. Paper presented at the American Association of Applied Linguistics, Denver, CO, 21–24 March 2009.

Shizuka, T. (2007). *Kiso Kara Fukaku Rikai Suru Rasshu Moderingu [Rasch Modelling for Objective Measurement]*. Osaka: Kansai University Press.

Stadthagen-Gonzalez, H. and Davis, C. J. (2006). The Bristol Norms for age of acquisition, imageability and familiarity. *Behavior Research Methods*, *38*, 598–605.

Wesche, M. and Paribakht, T. S. (1996). Assessing second language vocabulary knowledge: depth vs. breadth. *Canadian Modern Language Review*, *53*(1), 13–40.

West, M. (1953). *A General Service List of English Words*. London: Longman.

Yokokawa, H. (Ed.) (2006). *Nihonjin Eigo Gakushusha No Eitango Shinmitsudo: Mojihen [Japanese EFL Learners' Familiarities with English Words: Written Words]*. Tokyo: Kuroshio.

appendix 6.1

Word	Logit	Word	Logit	Word	Logit
a	−5.70	accumulate	2.76	admit	−0.66
abandon	2.04	accurate	2.24	adopt	0.20
able	−4.46	accuse	1.88	adult	−4.94
about	−5.70	accustom	1.01	advance	−1.96
above	−1.46	ache	−0.38	advantage	−1.16
abroad	−2.95	achieve	−0.30	adventure	−2.28
absence	−0.38	acknowledge	1.64	advertise	0.72
absent	−1.58	acquire	1.84	advertisement	1.12
absolute	1.58	across	−5.66	advice	−5.70
absolutely	1.29	act	−5.70	advocate	3.67
abstract	2.55	actual	−0.59	aeroplane	1.94
academy	1.06	adapt	0.16	affair	0.73
accept	−1.07	add	−5.68	affect	0.47
access	−0.42	address	−5.70	afford	0.84
accident	−2.95	adequate	2.55	afraid	−2.95
accommodate	3.80	adjacent	4.47	after	−5.69
accompany	1.84	adjust	1.16	afternoon	−5.70
accord	1.70	administrate	3.20	again	−5.70
account	0.20	admire	−0.31	against	−2.11

continued

Word	Logit	Word	Logit	Word	Logit
age	−5.70	anticipate	2.98	assess	3.20
agent	0.55	anxiety	2.06	assign	1.94
aggregate	4.05	anxious	0.14	assist	−0.17
ago	−5.69	any	−5.70	association	0.90
agree	−5.70	apart	−2.11	assume	1.64
agriculture	−0.59	apologize	−0.31	assure	2.04
ahead	−0.99	apology	1.07	astonish	1.94
aid	1.64	apparent	1.84	astonishment	2.12
aim	−0.18	appear	−5.67	at	−5.70
air	−5.70	append	4.48	attach	1.26
airplane	−4.46	applaud	3.73	attack	−2.69
albeit	4.79	applause	3.81	attain	2.65
alike	−0.66	apple	−3.28	attempt	1.01
alive	−2.94	apply	−0.74	attend	−1.96
all	−5.70	appoint	−1.70	attention	−2.68
allocate	6.95	appreciate	1.06	attentive	2.91
allow	−2.11	approach	−1.57	attitude	−0.69
almost	−3.28	appropriate	2.24	attract	−0.11
alone	−5.70	approval	2.70	attraction	−0.99
along	−1.96	approve	1.70	attractive	0.20
aloud	1.24	approximate	2.76	attribute	2.34
already	−5.70	April	−5.70	audience	−3.73
also	−5.70	arbitrary	4.97	August	−5.70
alter	2.14	arch	0.02	aunt	−2.69
alternative	1.94	area	−4.96	author	−2.11
although	−2.94	argue	0.26	authority	1.26
altogether	0.61	argument	0.55	automate	2.34
always	−4.46	arise	0.44	autumn	−1.46
ambiguous	3.79	arm	−5.70	available	−0.56
ambition	1.07	army	−1.16	avenue	1.12
amend	4.63	around	−5.68	average	−2.28
among	−1.70	arrange	−1.16	avoid	−1.07
amongst	3.42	arrangement	−0.24	avoidance	1.70
amount	−0.90	arrest	1.35	awake	−1.16
amuse	−0.24	arrive	−5.70	aware	0.58
analogy	3.32	arrow	−0.18	away	−3.28
analyse	1.16	art	−5.70	awkward	3.05
ancient	−0.99	article	−0.11	axe	3.65
and	−5.70	artificial	1.18	baby	−5.70
anger	−1.58	as	−3.73	back	−5.70
angle	−0.90	ash	1.18	bad	−5.70
angry	−4.46	ashamed	−0.05	bag	−5.70
animal	−5.70	aside	0.90	baggage	−2.46
annoy	1.12	ask	−5.70	bake	−0.17
annual	1.25	asleep	−0.82	balance	−3.28
another	−4.46	aspect	1.36	ball	−5.70
answer	−5.70	assemble	2.87	band	−0.74

continued

Word	Logit	Word	Logit	Word	Logit
bank	−4.46	bias	4.19	breathe	−1.07
bar	−1.57	bicycle	−5.70	bribe	3.34
barber	0.55	big	−5.70	brick	3.19
bare	0.61	bill	−1.57	bridge	−3.72
bargain	−0.82	billion	−1.58	brief	−0.42
barrel	3.57	bind	1.29	bright	−2.11
base	−2.95	bird	−5.70	bring	−4.46
basin	3.98	birth	−4.46	broad	0.20
basket	−4.46	bit	−1.57	broadcast	−0.52
bath	−2.95	bite	−0.05	brother	−5.69
bathe	1.82	bitter	−1.26	brother-in-law	0.95
battle	−2.69	black	−5.70	brown	−2.47
bay	0.61	blade	2.64	brush	0.14
be	−5.70	blame	0.72	bucket	1.47
beak	3.27	bless	0.14	build	−5.68
beam	0.08	blind	0.02	bulk	4.97
bean	−0.24	block	−2.28	bunch	3.12
bear	−2.69	blood	−5.66	bundle	4.66
beard	2.12	blow	0.02	burn	−2.11
beast	−0.37	blue	−5.69	burst	0.38
beat	−1.07	board	−0.99	bury	0.78
beauty	−4.46	boast	2.50	bus	−5.68
because	−5.70	boat	−3.73	bush	1.18
become	−5.70	body	−5.70	business	−5.70
bed	−5.70	boil	−2.95	busy	−5.70
before	−5.70	bold	1.35	but	−5.70
beg	1.35	bond	2.04	butter	−1.36
begin	−5.70	bone	−1.26	button	−0.98
behalf	3.43	book	−5.70	buy	−5.70
behave	−0.18	border	−2.94	by	−4.46
behaviour	−0.38	borrow	−3.71	cage	0.61
behind	−2.47	both	−5.68	cake	−5.68
being	−2.69	bottle	−5.70	calculate	1.12
believe	−5.70	bottom	−2.11	call	−5.70
bell	−2.69	boundary	3.65	calm	0.02
belong	−2.69	bow	−0.05	camera	−5.68
below	−0.82	bowl	−1.25	camp	−2.69
belt	−1.95	box	−5.70	can	−5.70
bend	1.29	boy	−5.70	canal	0.72
beneath	2.57	brain	−1.96	cap	−3.28
benefit	−0.84	branch	−0.45	capable	1.16
berry	0.72	brass	1.88	capacity	−0.06
beside	−1.69	brave	0.38	cape	2.84
best	−5.70	bread	−2.68	capital	−0.98
better	−5.70	break	−3.28	captain	−2.46
between	−5.70	breakfast	−5.70	car	−5.70
beyond	−0.38	breath	−2.69	card	−3.72

continued

Word	Logit	Word	Logit	Word	Logit
care	−4.46	circle	−2.69	comment	−0.56
carriage	1.64	circumstance	1.84	commerce	2.06
carry	−5.70	cite	2.24	commission	3.32
cart	0.26	city	−5.70	commit	1.84
case	−4.46	civil	−0.18	committee	0.84
castle	−1.96	civilise	2.19	commodity	4.63
cat	−3.73	claim	−0.52	common	−3.27
catch	−5.70	clarify	3.92	communicate	−1.58
category	−0.29	class	−5.70	community	−1.00
cattle	1.35	classic	−1.17	companion	0.38
cause	−3.26	classify	2.12	company	−5.70
caution	1.29	clause	4.79	compare	−0.59
cave	1.12	clay	2.98	compatible	4.48
cease	1.93	clean	−5.70	compensate	3.55
cent	−0.38	clear	−4.46	compete	1.35
centimetre	−0.18	clerk	0.32	compile	5.57
centre	0.55	clever	−0.99	complain	−0.66
century	−5.70	cliff	3.42	complement	3.09
ceremony	−5.68	climb	−1.46	complete	−1.26
certain	−1.46	clock	−4.45	complex	−1.58
chain	0.67	close	−5.70	complicated	0.32
chair	−5.68	cloth	−2.11	component	3.80
chalk	1.01	cloud	−1.46	compose	1.35
challenge	−4.96	club	−5.70	compound	4.19
chance	−5.70	coal	1.07	comprehensive	2.65
change	−5.70	coarse	3.12	comprise	4.63
channel	−0.42	coast	−0.11	compute	2.34
chapter	−0.29	coat	−2.47	conceive	2.98
character	−5.70	code	0.37	concentrate	0.87
charge	−1.16	coffee	−5.70	concept	0.77
charm	0.20	coherent	4.80	concern	0.20
chart	0.97	coin	−4.46	conclude	1.06
cheap	−5.65	coincide	3.43	concurrent	4.80
cheat	1.41	cold	−5.70	condition	−3.28
check	−3.28	collapse	2.34	conduct	1.35
cheer	−1.07	collar	1.29	confer	4.33
cheese	−1.70	colleague	2.76	confess	2.50
chemical	−1.57	collect	−3.28	confidence	1.01
cheque	2.50	college	−5.70	confine	3.32
chest	0.14	colony	0.61	confirm	2.55
chicken	−3.71	colour	−1.07	conflict	2.44
chief	−1.07	comb	1.29	conform	2.55
child	−5.70	combine	1.35	confuse	−0.24
chimney	3.05	come	−5.70	congratulate	−3.27
choose	−5.70	comfort	−0.11	connect	−1.16
Christmas	−5.70	command	0.38	conquer	1.70
church	−5.66	commence	3.55	conscience	2.44

continued

Word	Logit	Word	Logit	Word	Logit
conscious	1.70	cough	−0.11	dad	−3.26
consent	1.26	could	−5.70	damage	−3.73
consequent	2.98	council	2.31	damp	0.72
consider	−2.11	count	−5.68	dance	−5.70
considerable	1.74	country	−5.68	danger	−5.69
consist	−0.69	couple	−1.82	dare	1.58
constant	1.35	courage	−0.31	dark	−5.70
constitute	1.84	course	−1.70	data	−1.00
constrain	4.63	court	−0.59	date	−3.73
construct	1.55	cousin	−0.59	daughter	−5.70
consult	1.84	cover	−5.67	day	−5.70
consume	1.55	cow	−1.95	dead	−3.71
contact	−0.69	coward	2.44	deaf	1.18
contain	−0.90	crack	2.70	deal	−0.31
contemporary	1.84	crash	−2.11	dear	−1.70
content	0.72	cream	−2.28	debate	0.27
context	2.55	create	−2.10	debt	1.01
continue	−5.70	creature	−1.46	decade	0.58
contract	2.76	credit	−0.84	decay	2.84
contradict	3.67	creep	2.12	deceive	1.41
contrary	2.65	crime	−0.59	December	−5.68
contrast	0.68	criteria	5.15	decide	−5.70
contribute	0.97	critic	2.19	declare	1.70
control	−5.70	crop	0.67	decline	1.16
controversy	4.06	cross	−5.68	decrease	−1.46
convene	4.79	crowd	−1.25	deduce	4.62
convenience	−2.11	crown	0.44	deed	2.19
conversation	−0.98	crucial	4.48	deep	−5.70
converse	2.65	cruel	1.53	deer	1.12
convert	2.55	crush	−0.90	defeat	1.82
convince	2.34	cry	−5.70	defend	−0.59
cook	−5.70	cultivate	1.64	define	1.54
cool	−5.70	culture	−4.95	definite	2.24
cooperate	1.35	cup	−4.45	degree	−0.59
coordinate	2.76	cure	−0.74	delay	0.95
copper	3.34	curious	0.84	delicate	−1.58
copy	−5.70	curl	1.41	delight	−0.11
core	0.87	currency	1.94	deliver	−0.82
cork	2.70	current	1.12	demand	−0.11
corn	−0.66	curse	1.24	demonstrate	1.06
corner	−5.69	curtain	−0.05	denote	4.19
corporate	1.65	curve	−0.11	deny	0.47
correct	−2.11	cushion	2.38	depress	2.87
correspond	2.76	custom	−2.11	derive	3.20
cost	−4.46	customer	−5.65	descend	2.84
cottage	0.32	cut	−5.70	describe	−0.31
cotton	−1.82	cycle	−1.17	desert	−1.58

continued

Word	Logit	Word	Logit	Word	Logit
deserve	2.12	disturb	1.88	earth	−5.70
design	−1.57	ditch	4.26	ease	0.20
desire	−1.26	dive	−0.44	east	−3.73
desk	−5.68	diverse	3.20	easy	−5.70
despair	1.70	divide	−0.24	eat	−5.70
despite	1.35	do	−5.70	economy	−1.82
destroy	−1.96	doctor	−5.70	edge	0.02
detail	−0.66	document	0.97	edit	2.04
detect	2.76	dog	−5.70	educate	−1.69
determine	0.49	dollar	−1.82	effect	−2.11
develop	−2.95	domain	2.98	efficient	1.29
deviate	5.58	domestic	−1.00	effort	−1.46
device	1.74	dominate	2.34	egg	−5.70
devil	−2.46	donkey	1.35	eight	−5.70
devote	1.16	door	−5.70	either	−2.28
diamond	−2.11	dot	−0.05	elastic	4.66
dictionary	−5.69	double	−3.27	elder	0.02
die	−4.45	doubt	−2.11	elect	−0.38
difference	−5.70	down	−5.70	electric	−1.36
differentiate	4.05	dozen	0.72	element	−0.42
difficult	−5.70	draft	2.76	elephant	−5.70
dig	0.90	drag	−1.46	eleven	−3.73
dimension	3.43	drama	−1.82	eliminate	2.87
diminish	2.87	draw	−2.47	else	−3.73
dinner	−5.68	drawer	1.82	emerge	1.94
dip	3.04	dream	−5.70	emphasis	1.55
direct	−1.26	dress	−3.73	empire	1.29
dirt	2.00	drink	−5.70	empirical	6.96
disappoint	−0.66	drive	−5.70	employ	−1.07
discipline	2.44	drop	−1.58	empty	−2.69
discover	−2.69	drown	0.26	enable	−0.18
discrete	3.92	drum	−0.98	enclose	2.06
discriminate	3.43	dry	−5.69	encounter	2.24
discuss	−3.73	duck	−0.05	encourage	−0.66
disease	−0.52	due	−0.52	end	−5.70
disgust	2.98	dull	0.72	enemy	−0.90
dish	−3.26	duration	4.63	energy	−4.96
dismiss	2.70	during	−3.73	enforce	2.65
displace	2.65	dust	−2.10	engine	−2.28
display	−0.69	duty	−0.52	English	−5.70
dispose	3.43	dynamic	0.16	enhance	4.33
distance	−2.94	each	−5.70	enjoy	−5.70
distinct	2.34	eager	1.18	enormous	0.97
distinguish	1.18	ear	−5.68	enough	−5.70
distort	4.05	early	−5.67	ensure	2.65
distribute	1.45	earn	−1.36	enter	−5.68
district	1.82	earnest	1.47	entertain	−0.24

continued

Word	Logit	Word	Logit	Word	Logit
entire	1.35	experience	−3.26	fear	−0.74
entity	3.92	experiment	0.32	feast	3.49
envelope	1.53	expert	0.05	feather	0.90
environment	−1.18	explain	−2.28	feature	0.77
envy	0.61	explicit	3.92	February	−5.70
equal	−2.11	explode	1.82	federal	4.19
equate	3.20	exploit	3.32	fee	0.58
equip	1.74	explore	0.61	feed	−1.16
equivalent	2.65	explosion	1.76	feel	−5.70
erode	4.97	export	−1.17	fellow	0.44
error	−2.10	expose	2.14	female	−1.96
escape	−2.47	express	−1.36	fence	−1.35
especial	−0.44	extend	0.67	fever	−1.46
essence	0.08	external	2.55	few	−5.66
essential	−0.90	extra	−0.82	field	−2.47
establish	0.37	extract	3.20	fierce	3.27
estate	2.04	extraordinary	1.76	fight	−2.95
estimate	0.97	extreme	1.76	figure	−1.26
ethic	2.65	eye	−5.70	file	−0.69
ethnic	−0.29	face	−5.70	fill	−1.69
evaluate	3.09	facilitate	4.96	film	−3.72
even	−4.46	fact	−4.46	final	−2.46
evening	−5.70	factor	−1.37	finance	1.16
event	−5.70	factory	−5.70	find	−5.70
eventual	2.14	fade	2.25	fine	−4.46
ever	−5.67	fail	−1.58	finger	−5.70
every	−5.70	faint	0.49	finish	−5.70
evident	1.26	fair	−1.16	finite	3.43
evil	0.44	faith	0.20	fire	−4.46
evolve	2.87	fall	−4.45	firm	0.72
exact	−0.11	false	−0.37	first	−5.70
examination	−1.46	familiar	−1.96	fish	−5.70
example	−5.70	family	−5.70	fit	−5.70
exceed	2.24	famous	−4.46	five	−5.70
excellent	−2.47	fan	−2.11	fix	−1.69
except	−0.18	fancy	0.61	flag	−5.65
excess	2.50	far	−3.72	flame	−1.07
exchange	−2.95	farm	−3.27	flash	−2.27
excite	−1.69	farther	−0.82	flat	−0.98
exclude	1.84	fashion	−3.72	flavor	−0.38
excuse	−1.58	fast	−5.70	flesh	−1.16
exercise	−2.94	fasten	0.95	flexible	2.24
exhibit	1.64	fat	−2.47	float	0.55
exist	−0.38	fate	1.01	flood	0.55
expand	1.55	father	−3.71	floor	−5.67
expect	−0.66	fault	−0.38	flour	0.08
expense	0.61	favour	−0.05	flow	−0.31

continued

Word	Logit	Word	Logit	Word	Logit
flower	-5.70	fundamental	0.77	grateful	-0.18
fluctuate	5.82	funeral	2.12	grave	1.64
fly	-4.46	fur	1.12	grease	3.81
focus	-1.36	furnish	2.84	great	-5.69
fold	1.70	furniture	-0.66	greed	2.06
follow	-1.96	furthermore	0.87	green	-5.70
fond	1.01	future	-4.46	greet	-0.18
food	-5.70	gain	-1.07	grey	0.26
fool	-1.26	gallon	2.31	grind	3.73
foot	-4.44	game	-5.70	ground	-4.45
for	-4.46	gap	-0.99	group	-4.46
forbid	2.38	garage	-0.82	grow	-4.46
force	-1.26	garden	-5.70	guarantee	1.55
foreign	-4.45	gas	-2.95	guard	-0.59
forest	-3.27	gate	-5.68	guess	-2.47
forget	-5.70	gather	-1.96	guest	-4.45
forgive	-0.24	gay	0.78	guide	-2.69
fork	-0.90	gender	-0.17	guideline	0.87
form	-3.28	general	-1.57	guilty	0.14
formal	-1.46	generate	0.58	gun	-3.26
format	2.65	generation	-2.11	habit	-1.70
former	-0.31	generous	1.24	hair	-4.46
formula	2.98	gentle	-2.69	half	-5.70
forth	-2.11	get	-5.70	hall	-3.28
forthcoming	4.63	gift	-5.70	hammer	0.84
fortune	-1.46	girl	-5.69	hand	-5.70
forward	-1.46	give	-5.70	handkerchief	-1.58
found	-0.69	glad	-5.69	handle	-1.82
foundation	-0.55	glass	-5.68	hang	-0.59
four	-5.70	globe	-0.42	happen	-5.70
frame	-0.90	glory	0.95	happy	-5.70
framework	3.67	go	-5.70	harbor	0.32
free	-5.70	goal	-4.95	hard	-5.70
freeze	-2.27	goat	2.31	hardly	-2.11
frequent	0.61	god	-5.69	harm	-0.11
fresh	-5.67	gold	-4.46	harvest	0.73
Friday	-5.70	good	-5.70	haste	1.88
friend	-5.70	govern	0.78	hat	-3.73
fright	-0.98	grace	2.19	hate	-2.28
from	-4.46	grade	-1.36	have	-5.70
front	-4.46	gradual	1.29	hay	3.65
fruit	-3.28	grain	2.00	he	-5.70
fry	-0.59	gram	-0.37	head	-5.69
full	-4.46	grammar	-1.26	heal	1.24
fun	-3.72	grand	-0.05	health	-5.70
function	0.48	grant	2.55	heap	3.57
fund	1.45	grass	-1.70	hear	-5.70

continued

Word	Logit	Word	Logit	Word	Logit
heart	−3.28	hut	−0.24	influence	−1.82
heat	−2.69	hypothesis	3.20	inform	−0.31
heaven	−5.69	I	−5.70	infrastructure	4.05
heavy	−5.69	ice	−5.68	inherent	3.43
height	−0.45	idea	−5.70	inhibit	2.24
hello	−5.70	ideal	0.32	initial	0.37
help	−5.70	identical	1.74	initiate	2.76
hence	4.06	identify	0.58	injure	−0.84
here	−5.70	ideology	2.34	ink	−2.69
hesitate	0.55	idle	−0.59	inn	2.38
hide	−1.46	if	−5.70	innovate	3.92
hierarchy	3.67	ignorant	1.45	input	0.77
high	−4.46	ill	−2.93	inquire	2.50
highlight	1.45	illustrate	1.35	insect	−0.45
hill	−5.67	image	−4.96	insert	2.44
hinder	2.77	imagine	−3.73	inside	−2.47
hire	0.02	imitate	1.53	insight	1.74
history	−5.70	immediate	0.90	inspect	2.98
hit	−4.46	immense	3.49	instance	0.87
hold	−5.65	immigrate	1.25	instant	−0.52
hole	−2.69	impact	−1.58	instead	−1.57
holiday	−5.70	implement	4.19	institute	2.55
hollow	3.26	implicate	3.80	instruct	1.35
holy	0.73	implicit	4.63	instrument	0.67
home	−5.70	imply	1.84	insult	1.76
honest	−2.28	important	−4.46	insure	1.94
honour	1.12	impose	2.65	integral	3.55
hook	1.07	impossible	−3.73	integrate	3.55
hope	−5.70	improve	−0.74	integrity	4.05
horizon	−0.99	in	−5.70	intelligent	−0.56
horse	−4.45	incentive	4.05	intend	0.61
hospital	−5.69	inch	−1.26	intense	2.44
host	−0.98	incidence	2.87	interact	2.55
hot	−5.70	incline	2.76	interest	−4.46
hotel	−5.70	include	−1.82	interfere	1.64
hour	−5.70	income	−0.42	intermediate	3.67
house	−5.68	incorporate	3.67	internal	1.55
how	−4.46	increase	−2.68	international	−5.67
however	−4.46	indeed	0.72	interpret	1.45
human	−5.70	independent	−2.28	interrupt	1.58
humble	3.19	index	0.97	interval	0.77
hundred	−5.69	indicate	2.04	intervene	2.98
hunger	−2.68	individual	0.16	into	−5.70
hunt	−1.96	induce	3.67	intrinsic	4.19
hurry	−5.65	industry	−1.82	introduce	−5.67
hurt	−0.98	inevitable	2.55	invent	0.14
husband	−5.70	infer	3.67	invest	2.34

continued

Word	Logit	Word	Logit	Word	Logit
investigate	1.74	labour	1.74	light	−5.68
invite	−0.90	lack	−2.11	like	−5.70
invoke	4.97	ladder	2.31	likely	−1.82
involve	0.97	lady	−3.73	likewise	3.32
inward	4.45	lake	−5.70	limb	3.90
iron	−1.96	lamp	−1.69	limit	−3.73
island	−5.70	land	−3.72	line	−5.70
isolate	1.45	landlady	3.12	link	−0.06
issue	−0.55	landlord	3.81	lip	−2.94
it	−5.70	language	−5.70	liquid	0.26
item	−1.36	large	−5.70	list	−2.69
January	−5.70	last	−5.70	listen	−5.70
jaw	3.19	late	−5.70	literature	−0.51
jealous	1.01	latter	−0.05	litre	2.38
jewel	−1.36	laugh	−3.28	little	−5.70
job	−4.95	law	−3.73	live	−5.70
join	−5.70	lay	−1.57	load	−0.24
joint	−0.11	layer	1.26	loaf	2.91
joke	−5.70	lazy	−0.05	loan	0.26
journal	−0.06	lead	−3.28	local	−3.73
journey	−0.38	leaf	−1.69	locate	−0.42
joy	−2.28	lean	0.44	lock	−2.69
judge	−3.73	learn	−3.73	lodging	3.90
juice	−1.82	least	−0.99	log	1.70
July	−5.70	leave	−4.46	logic	1.84
jump	−5.70	lecture	−1.00	lone	0.38
June	−5.70	left	−5.70	long	−5.70
just	−5.70	leg	−2.94	look	−5.70
justice	−0.90	legal	0.87	loose	−1.16
justify	0.77	legislate	4.48	lord	2.31
keep	−5.70	lend	−1.46	lose	−5.70
key	−5.70	length	−1.36	loss	−2.28
kick	−2.69	less	−2.95	lot	−4.45
kill	−5.70	lessen	−0.04	loud	−0.82
kilogram	−4.46	lesson	−5.69	love	−5.70
kilometre	−2.69	let	−3.28	low	−3.72
kind	−4.46	letter	−5.70	loyal	0.14
king	−5.67	level	−3.71	luck	−1.82
kiss	−5.68	levy	5.83	lump	0.02
kitchen	−5.70	liberal	2.76	lunch	−5.70
knee	−0.90	liberty	−0.11	lung	1.58
kneel	3.05	library	−5.70	machine	−5.70
knife	−4.46	licence	−2.46	mad	−0.11
knock	−2.28	lid	4.16	mail	−4.45
knot	3.12	lie	−2.28	main	−5.70
know	−5.70	life	−5.70	maintain	−0.30
label	0.68	lift	−2.11	major	−4.96

continued

Word	Logit	Word	Logit	Word	Logit
make	−5.70	mere	0.14	morning	−5.70
male	−0.82	merry	0.78	most	−5.70
man	−5.70	message	−5.68	mother	−5.70
manage	−1.26	metal	−0.82	motion	−0.66
manipulate	4.06	method	−0.30	motive	1.26
manner	−5.70	metre	1.70	motor	−1.57
manual	−0.42	middle	−5.68	mountain	−5.70
manufacture	−0.38	might	−2.69	mouse	−2.47
many	−5.70	migrate	3.55	mouth	−4.46
map	−5.70	mild	−0.99	move	−5.70
march	−2.28	mile	−3.27	Mrs	−4.44
margin	4.06	military	1.16	much	−4.46
mark	−3.72	milk	−5.70	mud	1.41
market	−4.46	mill	2.31	multiply	2.77
marry	−5.68	millilitre	2.12	murder	−0.45
mass	−0.17	millimetre	0.44	music	−5.70
master	−2.69	million	−3.27	must	−5.70
mat	−0.31	mind	−5.66	mutual	3.09
match	−2.11	miner	0.55	mystery	−2.69
material	−0.52	mineral	−0.24	nail	−2.11
matter	−2.28	minimal	3.20	name	−5.70
mature	2.34	minimise	2.04	narrow	−0.18
maximise	2.24	minimum	−1.37	nation	−1.82
may	−4.46	minister	0.44	native	−3.73
maybe	−5.70	ministry	3.20	nature	−4.45
meal	−2.68	minor	−0.56	near	−5.70
mean	−5.70	minute	−5.68	neat	2.00
meantime	3.12	miserable	0.72	necessary	−3.73
meanwhile	2.31	miss	−4.46	neck	−4.43
measure	−0.99	mistake	−5.70	need	−5.70
meat	−3.71	mister	−0.98	needle	0.95
mechanic	−0.99	mix	−5.69	negate	4.19
mechanism	0.16	mode	0.05	neglect	1.12
media	−0.84	model	−5.69	neighbour	−2.47
mediate	3.80	modern	−5.67	neither	−1.96
medical	−1.18	modest	1.82	nephew	1.24
medicine	−3.28	modify	2.14	nest	1.18
medium	−0.42	moment	−5.66	net	−1.58
meet	−5.70	Monday	−5.70	network	−0.84
melt	0.20	money	−5.70	neutral	2.14
member	−5.70	monitor	−0.06	never	−5.70
memory	−5.70	monkey	−5.70	nevertheless	1.45
mend	1.76	month	−5.70	new	−5.70
mental	−1.18	moon	−5.68	next	−5.70
mention	0.14	moral	−1.07	nice	−3.73
merchant	2.00	more	−5.70	niece	1.76
mercy	1.94	moreover	−0.17	night	−5.70

continued

Word	Logit	Word	Logit	Word	Logit
nine	−5.70	oh	−4.45	pair	−2.28
no	−5.70	oil	−4.46	pale	0.67
noble	0.95	old	−5.70	pan	0.14
noise	−3.73	omit	3.19	panel	1.07
none	−1.26	on	−5.69	paper	−5.70
nonetheless	2.65	once	−4.46	paradigm	5.15
nonsense	0.32	one	−5.70	paragraph	−2.10
noon	−3.26	ongoing	3.67	parallel	1.45
nor	−0.59	only	−5.70	parameter	2.14
norm	4.06	onto	2.00	parcel	3.81
normal	−1.82	onwards	4.55	pardon	−1.46
north	−4.46	open	−5.70	parent	−1.82
nose	−3.28	operate	−0.90	park	−5.69
not	−4.46	opinion	−2.47	part	−5.70
note	−4.46	opportunity	−0.59	participate	0.97
notice	−3.71	oppose	0.67	particular	−0.18
notion	1.64	opposite	−0.59	partner	−1.17
notwithstanding	5.15	option	0.58	party	−5.70
noun	2.77	or	−5.70	pass	−5.66
November	−5.69	orange	−3.28	passage	−0.24
now	−5.70	order	−5.67	passenger	−1.26
nuclear	0.16	ordinary	−0.31	passive	2.34
nuisance	3.57	organ	−0.11	past	−5.69
number	−5.70	organize	−0.66	paste	1.64
nurse	−5.67	orient	1.84	path	0.90
nut	1.88	origin	−1.16	patient	−0.99
oar	4.45	ornament	3.12	patriotic	3.81
obey	−0.11	other	−4.46	pattern	−2.11
object	−1.69	otherwise	−0.52	pause	0.90
objective	1.45	ought	−0.24	paw	3.90
observe	0.84	out	−5.70	pay	−5.70
obtain	1.26	outcome	1.64	peace	−5.70
obvious	0.47	outline	0.26	pearl	1.41
occasion	0.44	output	2.55	peculiar	2.84
occupy	1.26	over	−5.70	pen	−5.68
occur	−0.84	overall	2.87	pencil	−5.68
ocean	−3.72	overcome	−0.44	penny	1.82
October	−5.67	overflow	2.84	people	−5.70
odd	1.26	overlap	2.87	per	−0.74
of	−4.46	overseas	−0.17	perceive	2.76
off	−4.44	owe	−0.44	percent	−4.95
offend	0.44	own	−3.28	perfect	−5.70
offer	−2.95	pack	−2.95	perform	−0.82
office	−5.70	pad	1.94	perhaps	−1.58
official	−2.69	page	−4.46	period	−1.37
offset	3.55	pain	−2.94	permanent	0.32
often	−5.70	paint	−5.70	permit	0.20

continued

Word	Logit	Word	Logit	Word	Logit
persist	2.24	pose	1.16	prison	0.84
person	−5.70	position	−5.70	private	−3.27
perspective	3.32	positive	−1.58	probable	0.72
pet	−3.73	possess	0.95	problem	−5.70
phase	2.65	possible	−5.70	proceed	2.44
phenomenon	0.47	post	−4.44	process	−1.18
philosophy	0.97	postpone	−0.05	procession	3.12
photograph	−3.73	pot	−2.28	produce	−5.66
physical	−0.69	potential	0.87	product	−1.16
pick	−2.28	pour	0.67	production	−1.16
picture	−5.70	powder	−1.69	profession	−0.45
piece	−4.45	power	−5.70	professional	−2.11
pig	−3.27	practical	0.02	profit	0.73
pigeon	2.31	practice	−4.46	programme	−0.66
pile	2.77	practitioner	4.48	progress	−0.52
pin	−0.66	praise	0.61	prohibit	1.94
pinch	−0.44	pray	0.14	project	−2.11
pink	−5.70	preach	5.01	promise	−3.73
pint	0.20	precede	3.55	promote	0.77
pipe	0.20	precious	−1.36	prompt	3.90
pity	0.32	precise	2.87	pronounce	0.08
place	−4.46	predict	2.14	proper	0.95
plain	−0.04	predominant	5.15	property	1.82
plan	−4.46	prefer	−1.26	proportion	0.87
plane	−2.11	prejudice	2.38	propose	−1.16
plant	−4.46	preliminary	4.19	prospect	1.94
plaster	4.65	prepare	−1.69	protect	−1.36
play	−5.70	present	−3.28	protocol	5.15
please	−4.46	preserve	1.41	proud	−0.90
plenty	1.06	president	−1.46	prove	−0.31
plough	4.77	press	−1.46	provide	−0.31
plural	5.01	pressure	−2.11	psychology	0.87
plus	−1.18	presume	2.65	public	−3.73
pocket	−5.69	pretend	0.67	publication	2.44
poem	−5.69	pretty	−5.70	publish	−1.18
point	−5.70	prevent	0.02	pull	−1.82
poison	−1.58	previous	1.45	pump	2.50
police	−5.69	price	−3.73	punctual	2.19
policy	−1.57	pride	−2.47	punish	1.18
polish	0.90	priest	2.91	pupil	1.82
polite	−0.59	primary	1.35	purchase	2.14
political	0.02	prime	2.24	pure	−1.70
pool	−2.94	principal	0.77	purple	−2.11
poor	−5.70	principle	1.45	purpose	−1.46
popular	−5.70	print	−5.67	pursue	1.84
population	−3.73	prior	3.09	push	−2.68
portion	2.65	priority	3.43	put	−5.70

continued

Word	Logit	Word	Logit	Word	Logit
puzzle	-2.95	record	-2.47	reserve	0.14
qualify	1.35	recover	0.16	reside	3.55
qualitative	2.98	red	-5.70	resign	1.82
quality	-2.69	reduce	-0.66	resist	1.35
quantity	0.32	refer	1.01	resolve	1.45
quarrel	0.90	refine	3.20	resource	0.87
quart	2.98	reflect	0.61	respect	-3.72
quarter	-2.94	refresh	-1.36	respond	0.47
queen	-5.67	refuse	-0.59	responsible	-0.11
question	-5.68	regard	0.44	rest	-3.73
quick	-2.68	regime	4.06	restaurant	-5.69
quiet	-2.47	region	0.16	restore	2.65
quite	-1.58	register	1.55	restrain	3.92
quote	2.87	regret	0.08	restrict	2.65
rabbit	-5.69	regular	-2.69	result	-2.11
race	-5.67	regulate	2.65	retain	2.24
radical	2.76	reinforce	3.20	retire	-1.82
radio	-3.73	reject	1.55	return	-5.68
rail	0.38	rejoice	3.42	reveal	1.64
rain	-5.66	relation	-0.74	revenge	-0.90
raise	-2.28	relax	-2.46	revenue	3.32
rake	2.25	release	-0.30	reverse	0.27
random	-1.82	relevant	3.55	review	0.32
range	1.26	relieve	1.29	revise	4.19
rank	-1.26	religion	0.26	revolution	-1.82
rapid	0.55	reluctance	2.76	reward	1.07
rare	-1.46	rely	-0.17	ribbon	-0.74
rate	-1.70	remain	-1.16	rice	-3.73
rather	-1.96	remark	0.02	rich	-5.70
ratio	3.43	remedy	3.12	rid	1.24
rational	2.76	remember	-5.70	ride	-4.45
raw	-0.17	remind	-0.74	right	-5.66
ray	0.50	remove	0.05	rigid	3.92
razor	3.12	rent	-1.16	ring	-5.68
reach	-2.69	repair	-0.74	ripe	2.64
react	0.27	repeat	-5.70	rise	-5.69
read	-5.70	replace	-0.38	risk	-2.95
ready	-4.45	reply	-0.24	rival	0.02
real	-5.70	report	-3.73	river	-5.70
realize	-2.28	represent	0.67	road	-5.70
really	-5.69	reproduce	0.90	roar	3.57
reason	-4.46	republic	2.00	roast	1.82
receipt	1.53	reputation	3.05	rob	-0.05
receive	-2.69	request	-3.71	rock	-4.44
recent	-0.99	require	0.47	rod	2.12
recognize	-0.52	rescue	-1.26	role	-1.00
recommend	-0.05	research	-4.95	roll	-2.11

continued

Word	Logit	Word	Logit	Word	Logit
roof	−1.16	scheme	3.32	sex	−4.95
room	−5.70	school	−5.70	shade	0.20
root	−0.98	science	−5.70	shadow	−3.72
rope	−0.66	scissors	1.47	shake	−5.66
rot	2.70	scold	1.18	shall	−2.46
rough	−0.52	scope	1.94	shallow	2.19
round	−1.70	scorn	1.70	shame	0.08
route	0.58	scrape	3.49	shape	−3.27
row	0.32	scratch	−0.24	share	−2.94
royal	−0.31	screen	−4.44	sharp	−1.26
rub	1.53	screw	1.18	she	−5.70
rubber	1.29	sea	−5.70	sheep	−1.16
rubbish	3.42	search	−5.66	sheet	−1.82
rude	0.44	season	−5.70	shelf	1.29
rug	3.34	seat	−5.70	shell	0.38
ruin	1.82	second	−5.70	shelter	−0.38
rule	−5.70	secret	−5.67	shield	1.07
run	−5.70	secretary	−0.52	shift	0.37
rush	−1.82	section	−0.42	shilling	3.73
rust	3.57	sector	2.44	shine	−5.67
sacred	2.38	secure	2.76	ship	−3.28
sacrifice	2.12	see	−5.70	shirt	−0.82
sad	−5.69	seed	0.14	shock	−3.72
saddle	0.84	seek	0.05	shoe	−1.96
safe	−5.67	seem	−5.66	shoot	−2.28
sail	−0.31	seize	0.26	shop	−3.73
sake	1.01	seldom	−0.74	shore	0.61
salary	−2.11	select	−2.10	short	−5.70
sale	−2.95	self	−2.47	should	−4.46
salt	−1.16	sell	−5.68	shoulder	−4.45
same	−5.70	send	−5.70	shout	−2.11
sample	−3.73	sense	−2.11	show	−5.68
sand	−0.45	sensitive	0.08	shower	−2.47
satisfy	−0.74	sentence	−2.11	shut	0.08
Saturday	−5.70	separate	−1.82	sick	−5.70
sauce	0.61	September	−5.70	side	−5.70
saucer	2.70	sequence	2.76	sight	−1.96
save	−4.46	series	−0.06	sign	−3.28
saws	0.00	serious	−2.95	signal	−2.11
say	−5.70	serve	−0.31	significant	1.26
scale	−0.74	service	−2.68	silence	−1.96
scarce	1.47	set	−5.66	silk	−2.28
scatter	2.31	settle	0.49	silver	−4.45
scenario	1.65	seven	−5.70	similar	−3.71
scene	−1.36	several	−2.46	simple	−5.70
scent	2.57	severe	0.78	simulate	1.74
schedule	−2.46	sew	1.24	since	−5.70

continued

Word	Logit	Word	Logit	Word	Logit
sincere	2.19	sorry	−5.70	status	0.37
sing	−4.46	sort	0.08	stay	−5.70
single	−4.46	soul	−2.69	steady	0.32
sink	0.55	sound	−5.70	steam	0.14
sir	−0.90	soup	−3.73	steel	−0.24
sister	−5.70	sour	0.84	steep	3.12
sit	−5.70	source	−1.17	steer	3.49
site	0.27	south	−5.70	stem	2.64
situation	−4.46	sow	2.44	step	−5.70
six	−5.70	space	−5.70	stick	−1.96
size	−5.69	spade	1.35	stiff	3.49
skill	−5.68	spare	−0.38	still	−4.46
skin	−3.27	speak	−5.70	sting	3.57
skirt	−1.36	special	−5.70	stir	3.05
sky	−5.70	specific	1.74	stock	−0.59
slave	1.58	specify	2.98	stocking	−0.98
sleep	−5.70	speed	−5.70	stomach	−1.82
slide	−0.11	spell	−2.47	stone	−5.70
slight	0.38	spend	−4.45	stop	−5.70
slip	−1.26	sphere	2.55	store	−5.70
slope	1.24	spill	2.50	storm	−2.28
slow	−5.70	spin	−0.17	story	−5.70
small	−5.70	spirit	−1.82	stove	−0.37
smell	−5.67	spit	3.12	straight	−3.28
smile	−5.70	spite	1.12	straightforward	3.43
smoke	−5.70	splendid	2.38	strange	−2.95
smooth	−1.70	split	0.78	strap	0.95
snake	−5.65	spoil	1.07	strategy	1.84
snow	−5.69	spoon	−2.28	straw	0.50
so	−5.70	sport	−3.73	stream	−0.18
so-called	2.24	spot	−2.69	street	−5.68
soap	−0.99	spread	−1.36	strength	−0.74
social	−1.96	spring	−5.70	stress	−1.37
society	−2.11	square	−1.69	stretch	−1.96
sock	1.35	stable	2.04	strict	1.18
soft	−5.69	staff	−1.69	strike	−1.07
soil	−0.24	stage	−4.45	string	2.44
soldier	−0.05	stain	2.50	strip	0.78
sole	2.76	stairs	0.08	stripe	−0.17
solemn	4.07	stamp	−4.46	stroke	1.94
solid	1.12	stand	−5.70	strong	−5.70
solve	−1.36	standard	−1.96	structure	0.58
some	−5.70	star	−3.72	struggle	0.67
somewhat	2.24	start	−5.70	study	−5.70
son	−5.70	state	−1.26	stuff	−0.58
soon	−5.70	station	−5.69	stupid	−0.31
sore	2.25	statistic	3.20	style	−1.82

continued

Word	Logit	Word	Logit	Word	Logit
subject	−3.27	sympathy	0.72	then	−5.70
submit	2.04	system	−4.46	theory	−0.56
subordinate	5.35	table	−5.69	there	−5.68
subsequent	3.20	tail	−0.98	thereby	3.09
subsidy	4.19	tailor	2.12	therefore	−1.07
substance	1.29	take	−4.46	thesis	4.19
substitute	2.24	talk	−5.70	they	−5.70
succeed	−2.28	tall	−3.72	thick	−0.18
successor	1.26	tame	2.84	thief	−0.05
such	−5.70	tap	0.84	thin	−1.82
suck	2.63	tape	−1.18	thing	−5.70
sudden	−4.44	target	−1.58	think	−5.70
suffer	−0.38	task	0.37	thirst	1.24
sufficient	1.74	taste	−3.72	thirteen	−5.70
sugar	−5.69	tax	−1.36	thirty	−5.70
suggest	−2.47	taxi	−4.46	this	−5.70
suit	−1.36	tea	−5.70	thorn	5.01
sum	0.68	teach	−5.70	thorough	0.44
summary	−0.83	team	−2.11	though	−2.11
summer	−5.70	tear	−5.67	thousand	−4.46
sun	−5.70	technical	−0.69	thread	1.47
Sunday	−5.70	technique	−2.11	threat	1.35
supper	0.61	technology	−2.46	three	−5.70
supplement	0.68	telegraph	1.53	throat	0.73
supply	−0.90	telephone	−5.70	through	−3.27
support	−4.46	tell	−5.70	throw	−2.11
suppose	−0.38	temper	0.61	thumb	0.61
sure	−4.46	temperature	−1.70	thunder	−0.05
surface	−1.46	temple	−0.51	Thursday	−5.70
surprise	−5.70	temporary	1.64	thus	−0.66
surround	−0.82	tempt	2.00	ticket	−5.70
survey	1.16	ten	−5.70	tide	2.06
survive	−0.84	tend	−0.74	tidy	2.84
suspect	0.38	tender	1.76	tie	−1.82
suspend	1.84	tense	0.87	tight	−0.99
sustain	3.09	tent	−0.82	till	−1.96
swallow	−0.59	term	−2.46	time	−5.70
swear	2.63	terminate	2.65	tin	2.50
sweat	−1.16	terrible	−2.11	tip	0.78
sweep	2.06	test	−5.70	tire	−0.18
sweet	−4.46	text	−2.11	title	−4.45
swell	3.19	than	−5.70	to	−5.70
swim	−5.68	thank	−5.65	tobacco	−1.96
swing	−1.46	that	−5.70	today	−5.70
sword	2.00	the	−5.70	toe	−0.31
symbol	−2.11	theatre	1.24	together	−5.70
sympathetically	2.57	theme	0.16	tomorrow	−5.70

continued

Word	Logit	Word	Logit	Word	Logit
ton	0.20	tube	−0.38	veil	2.91
tongue	−1.26	Tuesday	−5.70	verb	0.67
tonight	−4.46	tune	1.64	verse	3.27
too	−5.70	turn	−5.68	version	−0.18
tool	−1.58	twelve	−5.70	very	−5.70
tooth	−1.96	twenty	−5.70	vessel	3.19
top	−5.70	twist	0.14	via	3.80
topic	−2.11	two	−5.70	victory	−3.72
total	−5.70	type	−5.70	view	−5.70
touch	−5.70	typical	0.08	village	−2.95
tough	−0.74	ugly	1.18	violate	2.24
tour	−0.74	ultimate	1.84	violent	−0.51
toward	−0.52	umbrella	−5.70	virtual	0.87
towel	0.95	uncle	−4.45	virtue	1.58
tower	−2.27	under	−5.70	visible	1.26
town	−5.70	undergo	2.34	vision	−1.37
toy	−4.45	underlie	2.34	visit	−5.70
trace	1.84	understand	−5.70	visual	0.16
track	−1.26	undertake	2.04	voice	−5.70
trade	−1.58	unfortunate	−1.16	volume	−1.37
tradition	−1.82	uniform	−1.37	voluntary	1.16
train	−5.70	unify	3.09	vote	0.08
transfer	1.26	union	0.44	vowel	4.25
transform	1.64	unique	−1.82	voyage	−1.57
transit	2.87	unit	−0.74	wage	1.94
translate	−0.59	unite	−0.51	waist	1.30
transmit	2.87	universe	−0.59	wait	−5.70
transport	−0.06	university	−5.70	wake	−2.47
trap	−0.66	unless	−1.07	walk	−5.70
travel	−4.46	until	−5.68	wall	−5.68
tray	1.88	up	−4.46	wander	−0.24
treasure	−1.16	upon	−0.74	want	−5.70
treat	−1.07	upper	1.01	war	−5.70
tree	−5.68	upright	2.44	warm	−2.11
tremble	3.81	upset	0.26	warn	−2.11
trend	0.77	urge	1.94	wash	−2.47
trail	1.47	use	−5.70	waste	−1.16
tribe	1.82	usual	−3.73	watch	−5.70
trick	−1.82	utilise	3.92	water	−5.70
trigger	3.31	vain	0.78	wave	−3.72
trip	−2.69	valid	4.33	wax	−1.07
trouble	−5.70	valley	0.38	way	−5.70
truck	−0.66	value	−2.69	we	−5.70
true	−3.73	variety	−1.58	weak	−2.47
trunk	−0.58	various	−1.36	wealth	−1.16
trust	−1.96	vary	1.26	weapon	−1.58
try	−5.70	vehicle	1.55	wear	−5.67

continued

Word	Logit	Word	Logit	Word	Logit
weather	−3.71	white	−5.70	woman	−5.70
weave	1.18	who	−5.70	wonder	−4.46
Wednesday	−5.69	whole	−2.28	wood	−5.69
weed	2.50	why	−5.70	wool	−1.58
week	−5.70	wicked	2.91	word	−5.70
weigh	−0.24	wide	−5.69	work	−5.70
weight	−3.73	widespread	1.64	world	−5.70
welcome	−5.70	widow	0.95	worm	−0.18
welfare	1.94	wife	−5.70	worry	−3.73
well	−5.70	wild	−4.46	worse	−2.11
west	−2.95	will	−5.70	worship	1.76
western	−1.46	willing	0.14	worth	−1.96
wet	−2.69	win	−5.70	would	−5.70
what	−5.70	wind	−4.46	wound	1.12
wheat	2.31	window	−5.70	wrap	0.26
wheel	0.32	wine	−2.69	wreck	4.77
when	−5.70	wing	−2.47	wrist	1.76
where	−5.70	winter	−5.70	write	−5.70
whereas	2.87	wipe	1.47	wrong	−4.46
whereby	4.80	wire	0.20	year	−5.70
whether	−2.47	wise	−1.69	yellow	−5.70
which	−4.46	wish	−5.70	yes	−5.70
while	−3.28	with	−5.70	yet	−5.70
whip	2.70	within	−1.25	yield	1.88
whisper	−1.69	without	−4.46	you	−5.70
whistle	2.57	witness	1.88	young	−5.70
				zero	−4.46

appendix 6.2

Items exceeding 1.5 in outfit mean square

Word	Infit mean sq.	Outfit mean sq.	Logit	Error
Brother-in-law	1.39	1.96	0.95	0.24
Bucket	1.47	1.92	1.47	0.24
Highlight	1.22	1.88	1.45	0.31
Flour	1.41	1.85	0.08	0.25
Pigeon	1.43	1.82	2.31	0.25
Drawer	1.5	1.78	1.82	0.24
Theatre	1.42	1.76	1.24	0.24
Metre	1.42	1.71	1.7	0.24
Scenario	1.34	1.69	1.65	0.31
Ugly	1.33	1.68	1.18	0.24
Induce	1.28	1.67	3.67	0.35
Despite	1.42	1.66	1.35	0.31

continued

Word	Infit mean sq.	Outfit mean sq.	Logit	Error
Annual	1.37	1.64	1.25	0.31
Widow	1.34	1.63	0.95	0.24
Gay	1.31	1.62	0.78	0.24
Chimney	1.43	1.62	3.05	0.27
Greet	1.39	1.6	−0.18	0.26
Wrist	1.37	1.6	1.76	0.24
Minimise	1.29	1.6	2.04	0.32
Funeral	1.43	1.6	2.12	0.25
Paste	1.4	1.59	1.64	0.24
Worship	1.41	1.59	1.76	0.24
Prime	1.33	1.58	2.24	0.32
Litre	1.49	1.58	2.38	0.25
Rub	1.41	1.57	1.53	0.24
Rake	1.5	1.57	2.25	0.25
Commence	1.41	1.57	3.55	0.35
Roast	1.48	1.56	1.82	0.24
Automate	1.42	1.56	2.34	0.32
Straightforward	1.34	1.56	3.43	0.34
Bake	1.39	1.55	−0.17	0.26
Supper	1.27	1.55	0.61	0.24
Cattle	1.32	1.55	1.35	0.24
Military	1.32	1.54	1.16	0.31
Sword	1.18	1.54	2	0.25
Thread	1.41	1.53	1.47	0.24
District	1.33	1.53	1.82	0.24
Stain	1.43	1.53	2.5	0.26
Holy	1.39	1.52	0.73	0.24
Polish	1.32	1.52	0.9	0.24
Shallow	1.34	1.52	2.19	0.25
Rid	1.19	1.51	1.24	0.24
Goat	1.41	1.51	2.31	0.25

7
an alternative approach to rating scale development
abdul halim abdul raof

introduction

A rating scale is undeniably an important tool in language assessment. Rating scales are normally used by teachers (or testers) when assessing the written or spoken performance of a learner (or a test candidate) to make decisions on the level that best describes the individual. But what constitutes a rating scale? Possibly the most useful definition of a rating scale is that it is:

> a scale for the description of language proficiency consisting of a series of constructed levels against which a language learner's performance is judged...typically such scales range from zero mastery through to an end-point representing the well-educated native speaker. The levels or bands are commonly characterised in terms of what subjects can do with the language (tasks and functions which can be performed) and their mastery of linguistic features (such as vocabulary, syntax, fluency and cohesion). (Davies et al., 1999: 153–154)

A rating scale, therefore, offers the teacher or tester a series of descriptors of certain criteria arranged hierarchically to show the differing levels of performance. However, in discussing the criteria and levels of a rating scale, we are faced with some intriguing but fundamental questions – "What criteria to use?", "Who decides what criteria to use?", "Where do the criteria come from?", "How many levels should there be?" and "What form should the scale take?": another question that is extremely relevant, given the recent trend towards language tests that are less general in focus and more specific, in that they are designed to tell us about a learner's ability to perform linguistically in a specific language use domain (such as business or academic). Unfortunately, to date there have been very few research studies undertaken with a focus on matters related to how rating scales are developed, let alone how a scale might be designed for use in a test of language for a specific use domain. Thus, it is the intention of this paper to propose an approach to rating scale construction and to describe the different stages involved in the development of a specific-purpose rating scale for the assessment of a spoken performance.

To set the scene, the following section will present a brief discussion on rating scale development, which distinguishes between two approaches, a priori and empirical.

rating scale development

We may reasonably say that the development of rating scales to date has been carried out, on the whole, using a priori decisions based on what developers believe to be aspects of language proficiency that define a preset number of bands within a scale and based on the developer's experience of working with second language learners.

This view is supported by North and Schneider (1998), who argue that existing scales have been produced by appeal to intuition and to those scales that are already in existence, rather than to theories of linguistic description or of measurement. North (2000: 207–211) categorises this approach of scale production into three methods: the intuitive method, the qualitative method and the quantitative method.

the intuitive method

This method does not require any structured data collection, just the principled interpretation of experience. In addition to experience, the developer may also refer to existing rating scales, curriculum documents or other relevant materials when devising the scale (Luoma, 2004: 83). Depending on which method is being used (see Table 7.1), the scale may go through several revisions before an agreed final version is proposed.

In the past, this methodology dominated scale production, with the Foreign Services Institute (FSI – the original analytical rating scale for speaking) and the widely used American Council on the Teaching of Foreign Languages (ACTFL) scales being classic examples. These scales, in turn, have been influential from the mid-1950s (in the case of the FSI) to the present day (see Clark and Clifford, 1988; McNamara, 1996).

Table 7.1   Rating scale construction – intuitive methods

Method	Description
Expert	Existing scales, curriculum documents and so on are consulted by the person writing the scale. May involve needs analysis of target group. The scale may be piloted and later revised.
Committee	Similar to "Expert" above but involving a development team and a consultants' group which comments on scale drafts.
Experiential	Similar to "Committee" above in that the framework still essentially relies on the experiences and/or expertise of the participants, but the process lasts longer within an institution and/ or specific assessment context and a "house consensus" develops.

There are three main methods that fall into this category: see Table 7.1 for details.

the qualitative method

This method is similar to the *Intuitive Method* in that the contents of the scale descriptors are developed intuitively (i.e. they are not based on actual data). The difference between the approaches is found in the way the final version of the scale is constructed. When the descriptors have been written they are presented in a random order to a group or groups of experts (raters, examiners or teachers who are familiar with the test context), who are expected to come to a consensus on a suitable ordering, which reflects increasing levels of achievement. The participants may also be asked to consider the wording of the descriptors and to suggest changes where they feel these are appropriate. In addition, they may be asked to use the newly formed scale to assess a set of performances in order to confirm that the scale is usable in practice. An example of a scale developed using this method is the IELTS scale (Alderson, 1991).

Turner and Upsher (1996) suggested an interesting alternative to the traditional scale. Their EBB scale, a rating scale that is empirically derived from samples of learner performance, defines boundaries between adjacent levels and requires making two or three binary choices about a performance being evaluated. Although it is empirical in nature, North (2000) categorises it as belonging to the qualitative method. An example of Turner and Upshur's scale is shown in Figure 7.1.

the quantitative method

In contrast to the qualitative method, the quantitative method involves a considerable amount of statistical analysis and careful interpretation

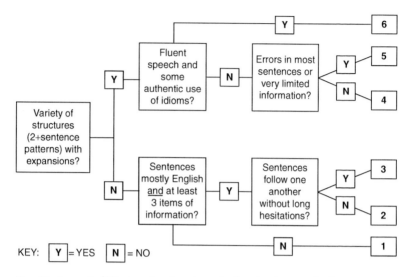

Figure 7.1 An example of EBB rating scale: rating scale procedure for audio pal (Turner and Upshur, 1996: 67)

of the results, an example being the work on the development of a scale for Arabic, using methods such as multidimensional scaling, by Chalhoub-Deville (1995).

In contrast to the approaches outlined briefly above, Fulcher (1987) advocates the development of rating scales through the study of what learners actually say; in other words, through the development of a corpus from which scales may be developed empirically. Fulcher analysed a corpus of candidate speech when constructing his scales for fluency and accuracy. The resultant scale included a five-band *Fluency* rating scale made up of band descriptors generated by the data, while two extreme levels, band 0 and band 6, were attached for additional range. A band description from the scale (Fulcher, 1993: 158–159) is provided below to serve as an example.

Band 1
The candidate frequently pauses in speech before completing the proposi-tional intention of the utterance, causing the interviewer to ask additional questions and/or make comments in order to continue the conversation. Utterances tend to be short, and there is little evidence of candidates taking time to plan the content of the utterance in advance of speaking. However, hesitation is frequently evident when the candidate has to plan

the utterance grammatically. This often involves the repetition of items, long pauses, and the reformulation of sentences.

Misunderstanding of the interviewer's questions or comments is fairly frequent, and the candidate sometimes cannot respond at all, or dries up part way through the answer. Single word responses followed by pauses are common, forcing the interviewer to encourage further contribution. It is rare for a band 1 candidate to be able to give examples, counter examples or reasons, to support a view expressed.

Pausing for grammatical and lexical repair is evident i.e. selection of a new word or structure when it is realised that an utterance is not accurate or cannot be completed accurately.

Candidates at band 1 may pause because of difficulty in retrieving a word, but when this happens will usually abandon the message rather than attempt to circumlocute. It is rare for a Band 1 candidate to express uncertainty regarding choice of lexis or the propositional content of the message. The message itself is often quite simple.

Fulcher's data-driven approach (1993) was a brave attempt at developing a rating scale that is empirically based, involving the use of actual data from a real test setting and culminating with the construction of a scale. Such an approach has apparent advantages over an a priori approach, which is overly dependent on theory and on the intuition and experiences of experts, with insufficient support from actual data and contextual parameters. However, the sheer breadth of description at each band level (234 words in the Band 1 descriptor shown here) meant that the scale was essentially unusable, due to the unlikelihood of finding candidates who matched each element described or more basically the difficulty met by the raters (and acknowledged by Fulcher) when trying simply to remember the contents of the scale when asked to apply it in the context of a test event.

the proposed approach

Thus far, I have looked at two main approaches to rating scale development. While these methods are used in scale development for tests of general proficiency, they could be applied in developing a scale for use in a specific language use domain. In contrast, the method suggested here has been devised specifically for such a test and involves occupational experts in the entire scale production process and from whom assessment criteria and band levels are derived. The approach is based on a study (Abdul Raof, 2002) carried out to discover the criteria and the number of levels identified within these criteria, which were used to assess a spoken performance for a specific working environment. Viewpoints of specialists who normally work in that environment and of ESP practitioners were examined. For this study, the Civil Engineering profession in Malaysia was selected as the specific working environment, or target language use domain, while the conference oral presentation genre made by specialists in the area was chosen as the spoken performance.

research context

Two groups of participants were involved in this study – the "Presenters" and the "Assessors". The former provided speech samples for use in the study while the latter assessed the speech samples. The first group of participants consisted of 25 Civil Engineering specialists who had presented papers at two conferences during the World Engineering Congress (WEC) held in Subang Jaya, Malaysia, in July 1999. Their presentations (research presentations, work in progress reports or innovations) served as speech samples used in this study. The specialists were Malaysian, the majority of them having between six and 15 years of experience in the field. The second group of participants were 32 Civil Engineering specialists who served as assessors or expert informants. Again, all were Malaysians who had had between 11 and 20 years of experience in the field. (Although ESP practitioners were also involved as assessors in the study, the focus of the discussion in this paper will be on the Civil Engineering specialists.)

procedures

The procedures carried out in this study involved four stepladder stages comprising six phases (see Figure 7.2). Each phase was carried out successively, with the exception of Phases II and III, which were carried out simultaneously. Each assessor participated in only one phase of the study.

Stage One was the "Scale Development" stage, which involved three phases: Phase I (the Pilot Study), Phase II (Ranking of Speech Samples) and Phase III (Comparing Pairs of Speech Samples). The assessors rated a number of videotaped speech samples, without the aid of a rating scale. They later participated in semi-structured interview sessions and described how they assessed the performances. In the next stage (Scale Drafting), the assessors involved served as expert informants providing feedback on the rating scale drafted from the outcome of Stage One. Stage Three was the "Scale Trials" stage, where a different group of

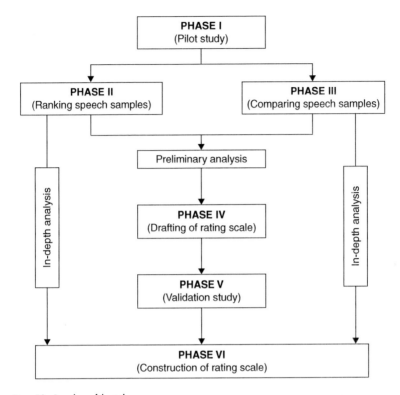

Figure 7.2 Procedures of the study

assessors rated a number of speech samples (the same ones as in Phase II and III) using the draft rating scale. They later participated in semi-structured interview sessions and provided feedback on how they had used the rating scale to come up with their judgements. They also commented on the ease and difficulty of using the scale.

The last stage was the "Scale Production" stage, involving Phase VI of the study. In this phase an in-depth analysis of the outcome of the earlier phases was carried out, focusing on the improvement of the draft rating scale. The specialists were consulted, from time to time, to seek their opinion and advice.

The outcome of the procedures described above was a draft rating scale, which is shown in Table 7.2. The rating scale is organised into four levels, with Level I being the highest level and Level IV the lowest. At each level all criteria are described, thus producing a matrix containing levels, criteria and their descriptors.

Table 7.2   Draft rating scale

Level	Delivery	Organisation	Subject matter
I	Visuals Legible, clear and presented in point form Personality Confident and relaxed Clear voice Interaction Communicates with audience, attracts audience's attention, receives response from audience Establishes and maintains good eye contact and posture. Good pacing.	Well-organised. Smooth flow of points. Good introduction. Presentation well outlined.	Good command of knowledge. Well-elaborated and supported with details. Topic is new, practical and relevant, and of interest to audience.
II	Visuals Legible and clear. Personality Shows confidence. Clear voice. Interaction Communicates with audience, maintains eye contact. Some reading from notes prepared.	Fairly well-organised and smooth flow of points. Presentation clearly outlined.	Shows command of knowledge. Clear explanation of points. Topic is of interest to audience.
III	Visuals A bit too detailed. Personality Lacks confidence. Interaction Reading from transparencies/slides. Little eye contact. At times blocking view of audience. Pacing is quite fast or slow.	Some elements of organisation. Flow of points not smooth. Presentation not well outlined.	Topic is simple and common.
IV	Visuals Not legible and too much detail. Personality Nervous and looks worried. Voice is monotonous and not clear. Interaction Passive. Reading word by word from screen. Not facing audience. Lacks eye contact. Poor pacing, rushing.	Poorly organised. Points not presented in an orderly manner.	Not elaborated clearly. Topic may be too detailed or specialised for audience to follow.

The scale consists of three main criteria – *Delivery, Organisation and Subject Matter. Delivery* has three further sub-criteria, namely *Visuals, Personality* and *Interaction*. The descriptor of *Visuals* includes legibility and form of the materials used. *Personality*, on the other hand, is described in terms of confidence and clarity of voice, while *Interaction* includes communication with audience, eye contact and pacing.

With regard to the second criterion, *Organisation*, its descriptor includes the flow of points and outlining, apart from organisation of the presentation itself. The descriptor of the third criterion, *Subject Matter*, includes mastery of knowledge presented, clarity of explanation and topic of presentation.

The phrases found in the draft scale were on the most part phrases and terms gathered from the Civil Engineering specialists. The descriptors, as can be seen, are all short, straightforward statements describing a presentation. Lengthy descriptors are sometimes associated with detailed, comprehensive listing of features of typical learners at a particular level. However, longer descriptors cannot be realistically referred to during an assessment process and are thus not favourable; see the reference to Fulcher (1993) above and the claim by North (2000: 207) that:

> A descriptor which is longer than a two-clause sentence cannot realistically be referred to during the assessment process. Teachers consistently seem to prefer short descriptors...teachers tended to reject or split descriptors longer than about 25 words.

Most of the statements in the draft scale (which was later subjected to systematic validation) are also positively constructed, with the exception of the ones at the lowest level, in line with the guidelines provided by North for formulating rating scale descriptors. Simplicity and practicality are evident in the descriptors above, further supporting the argument of North.

implications of the approach

This approach has a number of implications for test stakeholders. Each of these is elaborated below.

implications for test users

End-users of performance tests who depend on test results as an evaluation tool for recruitment and/or promotion purposes will be directly affected if the rating scale in use does not reflect the criteria used by people within that community when they evaluate a performance. A good example of this is recounted by McNamara (1996), who reports that his Occupational English Test examiners were most highly influenced by their perception of the grammatical accuracy of the test takers, even though there was no such criterion included on the scale they were using. A rating scale developed using the method described in this study would help end-users carry out their recruitment or promotional exercises with greater confidence, as it is more likely to result in a valid and reliable evaluation of the performance if it more accurately reflects the *actual* set of criteria used by the raters.

implications for test takers

Test takers suffer most from invalid or unreliable rating procedures, as their future can depend on their test results. Appropriate criteria and accurate estimates of level would allow a better evaluation of their capability in presenting their work. It is also likely that a test would benefit from a greater degree of face validity if the criteria used were based on actual rater criteria (specialist as opposed to ESP teacher) – presumably the test takers will either be aware of the need for such a procedure, or at least will appreciate the value of that procedure when it is made clear to them. So, we can look at the impact of scale development from the perspective of "fairness", validity and, as a scale developed in the way suggested here will be more likely to result in more consistent application, reliability.

implications for test developers (e.g. examination boards)

People who develop tests for use by educational institutions, governmental bodies and private sectors would benefit from the method described here. They need to consider criteria that are important from the viewpoints of their consumers in determining acceptable standards and practices. However, there are questions of cost, time and appropriateness of the development procedure, which will have to be addressed by the developer. Despite this limitation, the study broadens the scope of test validation to include the validity and appropriateness of the scale used. This aspect of test validity has not been reflected in the literature to date, though O'Sullivan (2002b) argues that it is relevant both to traditional views on validation and to the expanded multi-componential view of scoring system-related evidence of validity he proposes (as outlined by Weir and O'Sullivan in this book).

implications for testing, assessment and evaluation research

The study has provided additional evidence of the complexities involved in the rating process. The process is not just about raters making judgements on an individual's performance using a rating scale. It involves the background of raters, the criteria used, how the criteria are being used, the levels of attainment assigned, how the level assigning is done, the rating scale used and the validity and reliability of the scale, in addition to the many facets affecting a performance (see O'Sullivan, 1999, 2000, 2002a and O'Sullivan and Rignall, 2002 for an overview of these facets, their effects and interactions).

conclusion

The methodology advocated by this study marks an attempt to provide an alternative set of procedures for performance rating scale production to those that have traditionally been used in language testing. Although the methodology was aimed at producing a rating scale for one genre of spoken performance, it is adaptable in that it can be applied to the development of rating scales for other contexts, specific or general in nature. Unlike North's approach (1995a, b), this methodology was empirically based and utilised insights of specialists in the entire construction stage of the rating scale, and, while the approach was clearly influenced by the data-driven process described by Fulcher (1993), the scale produced is radically different in that it is both practical and usable. The approach also offers a practical operationalisation in a testing context of Bhatia's (1994: 26) observation that ESP teachers should "try to understand the conventions, the concerns, the intentions, and above all the environment in which decisions are taken by the expert members in the discourse community". This study has also striven to add to the scarce literature on the methodology of producing performance rating scales, adopting an empirically based approach to designing a methodology for rating scale production.

This study has demonstrated that a methodology for the development of rating scales can be realised empirically. It has, I believe, also opened up new avenues on the role of the "specialist" in the scale development and performance assessment process for tests of language for specific purposes. The study also lends empirical support to the notion of "indigenous" scales (as suggested by Jacoby, 1998; Jacoby and McNamara, 1999; Douglas, 2000 and Douglas and Myers, 2000) in the evaluation of specific-purpose performances. Collaboration with specific-purpose language use domain specialists right through the process (unlike previous research in which the specialists were only involved at certain stages of the process, e.g. beginning or end) is not impossible, and in fact adds greatly to the validity of the scale.

references

Abdul Raof, A. H. (2002). *The Production of a Performance Rating Scale: An Alternative Methodology.* Unpublished PhD thesis, The University of Reading.

Alderson, J. C. (1991). Bands and Scores. In C. J. Alderson and B. North (Eds), *Language Testing in the 1990s.* London: Modern English Publications and the British Council.

Bhatia, V. K. (1994). ESP and the world of professions: bridging the gap or making inroads? *ESP Malaysia, 2*(1), 19–31.

Chalhoub-Deville, M. (1995). Deriving oral assessment scales across different tests and rater groups. *Language Testing, 12*(1), 16–33.

Clark, J. L. D. and Clifford, R. T. (1988). The FSI/ILR/ACTFL proficiency scales and testing techniques. *Studies in Second Language Acquisition, 10,* 129–147.

Davies, A., Brown, A., Elder, C., Hill, K., Lumley, T. and McNamara, T. (1999). *Dictionary of Language Testing.* Cambridge: Cambridge University Press.

Douglas, D. (2000). *Assessing Languages for Specific Purposes.* Cambridge: Cambridge University Press.

Douglas, D. and Myers, R. (2000). Assessing the communication skills of veterinary students: whose criteria? In A. J. Kunnan (Ed.), *Fairness and Validation in Language Assessment: Selected papers from the 19th Language Testing Research Colloquium. Studies in Language Testing 9.* Cambridge: Cambridge University Press.

Fulcher, G. (1987). Tests of oral performance: the need for data-based criteria. *English Language Teaching Journal, 41,* 287–291.

Fulcher, G. (1993). *The Construction and Validation of Rating Scales for Oral Tests in English as a Foreign Language.* Unpublished PhD thesis, University of Lancaster.

Jacoby, S. (1998). *Science as Performance: Socializing Scientific Discourse through Conference Talk Rehearsals.* Unpublished doctoral dissertation, University of California, Los Angeles.

Jacoby, S. and McNamara, T. (1999). Locating Competence. *ESP Journal, 18*(3), 213–241.

Luoma, S. (2004). *Assessing Speaking.* Cambridge: Cambridge University Press.

McNamara, T. (1996). *Measuring Second Language Performance.* Longman: London and New York.

North, B. (1995a). The development of a common framework scale of descriptors of language proficiency based on a theory of measurement. In A. Huhta, V. Kohonen, L. Kurki-Suonio and S. Luoma (Eds), *Current Development and Alternatives in Language Assessment – Proceedings of LTRC'96.* Jyvaskyla: University of Jyvaskyla and University of Tampere.

North, B. (1995b). The development of a common framework scale of descriptors of language proficiency based on a theory of measurement. *System, 23*(4), 445–465.

North, B. (2000). The development of a common framework scale of language proficiency. S. Belanco (Series Ed.) *Theoretical Studies in Second Language Acquisition,* Vol. 8. Frankfurt: Peter Lang.

North, B. and Schneider, G. (1998). Scaling descriptors for language proficiency scales. *Language Testing, 15*(2), 217–262.

O'Sullivan, B. (1999). *TEEP Revision Project*. Reading: University of Reading.

O'Sullivan, B. (2000). Exploring gender and oral proficiency interview performance. *System, 28*, 373–386.

O'Sullivan, B. (2002a). Learner acquaintanceship and oral proficiency test pair-task performance. *Language Testing, 19*(3), 277–295.

O'Sullivan, B. (2002b). *Evidences of Reliability in the Oral Proficiency Test*. Paper presented as part of the Symposium 'Shifting Conceptions on Reliability'. Hong Kong: LTRC.

O'Sullivan, B. and Rignall. (2002). *Assessing the Value of Bias Analysis Feedback to Raters for the IELTS Writing Module*. IELTS Research Project Final Report.

Turner, C. E. and Upshur, J. A. (1996). Developing rating scales for the assessment of second language performance. *ARAL Series S. 13*, 55–79.

Upshur, J. A. and Turner, C. E. (1995). Constructing rating scales for second language tests. *ELT Journal, 49*(1), 3–12.

8
quantifying conversational styles in group oral test discourse

barry o'sullivan and fumiyo nakatsuhara

introduction

In this chapter, we will focus on the development and application of measures to quantify conversational styles in group oral tests. The approach taken is to modify a set of measures developed to quantify conversational styles in oral proficiency interviews (Young and Milanovic, 1992; Young, 1995; Kormos, 1999). The current popularity of the paired format has seen a rise in the number of research studies that have provided detailed insights into the discourse features found in this type of oral test (Galaczi, 2004; Nakatsuhara, 2004; Norton, 2005; May, 2007; Lazaraton and Davies, 2008; Brooks, 2009; Davies, 2009; May, 2009). In contrast, however, few studies have investigated how test takers interact in group oral tests (He and Dai, 2006; Van Moere, 2007; Nakatsuhara, 2009). Given the ongoing discussion concerning the impact on test scores of the co-construction of discourse in these test forms (McNamara, 1997; O'Sullivan, 2007), it would seem logical that we should strive to more fully understand how test takers interact with each other. This is particularly true of how they initiate and ratify topics, since it is at these junctures in the interaction that co-construction is most likely to be manifested.

In order to respond to this need, we set out first to develop a set of empirically based measures to quantify conversational styles in groups and then to apply these measures to describe conversational styles in group oral tests by comparing three different task types performed under two conditions (groups of three and four).

quantifying conversation

While "conversation" could be defined in a number of ways, van Lier (1989: 495) suggests that there seems to be broad agreement among researchers that conversation involves the following properties: "face-to-face interaction, unplannedness (locally assembled), unpredictability of sequence and outcome, potentially equal distribution of rights and duties in talk, and manifestation of features of reactiveness and mutual contingency". Because of limitations in the test data collected here, we will follow Young and Milanovic (1992), Young (1995) and Kormos (1999) and concentrate only on patterns of goal-orientation, interactional contingency and quantitative dominance. While modifying the methodologies of the above studies, this section will first describe the definitions and measures of the three chosen patterns. Second, it will explain why analytical units such as "t-unit" and "word" were chosen for different analyses. Third, the method of topic identification will be developed, based mostly on the literature but with several modifications to fit the present data.

measuring conversation styles

Goal-orientation involves "the speakers" attempts to realize certain internal goals or plans through the interaction" (Young and Milanovic, 1992: 405). Since conversation is related to "unplannedness (locally assembled)" and also to "equal distribution of rights and duties in talk", all interlocutors should ideally have an equal amount of initiative in this goal-oriented activity (van Lier, 1989: 495). Within the context of group oral testing, topic initiators are those who are goal-oriented and are likely to appropriate the role of chair in a group task. Thus, the measure of goal-orientation is the proportion of topics initiated by a test taker relative to the other test takers in the same group (expressed as a percentage). In Young and Milanovic's (1992) study on interview tests, the proportion of topic initiation was used to quantify a degree of interactional contingency. However, in the present study, it will be used as a measure of goal-orientation, as it seems more relevant to quantify "the speakers" attempts to realize certain internal goals or plans through the interaction" (ibid.: 405) in group oral discourse.

Interactional contingency refers to "a property of adjacent turns in dialogue in which the topic of the preceding turn is co-referential with the topic of the following turn" (Young and Milanovic, 1992: 405). If an utterance is contingent upon an immediately preceding utterance made by an interlocutor, we could describe the relationship of the two utterances as reactive, and such reactiveness is likely to be the key to successful topical continuity across conversational turns. In other words, reactiveness can be seen as a measure of interactional contingency. Therefore, the measure of the contingency used here is the proportion of topics initiated by other test takers in the same group that are ratified and become the topics of the subsequent turns of a test taker (expressed as a percentage). A topic is regarded as ratified if the topic initiation of participant A is followed by at least one "t-unit" (one clause plus any subordinate clauses) by participant B in which the same topic is continued. Topics during which one participant contributed only continuers or backchannels are not considered to be ratified (Young and Milanovic, 1992: 409–10; Young, 1995: 20; Kormos, 1999: 170). The dimensions of interactional contingency and goal-orientation could also reveal which of the four styles of dyadic interaction proposed by Jones and Gerard (1967) could most appropriately represent the interaction.

The third element, quantitative dominance, is also connected to "equal distribution of rights and duties in talk" (van Lier, 1989: 495). Dominance is defined as the tendency for one speaker to control the other speaker's conversational actions by various means (Young and Milanovic, 1992: 406). The multidimensional means for conversational dominance are most systematically classified by Itakura (2001) into sequential, participatory and quantitative dimensions. However, the analysis of dominance in this study focuses only on quantitative dominance. This is because sequential dominance (involving a tendency for one conversant to control the direction of an interaction, for example, with questions or topic initiation (Itakura, 2001: 1864)) in this study is dealt with as goal-orientation above. Additionally, participatory dominance (related to the restriction of speaking rights of the other conversant through interruption and overlap (ibid.: 1867)), seems to be controversial; although interruption and overlap could violate the interrupted speaker's right to maintain and complete the turn (Sacks et al., 1974), they may not necessarily be translated into controlling the other speaker's actions. Instead, they may, for instance, be employed to express interest and involvement in the other speaker's talk or conveying solidarity (Tannen, 1994). Hence, dominance here is measured in only one of the three senses: quantitative dominance, which refers to the level of contribution by the amount of talk (Itakura, 2001: 1870). As an indicator of quantitative dominance, the measure is the proportion of words spoken by a test taker relative to the other test takers in the same group (expressed as a percentage).

analytical units

The t-unit was chosen as the unit for measuring topic ratification for two reasons. First, since the t-unit, which is defined as "one main clause with all subordinate clauses attached to it" (Hunt, 1965), is based on syntactic criteria, it is simple to identify consistently, resulting in reliable analysis. Second, compared to other units, such as the c-unit or words used, the t-unit has more identifiable referential meaning and is therefore more suitable for analysing topical continuity (Young, 1995: 19). For example, both the c-unit and words used approaches would count minimum answers like "Yes" and "OK" as a unit even though they may not always contribute to topic continuation. Another type of measurement unit is the Analysis of Speech Unit (AS-unit (Foster et al., 2000)) developed to analyse speech primarily using syntactic criteria.) While this may at first appear to meet our requirements, the fact that it counts "irregular sentences" (Quirk et al., 1985: 838–853) such as "Yes" and "Oh poor woman" as a unit means that it will not always represent speakers' reactiveness.

While the t-unit is the most popular unit for the analysis of both written and spoken data, the literature has indicated that the definition, which was originally developed for analysing written work, is inadequate to deal with a full analysis of spoken discourse (Foster et al., 2000: 360). Therefore, in order to make it more compatible with speech data, this study will employ Young's (1995: 38) modified definition of the t-unit, which allows it to deal with the elliptical nature of the spoken language.

> The followings were counted as one t-unit each: "a single clause, a matrix plus subordinate clause, two or more phrases in apposition, and fragments of clauses reduced by ellipsis. . . . Elements not counted as t-units include backchannel cues such as mhm and yeah, and discourse boundary markers such as okay, thanks, or good. False starts were integrated into the following t-units.

In order to measure quantitative dominance, the word, which has been used with some success to measure quantitative dominance (Linell et al., 1988; Itakura, 2001; Galaczi, 2004), was chosen as the analytical unit. In spite of the fact that t-units, c-units and AS-units have been used to provide an estimate of quantity of talk (Young and Milanovic, 1992; Young, 1995; Kormos, 1999; Iwashita, 1998, 2001), they are not always accurate when estimating how much the person actually talks. For instance, a speaker could produce a high number of t-units which are very short (Galaczi, 2004: 86–87). In contrast, the number of words indicates more accurately the degree to which each speaker occupies the conversational floor in the sequence of utterances created mutually or in time (Itakura, 2001: 1870).

Additionally, filled pauses, laughter and false starts are excluded from the word count, and words that are cut off are included in the count only if it is clear what the word is. This is because, although these speech elements could also contribute to dominating the conversational floor, they do not directly contribute to the conversation. Moreover, the amount of "Uh huh", for example, greatly varies according to the person's individual speech style, and it could thus result in a skewed picture of how much the person actually talks.

topic identification

Finally, since topic is the key concept used to examine the degree of test takers' topic initiation and topic ratification, a framework to identify "goal-oriented topic shift" should first be clearly established. Here, topic shift does not refer to topic change, but, rather, means "topic development" to achieve the goal of the task. This is because, like most task-based speaking tests, the focus of candidates' talk when completing a task is specified in the task instructions. Therefore, candidates cannot dramatically change topics, for example, from "which camera to buy for the class to use" to "what you would like to eat tonight", as can happen in naturally occurring conversation. Since the analysis is aiming to identify who in a group is more goal-oriented by contributing to task completion, it is necessary to spot where local topics shift (or where topics develop) within a single global topic. However, whether the shift is at the global or local level, it is "an utterance which employs referents unrelated to prior talk in order to implicate a new set of mentionables" (Maynard, 1980: 280).

The identification of topics is far from simple, as "topic maintenance and shift are extremely complex and subtle" (Atkinson and Heritage, 1984: 165). It is also reported that even participants would recognise the topic of the conversation differently (Maynard, 1980). Nevertheless, there seems to be consensus among researchers that, instead of attempting to determine what a topic is about, judging where a topical notion commences and ends suffices for identifying a topic (Brown and Yule, 1983: 94–95). This approach to the analysis of discourse is based on the principle that is suggested by Garfinkel (1967: 28); *what* we are talking about cannot be distinguished from *how* we are speaking. Topics, therefore, can be identified by exploring "action" (what talk-in-interaction is doing) rather than "topicality" (what it is about) (Schegloff, 1990).

In fact, a number of conversation analysis (CA) studies have looked at how a topic is marked when it is closed and then another is initiated (e.g. Maynard, 1980; Button & Casey, 1984; Jefferson, 1984; Hobbs, 1990; Reichman, 1990; Jefferson, 1993; Drew and Holt, 1998; Antaki et al., 2000). For instance, Maynard (1980) noted the significance of pause in topic change. He argues that it is not the case that conversants run out of things to say and bring in a new topic in an unsystematic manner, but "silences are utilized as a resource to focus off the line of talk such that a topic change is invoked to restore continuous speaker transitions" (Maynard, 1980: 280). Therefore, the production of silence acts as a talk-in-interaction mechanism to wind down a topic. Button and Casey (1984) identified a particular type of topic-initiating utterance to invite co-participants to generate new topical materials. They term these utterances topic initial elicitors, prototypical instances of which are "What's new?" and "Anything else to report?" This linguistic device links with Maynard's study on pause, as topic initial elicitors repeatedly appear in the position where a flow of conversation on a prior topic is ending and there is a need to establish a new topic to maintain the conversational flow. In other CA studies, it has been revealed that some discourse markers such as "Okay" (often recurrently) emerge as devices to move towards closure of the interaction or closure of a topic, and in the latter case "Okays" are sometimes followed by a topic initial elicitor (Button, 1987; Beach, 1993).

Jefferson (1993) provides more insight into how topic shift is exercised by describing occurrences of other pre-shift tokens or topic-shift implicature that a conversation partner gives preceding a topic shift. For instance, minimal acknowledgement tokens (e.g. "yes", "yeah") may be recurrently observed immediately preceding a topic shift. Recipients may also shift topics after providing short assessments (e.g. "Oh lovely.", "That's good.") or elaborated commentaries (sometimes with figurative expressions) on the prior utterance (Jefferson, 1993; Drew and Holt, 1998; Antaki et al., 2000).

In the field of language testing, a few researchers have attempted to identify the location of topic shift using CA methodologies. Most of these studies focused on the asymmetrical interaction between an interviewer and an interviewee (Young and Milanovic, 1992; Young, 1995; Kormos, 1999). For them, topic shift refers to topic development (as defined in the present study) within the interactional constraints of the testing context. So, whether we are looking at an interview or a peer–peer test, the global topic in each phase of the test is normally predetermined according to the prescribed set of questions for interviewers or the task prompt card (e.g. lifestyle, recycling). Nevertheless, as long as the conversation is spontaneous talk-in-interaction, participants should follow systematic rules when shifting or developing topics, irrespective of whether the topic is locally or globally shifted, or whether the conversation is natural or institutional. For instance, incorporating CA findings, Young (1995: 19) uses the following criteria to identify topic shift:

> 1) explicit boundary markers such as 'alright', 'so', etc. 2) imperatives in the speech of the interviewer, such as 'Turn to page...' 3) long unfilled pauses 4) introduction of new information 5) rounding off by repetition or paraphrase in closing of a salient lexical item that was used to initiate the topic 6) framing moves such as 'Let's think about that passage for a moment, shall we?' 7) high pitch on a new lexical item as an indication of a topic opening 8) low pitch on the same item that opened a topic (or a paraphrase of it) as an indication of closing 9) explicit abandonment of a topic

Thus far, we have looked to the literatures of both CA and language assessment to see how each deals with issues of topic shift. Based on this overview and an examination of the actual interactions in small-scale pilot data (27 group oral test sessions), we have devised the following nine criteria which identify topic boundaries in order to identify occurrences of "goal-oriented topic shift" in group oral test discourse. The first six are the main criteria and can be seen as stand-alone, while the latter three criteria are used as sub-criteria which should co-occur together with main criteria. This is because gestures, pre-shift markers and long unfilled pauses (Sub-Criteria 7–9) by themselves are not sufficiently informative, as they could have functions other than indicating topic boundaries.

> *Main Criterion 1*: Sequence openers [unspecific] such as "what do you think?" in line 4 of (1) and "Any suggestions?" in line 7 of (2); this is especially used to elicit opinions from quiet group members by addressing their names, for example, "How about you, Mika?"

Example (1): Group of 4 (*A, B, C* and *D*), the free discussion task

1   C: My boyfriend is very poor. So, huh half ha(h)lf, I thi(h)nk.
[Huh
2   A: [huh huh Half half
3   (1.0)
4→C: What do you think?
5   D: Uh::, this is the first date,=
6   A: =[Yeah
7   B: =[Uh:
8   D: so (.) I think a girl expect him to pay?

Example (2): Group of 3 (*G, H* and *I*), the information-gap task

1   G: If you want to listen to music, you can listen to radio or any
[other
2   I: [We don't need that, huh
huh
3   huh [huh huh huh
4   G: [Huh huh huh huh you don't need to
5   H: [Huh huh huh   Yeh
6   (1.5)
7→ I: Any suggestions?
8   (.5)

Main Criterion 2: Sequence openers [specific] such as "shall we look, look at the opinions of others?" as shown in line 3 of (3), and "Intelligence, how about intelligence?" as in line 6 of (4).

Example (3): Group of 3 (*J, K* and *L*), the free discussion task

1   L: Yeh:::
2   (2.0)
3→K: Uh:::::::::: So so shall we look, look at the opinions of others?

Example (4): Group of 3 (*G, H* and *I*), the free discussion task

1   I: [That's very important thing, but not not probably not in
three most important qualities,
2   clear writings,
3   (1.0)
4   H: Uh
5   I: Yeh
6→G: Intelligence, how about intelligence?
7   H: Hu:: that's [difficult.
8   I: [That's important, I guess.

Note: Sequence openers [specific] specify topics to be discussed, while sequence openers [unspecific] allow the recipients to decide what to talk about. Young (1995) calls such utterances "framing moves", which is similar to "focusing moves" in Sinclair and Coulthard's (1992) terminology. However, this study names sequence opener [specific], as it describes the function most accurately to avoid confusion (Clift, 2007: personal communication).

Main Criterion 3: Using a new lexical item with *phonological stress* (also sometimes in <slow speed> or in LOUD VOICE), as in line 3 of (5), and sometimes with a deep inbreath (.h) as in line 3 of (6).

Example (5): Group of 4 (*A, B, C* and *D*), the ranking task

1   B: So, E E will be very good
2   D: Yes
3→B: but ah uh:: What are we going to *use* this camera for?
4   A: I don't know

Example (6): Group of 4 (*A, B, C* and *D*), the ranking task

1   A: We::ll yes
2   (1.0)
3→ B: Uh huh huh,.hh *Fairness* is the most important to me.
4   C: Uh
5   A: Uh::: in university?
6   B: A- a- well not not just university but in the: in the [world in general

Main Criterion 4: Explicitly announcing the introduction of new information; asking for permission to talk about something new (i.e. pre-sequence; Schegloff, 1980), as in line 4 of (7), and pointing out missing information that should be talked about, as in line 3 of (8).

Example (7): Group of 4 (*E, F, G* and *H*) the free discussion task

1   F: = I said I'm gonna pay all, but she said no [I'd like to pay as well,
2   H: [Yeah
3   F: so I just let her pay. Or=
4→ H: = Yeh Can I say something=
5   E: = Yeh, sur[e,
6   H: [I think that it's just important for him just to show that he wants to pay=

Example (8): Group of 4 (*E, F, G* and *H*), the free discussion task

1   G: Uh huh Yeah
2   F: Isn't it? Ability organize class, quite impor[tant
3→E: [It is, but we miss something really
4   important, <*enthusiasm for teaching*>
5   G: Oh
6   E: Because someone just sits there, [I'm gonna I'm gonna spend
50 minutes there

Main Criterion 5: Rounding off the previous topic by summarising what has been discussed; this often occurs with short assessments and/or commentaries, sometimes including repetition of salient lexical items that were used in the topic (lines 16–18 of (9)).

Example (9): Group of 3 (*J, K* and *L*), the free discussion task

1   J: First date=
2   L: =First, first date is important
3   J: Ye[h
(4–14: discussion of "how important the first date can be")
15 L: Yeh This is the first date decides from uh from uh:: his fu(h)
ture, [decides his future. Huh
16→K: [Yeh. First
17→ impression is very important.
18→ J: Yes, important.
19 K: As for the *equality*, I think=

Main Criterion 6: Closing a current topic explicitly by providing reasons for abandoning and terminating a topic (often signalling irrelevance of the current topic and abandoning topics, as in line 5 of Example (10)); repair is undertaken and topic-refocus is conducted.

Example (10): Group of 4 (*M, N, O* and *P*), the free discussion task

1   N: Its its depends on the sit- situation.
2   O: It depe(h)nds Huh huh huh
3   N: If (.5) the ba- if: (.5) the: if the day (.5) if if the day is friend's
birthday,
4   I think [uh
5→ P: [Yeh but this is a date. Huh [huh
6   N: [Yeh, Uh
7   (1.0)

8   P: Uh eh I don't know, if *he* asked that girl out, then eh uh maybe maybe he wants to pay,
9   or cover some of the cost, but if if the *girl* asked him to go o(h)ut with her, then uh why
10   should he cover the (.) uh cost?

Sub-Criterion 7: Using gestures to direct others' attention to something new, together with one or more main criteria, as in line 5 of (11).

Example (11): Group of 4 (*M, N, O* and *P*), the free discussion task

1   O: Just uh:: should be uh equal, even if it's the first first date (.5) dating.
2   P: Uh (.5) I think yeah he just shouldn't. It's matter of principle. [Huh huh
3   O: [Huh huh huh
4   What what do you think about that, other's suggestion about uh him? (.5) Ken?
5→   ((pointing out pictures))
Note: CA studies have reported that gaze direction (Goodwin, 1981) and hand gestures (Schegloff, 1984) play a salient role involved in the management of interaction.

Sub-Criterion 8: Pre-shift tokens such as "alright", "right" (Gardner, 2007), "so" (Raymond, 2004), "okay" (Button, 1987; Beach, 1993), "yeah", "then", "but", "anyway" etc. (Jefferson 1993), together with one or more main criteria, as seen in line 5 and 7 of the following example (12). Also see (2), (3), (4), (5) and (6) above.

Example (12): Group of 4 (*M, N, O* and *P*), the ranking task

1   M: =As a teacher=
2   P: =As a teacher. And more to do with his attitudes towards his profession.
3   O: Uh
4   (1.0)
5→   N: Right,
6   (.5)
7→   N: S(h)o:: (.5) huh huh wha(h)t d(h)o what do you think is the [mo(h)st (.) important? Huh
8   P: [Eh eh

Note: We categorise these tokens referring to only one of the functions, a pre-shift token. However, CA studies have found that each word can have many more functions. For instance, see Gardner (2007) for the use of "right", and see Raymond (2004) for the use of "so". Here, it is important to note that this study is a CA-informed study, but not a CA study, which much more closely analyses conversations.

Sub-Criterion 9: Long unfilled pauses (usually exceeding one second (Jefferson, 1989)), together with one or more main criteria, as in lines 4 and 6 of (13). Also see (1), (2), (3), (4), (6) and (12) above.

Example (13): Group of 3 (*D, E* and *F*), the ranking task
1   D: Well, so related to knowledge of subject, I think *intelligence* is important [too.
2   E: [Uh huh
3   F: Uh huh
4→(2.5)
5   F: %I see%
6→(3.0)
7   E: I don't think sense of humour is really important – OK, of course it's nice if the teacher
8   has got a sense of humour, the class will [be fun.

Although topic identification was primarily based on the formal markers in discourse listed above, it does not mean that semantic content is completely neglected when identifying topics. In fact, as well as these formal criteria, the semantic content is also examined to support whether it makes sense to mark topic boundaries where these linguistic features are signposted in the sequence. It is also worth noting that the constraint of the data within a test task completion sequence actually made topic identification more consistent. That is, most groups followed a similar structure of topic development, due to the nature of the given tasks. In the information-gap task, after exchanging information about cameras, they tended to discuss the types of camera, the budget and other special functions, and then moved on to determine which one to buy. The ranking task first required candidates to discuss ten items provided in the prompt card, one after another, and then they started selecting items according to the ideas raised in the previous exchanges. Compared with these two tasks, which had rather structured instructions to follow, the free discussion task showed a less systematic order of discussion, though the contents were often similar across groups. Thus, while formal markers were the main tools used to identify topic shift, semantic contents were also used to cross-check whether they co-supported the evidence of the topic boundaries. Additionally, for the purpose of this analysis, an old topic revisited was counted as another topic, because we assumed that the person who revisited the old topic must have done so in order to achieve the goal of the task.

reliability

Since topic identification plays an essential role in the analyses (related to the measures of *goal-orientation* and *interactive contingency*), inter-coder reliability was tested in two steps: in terms of 1) the topic boundary criteria and 2) the locations of topic boundaries, using data from the 27 pilot group tests referred to above. First, transcripts from three of these tests were given to a group of 14 researchers together with the above topic boundary criteria. These transcripts were divided into discrete topics, though the criteria used for topic identification were left blank. The 14 researchers were then asked to choose from the nine criteria. After the coding was provided individually, the outcomes were discussed in plenary. Despite minor differences at the beginning of this session, this group agreed that the set of criteria was an effective instrument. Secondly, with the purpose of examining the intercoder reliability on identifying topic boundary locations, the same three transcripts, as well as the topic boundary criteria, were given to another researcher with expertise in the analysis of spoken interactions. An overall agreement level of 91 per cent was recorded. After discussing all disagreements and reaching a consensus on which coding should be adopted, one of the current authors then coded all the transcripts.

applying the measures to quantifying group oral conversation

participants and tasks

A total of 269 Japanese upper-secondary students participated in the study. They worked in groups of three or four and were asked to respond to two of the three tasks (in a counterbalanced order): these were an information-gap task, a ranking task and a free discussion task.

First, *the information-gap task* is characterised as a three- or four-way task where information exchange is obligatory. The amount of information is equally distributed to all the participants, so that all test takers would be given equal opportunity to both request and provide information. The information exchange is followed by a discussion to make a convergent decision to select a single option. Second, *the ranking task* is an optional information exchange, or opinion-gap task, to make a convergent decision using shared information. Candidates are first asked to talk about ten shared items presented in the prompt card, and then to reach an agreed selection of three items out of all the items presented. Third, *the free discussion task* is also an optional information exchange, or opinion-gap task, where a convergent decision is required. However, this task provides candidates with only a topic to discuss, without a fixed set of procedures, and the outcome has unlimited possibilities depending on the candidates' input. Topics for the three tasks are which camera to buy for their class, using the class money (info-gap), which three qualities are the most important for a good high school teacher (ranking), and whether boys should pay all the costs for dates (free discussion). For more details of the task and topic selection, see Nakatsuhara (2009).

results

Table 8.1 shows descriptive statistics concerning the number of topics initiated and ratified and the number of words produced by individual test takers under the different conditions.

Here we can see that test takers tended to initiate more topics in the information-gap and ranking tasks than the free discussion task for both group sizes. This could be because the information-gap and ranking tasks provided test takers with fixed items to be discussed in order to complete these tasks, while the free discussion task required them to be creative in coming up with their own topics. Second, in terms of topic ratification there is a similar tendency, with slightly more topics being ratified in the information-gap and ranking tasks than in the free discussion task. Although it was a not a large trend, the free discussion task, where students could arrive at open outcomes, appears to have allowed test takers to be less reactive to each other. Third, test takers spoke almost twice as much in the information-gap task compared with the other tasks. While it was true that the information-gap task forced even the quietest students to talk about predetermined information in the prompt card due to the task requirement, this result is still somewhat surprising in terms of the amount of talk generated. However, since the length of time allowed for task completion was not controlled

Table 8.1   Descriptive statistics of the three conversational properties counted for individual test takers

Properties	Group size	Task types	N	Mean	Min	Max	SD
Topic initiation	Groups of 3	Info-gap	99	2.27	0	9	1.94
		Ranking	108	2.01	0	10	2.06
		Free discussion	81	1.31	0	7	1.52
	Groups of 4	Info-gap	64	2.31	0	9	2.14
		Ranking	68	1.93	0	9	2.20
		Free discussion	68	1.44	0	7	1.50
Topic ratification	Groups of 3	Info-gap	99	1.57	0	6	1.14
		Ranking	108	1.51	0	7	1.20
		Free discussion	81	1.17	0	4	0.96
	Groups of 4	Info-gap	64	1.53	0	8	1.61
		Ranking	68	1.60	0	6	1.34
		Free discussion	68	1.29	0	4	0.95
The amount of talk	Groups of 3	Info-gap	99	106.73	35	242	45.71
(in words)		Ranking	108	60.29	6	254	49.65
		Free discussion	81	43.70	2	177	34.65
	Groups of 4	Info-gap	64	110.08	29	381	59.20
		Ranking	68	52.93	0	155	35.63
		Free discussion	68	53.91	5	234	42.66

(only a minimum time was set for each test session), we should be careful in comparing performance across the three, as there was a tendency for the information-gap task to take significantly longer than the other tasks. On the other hand, as illustrated in Figures 8.1, 8.2 and 8.3, the two group sizes showed relatively similar patterns of mean scores for the number of topics initiated and ratified and the number of words in all the three tasks.

Lastly, the minimum and the maximum counts indicate that there was a significant discrepancy in the numbers of topics initiated and ratified by each candidate, and, most surprisingly, in the number of words each test taker uttered. For instance, while some candidates spoke as many as 254 words, others spoke as few as six words (in the ranking task performed by groups of three). This, in fact, should be seen as an indication of potential weakness in using some of these task types with particular test populations.

Three two-way between-groups ANOVAs were conducted to further explore whether there was any significant difference related to task type and group size in (i) the number of topics each test taker initiated, (ii) the number of topics each test taker ratified and (iii) the number of words

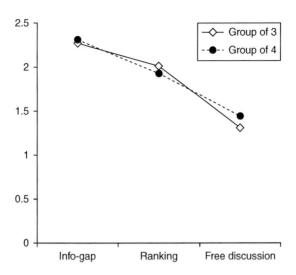

Figure 8.1 Topic initiation count

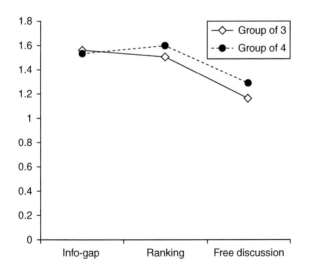

Figure 8.2 Topic ratification count

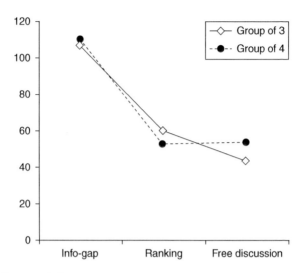

Figure 8.3 The amount of talk count

each test taker produced. Since Levene's tests of equality of error variances indicated that the variances of the dependent variables across the groups were not equal, we followed Pallant's (2001: 205) suggestion that a more stringent significant level of 0.01 should be set when interpreting the results.

Table 8.2 shows that there was a statistically significant main effect for task type on the number of topics each test taker initiated (F(2, 482) = 8.906, $p < 0.001$), although the effect size was small. Post hoc comparisons using the Tukey test indicated that the mean score for the information-gap task was significantly different from the free discussion task ($p < 0.001$). On the other hand, as shown in Table 8.3, group size and task type showed neither a significant main effect nor an interaction effect for topic ratification (again at the 0.01 level).

Table 8.4 shows the result for the amount of talk. There was a significant main effect for task type on the amount of talk that individual test takers produced (F(2, 482)=78.904, $p < 0.001$), and the effect size was large (eta squared (η^2)= 0.247). Post hoc comparisons using the Tukey test showed that the mean score for the information-gap task was significantly different from those of both the ranking task ($p < 0.001$) and the free discussion task ($p < 0.001$).

Table 8.2   Two-way between-groups ANOVAs on topic initiation (sig. level at 0.01)

Factor	F	df	p	Significance	Eta squared (η^2)	Effect
Group size	0.028	1	0.866	Non sig.	–	–
Task type	8.906	2	0.000	Sig.	0.036	small
Group size×Task	0.882	2	0.822	Non sig.	–	–

Table 8.3   Two-way between-groups ANOVAs on topic ratification (sig. level at 0.01)

Factor	F	df	p	Significance
Group size	0.292	1	0.589	Non sig.
Task type	3.545	2	0.030	Non sig.
Group size×Task	0.183	2	0.833	Non sig.

Table 8.4   Two-way between-groups ANOVAs on the amount of talk (sig. level at 0.01)

Factor	F	df	p	Significance	Eta squared (η^2)	Effect
Group size	0.243	1	0.622	Non sig.	–	–
Task type	78.904	2	0.000	Sig.	0.247	large
Group size×Task	1.508	2	0.222	Non sig.	–	–

conclusions

In this chapter we have attempted to achieve two things. First, we looked to the conversation analysis and language testing literatures and the actual data from the pilot test to establish a set of criteria that could be used to measure the conversational styles of candidates in group tests of speaking. Second, we applied the criteria identified to the data generated by a group of learners who participated in a research study in which three tasks were performed in groups of either three or four. We found that the combination of our analysis of the literatures with further exploration of the actual data allowed us to establish a practically useful set of criteria, which we feel will be of value to those researching task performance in applied linguistics in general and language testing in particular.

The application of the criteria to our data showed that, while the size of the group a candidate participated in did not appear to significantly impact on their conversational style, the task they were responding to did. This finding, we feel, has some significant implications for language test developers.

The most obvious implication is that our tests should employ a range of tasks where possible, as this is likely to allow individuals an opportunity to show their best level of performance at some point during the test. If a range of tasks is not possible, then it would appear that the type of information-gap task that we employed (including both information exchange and discussion phases) is most likely to generate language from all participants. However, the worrying finding that some individuals participated in these group activities with only a minimal linguistic contribution is of genuine concern, as the individuals concerned may not produce enough language for a reliable estimate of their ability to be made. This would seem to suggest that the inclusion of individual-focused tasks (interview or monologue) is vital to ensure that all candidates are allowed to show their highest level of ability. In particular cultures, such as that of the participants in this study, shyness and a reluctance to become involved in group-level tasks are perhaps more likely to occur than in others. The fact that there is likely to be a culture effect on task performance implies that the one-size-fits-all approach to testing oral language in large-scale international tests may be biased against candidates from these cultures, unless it is part of the construct to be measured. The very low levels of involvement in task performance found here imply that test developers need to develop more locally sensitive instruments if they are to be truly useful.

Another implication of our findings is on how oral language tests are scored. Here there are two issues. One relates to the criteria that are used by examiners and the other to the way multi-task tests are scored. At present, our rating scales tend not to overtly refer to conversational style, though there is typically some mention of how well candidates manage the discourse of task performance. Our findings suggest that the three patterns we included (i.e. goal-orientation, interactional contingency and quantitative dominance) are very likely to appear in test data and should be included in our ability descriptors.

O'Sullivan (2007) pointed out the need to award separate scores for each test task, arguing that a single score for performance on a number of tasks does not offer a true reflection of a candidate's true ability. While he was referring to the impact on performance of variables associated with a candidate's interlocutor, our findings reinforce his argument. If the conversational style of a candidate is affected by the nature of the task he or she is performing, then the score he/she is awarded by an examiner may vary. In many current tests, where a single score is awarded for performance on a set of tasks, we can never be certain what has influenced the examiner's decision to award a particular score. It may well be that the argument of the examination boards is correct (i.e. that examiners take an overview of performance on all tasks into consideration) or it may be that they are influenced by either good or poor performance on a particular task, and that a halo effect emerges, so that the overall score is overly influenced by this performance.

references

Antaki, C., Houtkoop-Steenstra, H. and Rapley, M. (2000). "Brilliant. Next question...": High-grade assessment sequences in the completion of interactional units. *Research on Language and Social Interaction*, *33*, 235–262.

Atkinson, J. M. and Heritage, J. (1984). *Structures of Social Action*. Cambridge; New York: Cambridge University Press.

Beach, W. A. (1993). Transitional regularities for "casual" "Okay" usages. *Journal of Pragmatics*, *19*, 325–352.

Brooks, L. (2009). Interacting in pairs in a test of oral proficiency: co-constructing a better performance. *Language Testing*, *26*, 341–366.

Brown, G. and Yule, G. (1983). *Discourse Analysis*. Cambridge: Cambridge University Press.

Button, G. (1987). Moving out of closing. In G. Button and J. R. E. Lee (Eds), *Talk and Social Organisation*. Clevedon/Philadelphia, PA: Multilingual Matters, pp. 101–151.

Button, G. and Casey, N. (1984). Generating topic: the use of topic initial elicitors. In J. M. Atkinson and J. Heritage (Eds), *Structures of Social Action*. Cambridge/New York: Cambridge University Press, pp. 167–190.

Davies, L. (2009). The influence of interlocutor proficiency in a paired oral assessment. *Language Testing*, *26*, 367–396.

Drew, P. and Holt, E. (1998). Figures of speech: figurative expressions and the management of topic transition in conversation. *Language in Society*, *27*, 495–522.

Foster, P., Tonkyn, A. and Wigglesworth, G. (2000). Measuring spoken language: a unit for all reasons. *Applied Linguistics*, *21*, 354–375.

Galaczi, E. (2004). *Peer–Peer Interaction in a Paired Speaking Test: The Case of the First Certificate in English*. Unpublished PhD thesis, Columbia University.

Gardner, R. (2007). The *Right* connections: acknowledging epistemic progression in talk. *Language in Society*, *36*, 319–341.

Garfinkel, H. (1967). *Studies in Ethnomethodology*. Englewood Cliffs, NJ: Prentice-Hall.

Goodwin, C. (1981). *Conversational Organisation: Interaction between Speakers and Hearers*. New York: Academic Press.

He, L. and Dai, Y. (2006). A corpus-based investigation into the validity of the CET-SET group discussion. *Language Testing, 23,* 370–401.

Hobbs, J. (1990). Topic drift. In B. Dorval (Ed.), *Conversational Organization and its Development.* Norwood, NJ: Ablex, pp. 3–22.

Hunt, K. (1965). *Grammatical Structures Written at Three Grade Levels.* Champaign, IL: National Council of Teachers of English.

Itakura, H. (2001). Describing conversational dominance. *Journal of Pragmatics, 33,* 1859–1880.

Iwashita, N. (1998). The validity of the paired interview in oral performance assessment. *Melbourne Papers in Language Testing, 5*(2), 51–65.

Iwashita, N. (2001). The effect of learner proficiency on interactional moves and modified output in nonnative-nonnative interaction in Japanese as a foreign language. *System, 29,* 267–287.

Jefferson, G. (1984). On stepwise transition from talk about a trouble to inappropriately next-position matters. In J. M. Atkinson and J. Heritage (Eds), *Structures of Social Action.* Cambridge/New York: Cambridge University Press.

Jefferson, G. (1989). Preliminary notes on a possible metric which provides for a 'standard maximum' silence of approximately one second in conversation. In D. Roger and P. Bull (Eds), *Conversation: An Interdisciplinary Perspective.* Clevedon: Multilingual Matters, pp. 166–196.

Jefferson, G. (1993). Caveat speaker: preliminary notes on recipient topic-shift implicature. *Research on Language and Social Interaction, 26,* 1–30.

Jones, E. E. and Gerard, H. B. (1967). *Foundations of Social Psychology.* New York: Wiley.

Kormos, J. (1999). Simulating conversations in oral proficiency assessment: a conversation analysis of role plays and non-scripted interviews in language exams. *Language Testing, 16*(2), 163–188.

Lazaraton, A. and Davies, L. (2008). A microanalytic perspective on discourse, proficiency, and identity in paired oral assessment. *Language Assessment Quarterly, 5,* 313–335.

van Lier, L. (1989). Reeling, writhing, drawing, stretching, and fainting in coils: oral proficiency interviews as conversation. *TESOL Quarterly, 23*(3), 489–508.

Linell, P., Gustavsson, L. and Juvonen, P. (1988). Interactional dominance in dyadic communication: a presentation of initiative-response analysis. *Linguistics, 26,* 415–442.

May, L. (2007). *Interaction in a Paired Speaking Test: The Rater's Perspective.* Unpublished PhD thesis, the University of Melbourne.

May, L. (2009). Co-constructed interaction in a paired speaking test: the rater's perspective. *Language Testing, 26,* 397–421.

Maynard, D. W. (1980). Placement of topic changes in conversation. *Semiotica, 30,* 263–290.

Nakatsuhara, F. (2004). *An Investigation into Conversational Style in Paired Speaking Tests.* Unpublished MA thesis, the University of Essex.

Nakatsuhara, F. (2009) *Conversational Styles in Group Oral Tests: How is the Conversation Co-constructed?* Unpublished PhD thesis, the University of Essex.

Norton, J. (2005). The paired format in the Cambridge speaking tests. *ELT Journal, 59,* 287–297.

O'Sullivan, B. (2007). *Modelling Performance in Tests of Spoken Language.* Frankfurt: Peter Lang.

Pallant, J. (2001). *SPSS Survival Manual*. Berkshire, NY: Open University Press.

Quirk, R., Greenbaum, S., Leech, G. and Svartvik, J. (1985). *A Comprehensive Grammar of the English Language*. Harlow: Longman.

Raymond, G. (2004). Prompting action: the stand-alone "so" in ordinary conversation. *Research on Language and Social Interaction, 37*, 185–218.

Reichman, R. (1990). Communication and mutual engagement. In B. Dorval (Ed.), *Conversational Organization and its Development*. Norwood, NJ: Ablex, pp. 23–48.

Sacks, H., Schegloff, E. A. and Jefferson, G. (1974). A simplest systematics for the organization of turn-taking for conversation. *Language, 50*(4), 696–735.

Schegloff, E. A. (1980). Preliminaries to preliminaries: "Can I ask you a question?" *Sociological Inquiry, 50*, 104–152.

Schegloff, E. A. (1984). 'On some gestures' relation to talk. In J. M. Atkinson and J. Heritage (Eds), *Structures of Social Action: Studies in Conversation Analysis*. Cambridge: Cambridge University Press, pp. 266–296.

Schegloff, E. A. (1990). On the organization of sequences as a source of "coherence" in talk-in-interaction. In B. Dorval (Ed.), *Conversational Organization and Its Development*. Norwood, NJ: Ablex, pp. 51–77.

Sinclair, J. and Coulthard, M. (1992). Towards an analysis of discourse. In M. Coulthard (Ed.), *Advances in Spoken Discourse Analysis*. London: Routledge.

Tannen, D. (1994). *Gender and Discourse*. Oxford: Oxford University Press.

Van Moere, A. (2007). *Group Oral Test: How does Task Affect Candidate Performance and Test Score?* Unpublished PhD thesis, Lancaster University.

Young, R. (1995). Conversational styles in language proficiency interview. *Language Learning, 45*(1), 3–42.

Young, R. and Milanovic, M. (1992). Discourse variation in oral proficiency interviews. *Studies in Second Language Acquisition, 14*, 403–424.

9
a case of testing L2 english reading for class level placement

anthony green

introduction

This chapter describes the development of the reading component of an innovative suite of placement tests designed to assist in assigning learners to English language classes at an appropriate level. The test was intended for use with learners at a wide range of levels of proficiency on courses delivered in a variety of teaching environments. As a case study of the design and pilot phases of a test development project it provides an account of some of the ways in which test purpose, theoretical considerations and practical constraints can each play a role in shaping the test emerging from such a process. It shows how decisions taken at each stage of development contribute to a validity argument supporting the use of the test (Bachman, 2005) and how this argument can be reviewed and revised as the test passes through phases of development en route to becoming fully operational.

The process of development is considered in relation to Weir's (2005a) socio-cognitive framework for test validation. This framework, devised to inform operational test development and validation processes, suggests five aspects of validity that need to be considered: cognitive, context, scoring, consequential and criterion-related. See Chapter 1 of this book, in which Weir and O'Sullivan describe a recently updated version of this framework.

the brief

To help in understanding the decisions taken with respect to the design of the test, it is important first to outline the brief given to the development team and the practical constraints that this imposed. The purpose of a test is the starting point in the design process and for any consideration of its validity. The team, working at the University of Bedfordshire, was asked to develop a test of reading skills as part of a battery of placement instruments to be used in British Council teaching centres worldwide to place students into suitable courses according to their level of proficiency.

Class placement is usually seen to be a relatively low stakes decision: one that does not have serious or irreversible consequences for the test taker (Hughes, 2003). A language learner placed into an unsuitable class can generally be moved to a more suitable one once the mistake has been acknowledged. Nonetheless, it is important to institutions to make as few such errors as possible, since learners may lose the motivation to study and so drop out of their course if they are placed into a class that they do not feel matches their needs.

The test-taking population would be very diverse. It was anticipated that around 100,000 placement tests would be administered each year to learners ranging in age from 14 to over 60 and from a wide variety of first language and educational backgrounds: some test takers would be highly educated professionals while others would still be at school. The courses were based on the six levels of the Common European Framework of Reference (CEFR) (Council of Europe, 2001) and the test would have to cover the full range of these from below A1 (i.e. the level of the starting language learner, which we termed A0) to C2 (also called "mastery" in the CEFR scheme).

Results would need to be instantly available so that potential students could immediately be offered a suitable course. As trained teaching staff might not always be available, the tests would need to be scored by clerical staff with no training in language teaching.

There would be limited time available for testing, so only a very brief reading test would be feasible. Other elements in the test battery would include an oral interview and tests of grammar and vocabulary, and these would also need to be accommodated. Time limitations negotiated with the client and with partners working on other components allowed for no more than 20–25 minutes of test takers' time to be spent on reading.

It was also felt to be important that test takers should not be presented with too many items that were either too easy or too difficult for them. If the test appeared too easy, they might become bored; if it seemed too difficult, they might lose heart. In either case, as potential customers, they might be deterred from enrolling for a course.

These requirements restricted the scope of the test in several important respects. The sheer diversity of the test-taking population implied that the tasks would need to reflect the most general purposes for reading at each level and that the content would need to be widely accessible and free of culturally specific references or assumptions.

As all tasks would need to be delivered within a strict time frame, the number of items would inevitably be circumscribed. The fewer the items in a test, the less reliable it is likely to be. Hence there was pressure to deliver as many items as possible within the time available. For this reason, items requiring lengthy instructions or extensive detailed reading were ruled out.

The time limitations provided a further incentive to deliver items that would match each test taker's level of ability. Answering large numbers of easy or difficult questions would take time and provide little useful information about a learner. Advanced level items targeting C2 would provide little information about whether a learner is at the A1 or B1 level of the CEFR, as learners at both of these levels would be very likely to get such items wrong. Items at the A2 level, on the other hand, might discriminate well between the two.

In order to make best use of the time available and to comply with the request to avoid presenting test takers with numbers of unnecessarily easy or difficult items, the team developed, in parallel with the tests, a set of pre-assessments or short screening instruments that might be used to ensure that students were directed to a full test form that would be suitable for their level. These included self-assessment checklists based on can-do statements from the CEFR, self-assessment in relation to texts representing the CEFR levels and brief c-tests based on graded texts. Centres were asked to select from these pre-assessments the format or combination of formats that appeared best suited to their context and to give sufficiently accurate results.

On this basis, prospective learners would be given an initial level estimate. They would then be directed to a test that would include three tasks at adjacent levels. A learner who was initially estimated to be at level B1 would therefore receive an A2, a B1 and a B2 task in the placement test while those estimated to be at C1 or C2 would receive the B2, C1 and C2 tasks.

The requirement for quick, objective scoring effectively limited the task formats to selected response items or to very short constructed response items with no more than a handful of plausibly correct answers. More open-ended formats (such as summary writing) that would require judgement on the part of markers would not be practical in these circumstances.

laying the theoretical foundations

It is widely held that the test developer faces two options when developing a placement test: basing test content either on a theory of language proficiency or on the learning objectives of the curriculum that students will study (Green and Weir, 2004; Brown, 2005). Hughes (2003: 14) suggests that accuracy of placement will depend on the use of tests that adequately reflect "the key features at different levels of the institution". In this case, there was no single curriculum in operation across the centres where the test would be used, but as the course levels were based on the CEFR it seemed most appropriate to take this as a starting point for the test design.

We have already seen that practical concerns limited the choices available to the test development team in devising suitable tasks and scoring procedures. Within these limitations we sought, in line with Weir's (2005a) socio-cognitive framework, to offer reading texts and associated tasks that would reflect salient differences between learners at the different CEFR levels in terms of the texts they might be able to access and the cognitive processes they might be able to engage.

In pursuing this goal, we faced an immediate obstacle. Although the CEFR provides some general guidance on the kinds of texts that might be accessible at each level, its shortcomings as a basis for test specifications have been well documented (Fulcher, 2004; Alderson, 2005; Weir, 2005b; McNamara and Roever, 2006). The performance level descriptions contained in the illustrative scales of the CEFR do not generally provide specific detail on aspects of context validity such as the range of vocabulary or grammatical complexity involved in texts suited to readers at different levels, or performance conditions such as the amount of time available for reading. Nor does the CEFR offer detailed guidance on cognitive validity: how readers at each level process the texts that they read and the degree of comprehension that they are able to achieve. This level of specification would need to be added by the team. In order to successfully target reading tasks at each CEFR level, we therefore needed first to establish what might characterise second language reading at the various levels.

Enright et al. (2000), building on suggestions made by Carver (1997), suggest that the reader's purposes for reading are a useful starting point for test development. They identify four:

(1) Reading to find information (or "search reading")
(2) Reading for basic comprehension (aiming for general comprehension or comprehension of [just] the major points in a text)
(3) Reading to learn (aiming to construct an organised representation of the text that includes major points and supporting details)
(4) Reading to integrate information across multiple texts.

For Khalifa and Weir (2009), fulfilling these purposes involves the reader in selecting a reading type such as *skimming, careful local reading* or *search reading*. Reading types vary on two dimensions:

(1) Scope of comprehension (contrasting local comprehension at the level of phrases and clauses with global reading at the level of the text and across texts);
(2) Pace of reading (contrasting expeditious with careful reading).

scope of comprehension

Global reading is directed at arriving at an overall understanding of a text or texts, while local reading is concerned only with understanding a limited portion such as a word, phrase or sentence. In reading for global comprehension, the main concern is with understanding the relationships between macrostructural propositions: ideas classically expressed at the level of the paragraph (Vipond, 1980). At global level, a reader may try to establish the macrostructure and the discourse topic of a text by *skimming* – reading selectively to obtain the gist, general impression and/ or superordinate idea of a text (Weir, 2005a; Khalifa and Weir, 2009) – or may seek to build an incremental representation of how the ideas in the text as a whole relate to each other through *careful global reading*.

Local comprehension refers to the understanding of propositions at the level of the sentence and the clause: the microstructure of a text. Cohen and Upton (2006) suggest that local comprehension is strongly associated with lexical, syntactic and semantic knowledge. It embraces *decoding (word recognition, lexical access* and *syntactic parsing)* and *establishing propositional meaning* at the clause and sentence level. Through local comprehension one may arrive at an understanding of the basic propositions made in a text, but not of their interrelationships. If too much of a reader's cognitive resource is required in order to achieve local comprehension, global comprehension is impaired – the reader can't see the wood for the trees.

pace of reading

Historically, the majority of studies of reading as a process have been concerned with *careful reading*: the extraction of complete meanings from presented material. However, as Rayner and Pollatsek (1989) acknowledge, careful reading models may have little to tell us about how skilled readers can cope with other reading behaviours such as the skimming for gist described above. For Khalifa and Weir (2009), careful reading can take place both at the local and at the global level. That is to say that a reader may read carefully in order to understand a clause, a sentence, part of a text, a complete text or a related collection of texts, but in all cases the approach to reading is based on slow, careful, linear, incremental reading for comprehension.

Contrasted with careful reading, expeditious reading is quick, selective and efficient. This includes the *skimming* that we have already encountered, as well as *scanning* a text to find specific words or phrases and *search reading* to locate information relating to a certain topic. Scanning involves reading to achieve very specific goals, such as finding certain words or phrases, and so requires only a local level of comprehension. Search reading differs from scanning in that no specific word or phrase is in focus and from skimming in that the search for information is guided by predetermined topics, so the reader does not necessarily have to establish a macro-propositional structure for the whole of the text. Skimming is global in scope as the objective is to form an overall representation of a text.

The wide range of reading models found in the second language literature suggest that when reading for different purposes readers may need to engage different cognitive processes, or to balance these processes in different ways. In developing the reading tests, as well as ensuring that the texts we employed would be suitable for the intended level of the test taker with respect to such contextual features as text length, lexical frequency, structural frequency, discourse mode and functional range, we also needed to consider carefully the *cognitive processing* required by test tasks to ensure that they would approximate to what readers do in non-test settings when they engage in different types of reading. The development team was concerned that the mental processes readers use in comprehending texts when engaging in different types of real life reading should be reflected when test takers processed the reading test tasks.

A language learner might need to engage only in careful local reading when encountering a short message or email. The message is understood if the basic propositions are successfully decoded. Expeditious local reading (scanning or search reading) is suitable when the reader has to quickly identify relevant information – such as finding out from a floor guide which area in a department store offers pens and notebooks. Often, in educational settings or other contexts in which the reader learns new information from a text, expeditious local reading is followed by careful reading: the student finds a section in a text book concerning a topic of interest and then reads this section carefully. Expeditious global reading is often sufficient to support a good level of comprehension when dealing with familiar topics, but careful global reading may be needed when dealing with texts that concern more complex or unfamiliar ideas. Key texts in an area of professional expertise will often require careful global reading: the relationship between ideas being as important to a full understanding of the text as the individual propositions expressed.

Having briefly discussed types of reading from a theoretical perspective, in the following section we examine how differences in reading processes relate to different levels of performance. To inform the test development process we examined the performance level descriptions provided in the CEFR – the levels to be targeted by the test – and considered Khalifa and Weir's (2009) suggestions on operationalising these levels for testing purposes.

CEFR levels and reading processes

In the CEFR there is no mention of differences in the pace of reading at levels A1 or A2, and it is argued in the literature that unskilled L2 readers are unable to adjust their processing when confronted with different purposes for reading (Koda, 2005). It seems appropriate that at the A1 and A2 levels a reader should only have to process information carefully. However, within these limitations, basic scanning tasks such as using "the *Yellow Pages*' to find a service or tradesman" and finding "specific, predictable information in simple everyday material such as advertisements, prospectuses, menus and timetables" become possible at the A2 level.

At the B1 level readers can carry out a simple form of what Enright et al. (2000) refer to as "reading to find information". Carver (1997) and Khalifa and Weir (2009) call this "search reading" – although, confusingly, it is referred to as "scanning" in the CEFR (Council of Europe, 2001: 70). If search reading of this kind appears at B1, expeditious global reading – skimming – is particularly associated with the C levels. By B2 learners are capable of "adapting style and speed of reading to different texts and purposes", but it is at C1 that we are told that a learner can "read quickly enough to cope with the demands of an academic course" (Council of Europe, 2001: 251).

Khalifa and Weir (2009) argue in any case that tasks requiring global understanding at the text level may be best suited to the C1 level and above because of the more demanding processing such tasks require. Inevitably, building a text-level representation also requires that the reader should decode a text and form an understanding at the propositional level as well. Skilled readers are, it is suggested, more likely to recognise changes of topic in a text; enrich their comprehension by bringing in general knowledge of the world or topic knowledge; and build meaning at a global (text) level rather than just at local (sentence) level. From the C1 level upwards readers should be able to answer items that test understanding of relationships between ideas in a text.

Of course, the pace of reading and scope of comprehension implicit in a reading task are not the only considerations in judging its difficulty. The level of the cognitive demands that a text makes on a reader will also depend on a number of what Enright et al. (2000) call text and task variables. Weir (2005a) and Khalifa and Weir (2009) refer to these as contextual parameters. These include text length, the time available for reading and the nature of the language used. Shorter texts with simpler vocabulary and simple sentence structures are likely to be easier to read than longer texts with infrequent vocabulary and complex sentence structure, although factors such as idiomaticity of language, genre and topic familiarity also contribute to difficulty.

In the CEFR, as in Khalifa and Weir's (2009) account of the Cambridge suite of CEFR-related tests, at lower levels vocabulary is restricted to the everyday, literal and concrete. The structures associated with the A1 level are "very basic phrases" and "very simple sentences" contained in texts such as "simple narratives and descriptions, straightforward instructions, directions and explanations", advertisements, prospectuses, menus and timetables and "standard routine letters and faxes (enquiries, orders, letters of confirmation etc.)".

As learners advance through the CEFR levels, they are gradually expected to deal with increasingly subtle uses of language that are indicative of the writer's attitude. Words may be less concrete and issues of polysemy may arise. Although the B2 learner is able to understand "the main ideas of complex text on both concrete and abstract topics, including technical discussions in his/her field of specialisation"

(CEFR: 24), more detailed understanding of "specialised articles and longer technical instructions" outside the learner's immediate field of interest is not available until levels C1 and C2 (CEFR: 27). At these higher levels, the relationship between propositions also becomes increasingly complex.

There is a progression in terms of sentence structure from short, simple sentences to long, complex sentences. Khalifa and Weir (2009) observe increasing complexity in verb forms through the levels of the examinations they analyse. The use of modals, conditionals, inversion and other structures become more common as texts at higher levels become more concerned with conveying feelings and opinions, persuading and hypothesising rather than dealing simply with the presentation of information as they do at lower levels. Referencing is one aspect of structure that Khalifa and Weir (2009) consider noticeably more challenging in higher-level texts, where a reader needs to engage in sometimes quite complex anaphoric resolution and be aware of the contribution of synonyms to text coherence.

initial consultation with teachers

Having derived from the literature salient differences between the kinds of texts that learners at different levels might be expected to access and the reading tasks that they might be expected to accomplish, the team drew up draft specifications operationalising these differences. In addition to the feedback provided through regular meetings with senior British Council staff, the team was keen to learn directly from teachers in the field whether they would agree with our interpretation of the CEFR levels and the kinds of texts and tasks that might allow us to discriminate between them.

A questionnaire was sent to British Council offices around the world to learn what task types teachers in these centres considered appropriate to learners at the different performance levels as they experienced them in their classes (see Table 9.1). We also provided samples of texts edited to our specifications and displaying a range of the features identified for each level. We asked the teachers to judge the suitability of these texts for learners in their classes.

Responses were received from 38 teachers working in 24 countries including Bangladesh, Cameroon, Colombia, Italy, Kuwait, South Korea and Thailand. A majority of respondents regarded the sample texts as being appropriate for the targeted level (see Table 9.2). Disagreement was highest at the A2 level (ten teachers regarded the text as too easy,

Table 9.1   Reading test task type options presented to British Council staff

Name	Description
Multiple choice question	Test takers are required to select the best choice from several options for each question or incomplete statement based on the understanding of the text. Questions/incomplete statements may appear before or after the text.
Short answer question	Short answer questions are generically those that require the test takers to write down answers in spaces provided on the question paper. Questions may appear before or after the text.
Multiple matching	In multiple matching, test takers may be required to choose the most suitable headings from a given "heading bank" for identified paragraphs or sections of a text, or for several texts. Alternatively , test takers are required to choose from paragraphs in a text the one(s) that contain(s) the necessary information for answering the questions or fit(s) the statement provided. At lower levels they may have to choose an option that completes a dialogue; match responses to utterances; match words with synonyms and so on.
Gap-filling summary	Test takers are required to fill in the gaps in notes or summary paragraphs of the text by using their own words, words from the text, or a bank of optional words according to the information provided in the text.
Cloze/selective deletion gap filling	Test takers are required to fill in single word gaps in a passage or select from a number of options provided for each gap. Random deletion every nth word or selective deletion according to a lexico-grammatical framework.
Sentence insertion	Test takers have to insert a number of sentences into the gaps in a text.
Paragraph insertion	Test takers have to insert a number of paragraphs appropriately into a gapped text.
C-test	Test takers are required to read through a text and complete every incomplete word in the text (usually second half of every second word deleted).
Cloze Elide	Test takers are required to read through a passage and underline all the foreign or irrelevant words that do not belong to the passage.
Information transfer	Test takers are required to transfer the textual information provided in a text into a non-verbal form by labelling or completing a diagram, table, grid and so on.
Sequencing	Test takers are required to put headings, paragraphs, statements and so on into the correct sequential order according to text or chronological order. Alternatively , test takers are required to reorder some statements to form a new paragraph.
Summarising	Test takers are asked to complete a summary of a text (one or two sentences of which are provided) by selecting additional sentences from a list that express the most important ideas in the passage...Distractors include ideas that either are not presented in the passage or are deemed to be minor ideas. Could be across texts too.

two as too difficult and 24 as appropriate to the level). The texts for the B2 to C2 levels were the least controversial, with 33 of 36 respondents regarding the B2 text and 32 of 35 the C1 and C2 texts as being appropriate to the relevant level.

With regard to task types, multiple choice questions were seen by the largest number of respondents to be *very suitable* for the lowest-level learners from A0 to A2 (Figure 9.1), but they were less likely to be

Table 9.2   British Council teacher judgements concerning suitability of sample texts for CEFR levels (*n* = 36)

Level	Too easy	Appropriate to level	Too difficult
A0	6	27	3
A1	10	24	2
A2	7	26	2
B1	7	26	3
B2	2	33	1
C1	2	32	1
C2	1	32	2

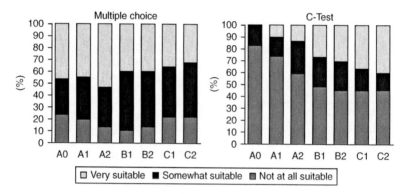

Figure 9.1   Teacher judgements of suitability of *Multiple Choice* and *C-Test* task types

regarded as *very suitable* at the higher levels. Most of the other formats included on the questionnaire were said to be better suited to higher than lower-level test takers. *Multiple matching, sentence* and *paragraph insertion, information transfer, sequencing, gap-filling summaries* and *summarising* (see Table 9.1) were all seen by the largest number to be *very suitable* for test takers at the B1 level or above. Short answer questions were regarded as *very suitable* by the largest number of respondents for the A2 level and above, but c-tests were not regarded as *very suitable* by a majority for any level of test takers (Figure 9.1).

Overall the exercise, although eliciting only a limited number of responses, appeared to confirm that the texts we had identified were suitable for the levels. Multiple choice items, which are widely familiar and offer the test taker a degree of support, appeared to be most suitable for lower-level learners, while a wider range of task types could be used with those at the A2 or B1 levels and above.

the task design phase

Following the literature review and initial consultation phases, team members worked to create tasks to operationalise the levels, incorporating what we had learned about the nature of the texts that learners might be able to access, the ways in which they might read them and the nature of the understandings that they might arrive at as a result of reading. Although initially the intention had been to include an A0 task, following the consultation exercise it was concluded that a separate test of reading at this level would be unnecessary, as learners are expected to understand only a limited range of isolated words and phrases. The kinds of exercise that might be possible (such as matching words to pictures) were to be included in any case in the test of vocabulary.

At A1, to address reading a "single phrase at a time, picking up familiar names, words and basic phrases and rereading as required" (CEFR: 69), a very simple message in postcard format was chosen (also reflecting the CEFR descriptor "can understand short, simple messages on postcards" (CEFR: 69)). The six three-option multiple choice questions (the first being an example) were all targeted at the sentence level and involved decoding skills.

At the A2 level, where the intention was to establish that test takers might be able to process "simple everyday material such as advertisements" (CEFR: 26), we first intended to use a brief advertisement with comprehension questions. Although our sample texts were generally judged to be level-appropriate, it proved difficult to find advertisements that seemed both authentic and equally accessible across cultures. In place of the advertisements, we used a very basic narrative. Test takers were required to sequence a series of seven sentences (the first being given as an example) to reconstruct a coherent text. This was intended to reflect a level of propositional comprehension adequate to support understanding of texts such as "short newspaper articles describing events" (CEFR: 69). To reconstruct the narrative, the test taker would need to be able to recover the relationships between the events in the story.

At B1, the CEFR suggests that learners should be able to "read straightforward factual texts on subjects related to his/her field and interest with a satisfactory level of comprehension" (CEFR: 69). To address this, the task at this level involved test takers filling seven gaps in a short passage on a concrete topic of general interest from a selection of 16 words provided in a box below the passage. The focus here was on features of coherence such as referencing and the relationships between proposi-tions at the local paragraph level. Again, as at all levels, the first answer was given as an example.

As learners progress through the CEFR levels they are able to proc-ess lengthier texts. While the design team wanted to include longer texts to reflect this, we were also aware that the time constraints would inevitably impose a limit on the amount of input that could reasonably be presented. The compromise solution was to use the same *text* for the three highest levels with *tasks* of increasing complexity representing the demands of each CEFR level as well as additional mini-texts to be used alongside this main text at the highest (C2) level.

As learners at B2 and above are said to be able to "understand articles and reports concerned with contemporary problems in which the writ-ers adopt particular stances or viewpoints" (CEFR: 27), texts with an argumentation rhetorical structure based around the advantages and disadvantages of a course of action (see Enright et al., 2000) were cho-sen for this B2–C2 text. Several texts with this rhetorical structure were sourced and evaluated by the members of the focus group, and those initially identified as being most appropriate were edited according to the text specifications previously established for each CEFR level and were analysed for compliance using a context validity checklist cover-ing features such as vocabulary frequency and range, grammatical com-plexity, coherence, abstractness of content and rhetorical organisation (see Weir et al., 2009).

The B2 task was designed to test reading comprehension at sentence level. It was intended that a successful test taker at B2 level would need to search read in order to locate relevant ideas, but would not, in finding the correct responses, need to comprehend the text as a whole by relating these ideas to each other. B2 items were designed such that each question could be linked with information explicitly presented in the text and appearing within a sentence. The test taker was asked to match seven of eight "subtitles" with the seven para-graphs in the text (the one additional subtitle served as a distractor). The topic sentences of each paragraph were explicit enough to enable direct matching using lexical cues (synonymy at the word or phrase level). Excluding the example, there were six matches for the test taker to make.

In line with our analysis of performance levels, the C1 task should require the reader to process the whole text and to form a macrostruc-ture of the main ideas. The test taker should not be able to complete the task simply by integrating a few isolated propositions from the text.

A popular format for assessing macrostructure formation is summary writing. However, summarisation requires extensive writing and, in addition to issues this raises about testing "reading comprehension" independently from writing skills, this would not be practical within the requirement for rapid, objective scoring set by the client.

The format selected involved test takers selecting summary statements based on parts of the text at the paragraph or multi-paragraph level. The summary statements were presented in random order and there were two additional statements to serve as distractors. The task required test takers first to identify the six correct statements and then to order them as the information appeared in the text. As the first one was given as an example, there were five summary statements to be chosen and ordered. Care was taken to avoid the use of direct word or phrase matching through synonymy.

The C2 task proved the most challenging of the three higher-level tasks to design, as there were no obvious precedents to draw on. The intention was to operationalise the combination of information across texts in line with the CEFR performance description "can understand a wide range of long and complex texts" (CEFR: 69) and Khalifa and Weir's (2009) observation that learners at the highest level are able to take information from multiple sources to build an integrated structure. Although some tests of English for academic purposes, such as the TOEFLibt (Educational Testing Service) or TEEP (University of Reading), include an essay based on combining information from listening and reading input texts, these are usually scored as writing tests rather than as indicators of reading or listening comprehension. Use of such an essay would, in any case, be precluded by the requirement for objective scoring. Therefore, we needed to isolate the processes involved in relating texts and to design an appropriate task to assess the ability to read across texts that could be scored quickly and objectively.

The literature suggests that, in reading across texts, the first step is to see the relation between the texts: to identify the information that is mutually relevant. Following discussion of a number of alternatives, the C2 task finally selected for inclusion in the test involved reading and understanding one main text and a number of mini-texts or short (60 to 120-word) extracts from texts on related topics. Test takers were required to decide, out of the seven paragraphs in the passage, which best related to each of the six mini-texts.

As one answer was given as an example, test takers would need to match five mini-texts with five related paragraphs from the six remaining in the main text. Thus one of the main text paragraphs served as a distractor, being unrelated to any of the mini-texts.

After sourcing suitable texts, members of the design team wrote prototype tasks. The most promising of these were chosen for further development. The tasks, texts and instructions were then edited in an iterative manner: team members submitted tasks for collective editing sessions where the tasks were reviewed for suitability, difficulty and fairness and suggestions were made for refinements. Following further individual work, additional sessions would be held until no further changes were indicated. During the earliest of these sessions, entire texts were rejected, but over time the sessions focused more on refining individual items. Once the group was satisfied with the tasks, two language testing experts who had not previously been directly involved in the test development evaluated the tests and suggested further (minor) revisions.

consultation on task design

By this stage, the development team had individually and collectively invested considerable time in close editing of the tasks and instructions, but this could not be sufficient to guarantee that our tests would identify the CEFR reading level of prospective learners. Further evidence would be needed that our judgements coincided with those of others with experience of the CEFR and with those of teachers in the centres that would use the tests. Even more importantly, we needed to establish that our tests had what Weir (2005a) terms *scoring validity*: that they could accurately and consistently discriminate between learners at different levels of ability. This could only be done by having language learners take the tests and analysing the results.

In a second round of consultation with British Council staff, the team invited comment on the tests. Teachers were asked to judge whether the texts and tasks were suited to the levels, whether instructions were clear and whether they could identify any other problems (such as potential bias against certain students). At every CEFR level the majority of these teachers felt that each of the tasks was "appropriate to the stated CEFR level": the percentage ranging from 59 per cent at the B2 level to 70 per cent at C1. The highest proportion responding "no" to this question was for the A1 level (13 per cent, perhaps reflecting the concern raised in some comments about the range of vocabulary) with none responding "no" at the B2 and A2 levels.

The third "not sure" option was selected by 41 per cent at the B2 level. This result for B2 may have reflected a degree of concern about the use of the single text to cover B2 to C2, as the text was, no doubt, rather challenging for the B2 learner. The development team considered that, although the text might not be understood in detail at B2, this level of comprehension would not be required by the task. The CEFR suggests that at B2 learners "can scan quickly through long and complex texts, locating relevant details" (CEFR: 70). Such learners may achieve "basic comprehension" of complex texts, but may not be able to use them for "reading to learn" in the sense used by Enright et al. (2000).

the piloting phase

At this point, the team was finally able to assemble sets of tasks into test forms. We were now in a position to collect the empirical evidence that would be needed to show that test takers were engaging different reading processes in arriving at their answers to the tasks, that these tasks represented levels of increasing difficulty (cognitive and context validity), that results were reliable (scoring validity) and that the task levels corresponded to the levels of the CEFR (criterion-related validity).

The tasks were piloted with groups of students from a range of backgrounds studying at British Council centres and other language schools in a variety of countries including Japan, the Netherlands, Spain and Turkey. In all, 1135 students each took one of three level-based versions of the test: one targeted at A1 and A2, the second at A2, B1 and B2 and the third at B2, C1 and C2. As the content of the test forms overlapped, all could be analysed as a single data set using Rasch analysis in order to place the results on a single measurement scale (see Bond and Fox, 2001).

In addition to taking the tests, those taking the highest-level test form (B2 to C2) also completed a brief questionnaire reporting on how they had arrived at their answers (see Tables 9.3 and 9.4). This questionnaire was intended to confirm whether the intended levels of processing identified by the development team were reflected in the ways in which the test takers responded to the tasks.

After the trialling, following recommendations in the draft *Manual for relating examinations to the Common European Framework of Reference for Languages* (Council of Europe, 2003), a standard setting panel was convened to determine the scores that should be used to decide which CEFR level students should be placed into.

test taker questionnaires

There were three major findings from this exercise, which differentiated between the three highest-level tasks (Table 9.3 and 9.4). Firstly,

Table 9.3   Extent of text required to locate answers

I found the answer...	B2 (%)	C1 (%)	C2 (%)
Within a single sentence	33.2	15.2	11.5
By understanding how information in the whole text fits together	43.9	61.5	43.9
By understanding how information in two different texts fits together	10.2	12.8	60.4

on the B2 task, analysis of variance showed that test takers were significantly ($p < 0.01$) more likely to attempt to match words from the question to words in the text (either the same words or similar words) and to read only certain sentences carefully. On the other hand, compared with the C1 and C2 tasks, significantly fewer test takers tried to read the whole text carefully or to connect information in different texts when responding to the B2 task.

Regarding the amount of text required to answer the questions (Table 9.3), significantly more test takers found the answers within a single sentence in the B2 task than in the C1 and C2 tasks. Thus, the B2 task, which was designed to test at the sentence level, seems to require test takers to match words that appeared in the question with exactly the same or similar words in the text or to read only certain sentences of the text slowly and carefully, while perhaps processing only a single sentence.

Secondly, while test takers read the whole text carefully (Q4) in both the C1 and C2 tasks, 61.5 per cent of the test takers found the answer by understanding how information in the whole text fits together (Q11) in the C1 task. This compares with 43.9 per cent in the B2 task and 40.6 per cent in the C2 task. The differences between the C1 task and the B2 and C2 tasks were statistically significant. This was in accordance with the test development team's intention, as the C1 task was designed to require test takers to create a macrostructure for the single text.

Thirdly, as shown in Table 9.4, when performing the C2 task, a significantly larger proportion of test takers (50.1 per cent) tried to connect information from one text with information in other texts (Q5) than when responding to the B2 task (25.5 per cent) or the C1 task (31.2 per cent). Furthermore, in the C2 task, significantly more test takers (60.4 per cent) reported finding answers by understanding how information in two different text(s) fits together (Q12) than in the B2 task (10.2 per cent) or the C1 task (12.8 per cent). These findings appeared to confirm

Table 9.4   Test taker questionnaire

To find the answer to the question, I tried to ...		B2 (%)	C1 (%)	C2 (%)
Q1	Match words that appeared in the question with exactly the same words in the text	35.8	22.6	21.7
Q2	Quickly match words that appeared in the question with similar or related words in the text	61.2	44.2	40.7
Q3	Read only certain sentences of the text slowly and carefully	37.2	30.9	26.9
Q4	Read the whole text slowly and carefully	27.1	47.8	41.9
Q5	Connect information from one text and compare with information in other texts	25.5	31.2	50.1

that, as intended, test takers performed the C2 task by combining information across texts.

analysis of test taker scores

Briefly, the results from these trials indicated that the tasks were performing in line with expectations. Point biserial correlations between individual items and section totals ranged from 0.38 to 0.89, indicating that all of the tasks were successfully discriminating between more and less able test takers. The intended hierarchy of task difficulty was also observed for all but the highest-level tasks: the A1 task proving easier than A2, which was in turn easier than B1, and so on up to the C1 level. However, the items targeted at C2 proved to be a little easier on average than the C1 items (see Table 9.5).

In effect, the pilot exercise confirmed that the tasks (with the exception of "C2") did increase in difficulty as intended. However, the results did not confirm that these levels of task difficulty matched the CEFR levels. Another approach to the data would be required to test this assertion.

CEFR linking exercise

As the test was intended to reflect the CEFR levels – a form of what Weir (2005a) calls *criterion related validity* – it was important to confirm whether the test tasks reflected these levels as they are generally interpreted. To further explore the relationship between the test and the CEFR and to set appropriate cut scores for entry into courses at each level, a standard setting panel of eight language teaching experts was convened. All had prior experience of the CEFR, and three had been involved with aspects of the test development.

Table 9.5   Scaled difficulty of tasks targeting each CEFR level

Item group	Number of Items	Mean p	Mean scaled difficulty	SD
A1	5	0.73	22.7	9.67
A2	6	0.58	38.7	12.70
B1	7	0.58	44.3	10.14
B2	6	0.72	54.5	8.76
C1	5	0.47	74.0	10.17
C2	5	0.56	69.6	3.40

Prior to the meeting, following recommendations made in the draft *Manual for Relating Examinations to the CEFR* (Council of Europe, 2003), each panellist completed a series of familiarisation tasks to refresh his or her knowledge of the CEFR. These included a review of the five illustrative CEFR scales for Reading: *Overall Reading Comprehension; Reading Correspondence; Reading for Orientation; Reading for Information and Argument; Reading Instructions* (CEFR: 69–71) and a ranking of nine reading testlets (texts with associated tasks). These nine testlets included six from the proposed test and three from materials provided by the Council of Europe to illustrate the CEFR levels for Reading (Council of Europe, 2005). These Council of Europe materials served as a check on the accuracy of the panellists' judgements.

In the first session of the meeting, the panellists discussed their judgements of the difficulty of the testlets in relation to the CEFR levels and discussed any disagreements until reaching a group consensus. In a second session, the panellists judged the difficulty of the individual test items to arrive at an agreement concerning the number of points on each testlet that a test taker would need to achieve to justify a recommendation that they enter a class at a higher level. In other words, how many points would a test taker have to achieve on the B2 testlet to justify a recommendation of immediate entry to a C1 reading class?

The panel session confirmed that the CEFR level of each testlet from A1 to C1was as intended by the test development team, but was unable to agree that the C2 level represented a greater challenge than C1. Interestingly, this lack of differentiation was also reflected in the results from trialling (see above). Rather than attempting to devise an alternative task for the C2 level, the solution adopted by the panel was to treat both C1 and C2 as parts of the same testlet and to set two cut scores for the combined score.

conclusions

Incorporating ongoing validation into the development process has allowed us to conclude that the levels of the tasks in the reading tests do, as intended, correspond to levels A2 to C2 of the CEFR, although it has also made it clear that differentiating between learners at the highest level must be based on their performance over the two C level tasks and not, as originally intended, on differentiation between C1 and C2 level tasks. The use of a theoretically grounded socio-cognitive approach to task construction and the standard setting procedures with British Council teachers and other experts mean that we can be confident that, despite the limited sampling of learners' reading skills that is possible within the time available for the test, users of the results should be able to locate students in appropriate classes in terms of their reading ability. In fact, the specification we have developed provides a more comprehensive account of the contextual and cognitive parameters for reading in a second language at the CEFR levels than was hitherto available.

The tasks were administered to over 1000 test takers in a number of countries to establish that their statistical properties were acceptable and that the cognitive processing to complete the tasks was as intended. The final versions of the tests were trialled operationally by the British Council around the world in the summer of 2008. It is hoped that a long-term commitment to research and development of the test will generate further evidence relating to its validity.

During the operational phase, the main focus for validation activity moves from contextual and cognitive validity to issues of criterion-related validity and consequential validity. Now that the test is being used to place students, further evidence can be gathered on how well it performs as a placement instrument. To investigate the test's criterion-related validity and to confirm that the new test provides the most effective available means of placing learners, comparisons can be made with the tests previously in use and with other forms of assessment used in British Council programmes.

In terms of consequential validity, levels of satisfaction with the placement decisions that result from the use of the test need to be researched to ensure that the test is fulfilling its purpose. Data on learner performance will continue to be collected to ensure that the test works equally well across the wide variety of settings for which it is intended and is not biased in favour of learners from a particular language background, age group or gender.

This chapter has provided a brief overview of one test development project. It has shown how a range of considerations inform decisions about test design and how the justification for such decisions can be investigated through processes of validation that draw on a range of sources of evidence. Such processes are necessarily fragmentary and dynamic: there is always scope for additional validation. In addition to the further work that is needed to demonstrate that the test is fit for its current purpose, over time the nature of the students, the teaching and the courses will change and validity studies will be needed to determine whether the test continues to be relevant. Such studies should then inform modification or revision of the test so that its use continues to result in appropriate placement decisions.

references

Alderson, J. C. (2005). *Diagnosing Foreign Language Proficiency.* London: Continuum.

Bachman, L. F. (2005). Building and supporting a case for test use. *Language Assessment Quarterly, 2*(1), 1–34.

Bond, T. and Fox, C. (2001). *Applying the Rasch Model: Fundamental Measurement in the Human Sciences.* Mahwah, NJ: Lawrence Erlbaum Associates.

Brown, J. D. (2005). Testing in language programs: a comprehensive guide to English language assessment (New edition). New York: McGraw-Hill College.

Carver, R. P. (1997). Reading for one second, one minute, or one year from the perspective of rauding theory. *Scientific Studies of Reading, 1*(1), 3–43.

Cohen, A. and Upton, T. (2006). *Strategies in Responding to the New TOEFL Reading Tasks* (TOEFL Monograph No. MS-33). Princeton, NJ: Educational Testing Service.

Council of Europe (2001). *Common European Framework of Reference for Languages: Learning, Teaching and Assessment.* Cambridge: Cambridge University Press.

Council of Europe (2003). *Relating Language Examinations to the Common European Framework of Reference for Languages: Learning, Teaching, Assessment (CEF), Manual: Preliminary Pilot Version* (DGIV/EDU/LANG 2003, 5). Strasbourg: Language Policy Division.

Council of Europe (2005). Pilot samples illustrating the European reference levels in English, French, German, Italian and Spanish. CD-ROM (DECS-LANG@coe.int). Strasbourg: Language Policy Division.

Enright, M. K., Grabe, W., Koda, K., Mosenthal, P., Mulcahy-Ernt, P. and Schedl, M. (2000). *TOEFL 2000 Reading Framework: A Working Paper.* TOEFL Monograph Series 17. Princeton, NJ: Educational Testing Service.

Fulcher, G. (2004). Deluded by artifices? The Common European Framework and harmonization. *Language Assessment Quarterly, 1*(4), 253–266.

Green, A. B. and Weir, C. J. (2004). Can placement tests inform instructional decisions? *Language Testing, 21*(4), 467–494.

Hughes, A. (2003). *Testing for Language Teachers* (2nd edition). Cambridge: Cambridge University Press.

Khalifa, H. and Weir, C. J. (2009). *Examining Reading: Research and Practice in Assessing Second Language Reading. Studies in Language Testing 29*. Cambridge: Cambridge University Press.

Koda, K. (2005). *Insights into Second Language Reading: A Cross-Linguistic Approach*. Cambridge: Cambridge University Press.

McNamara, T. and Roever, C. (2006). *Language Testing: The Social Dimension*. Malden, MA: Blackwell Publishing.

Rayner, K. and Pollatsek, A. (1989). *The Psychology of Reading*. Englewood Cliffs, NJ: Prentice-Hall.

Vipond, D. (1980). Micro- and macroprocesses in text comprehension. *Journal of Verbal Learning and Verbal Behavior, 19*, 276–296.

Weir, C. J. (2005a) *Language Testing and Validation: An Evidence Based Approach*. Basingstoke: Palgrave Macmillan.

Weir, C.J. (2005b). Limitations of the common European framework for developing comparable examinations and tests. *Language Testing, 22*(3) 281–300.

Weir, C. J., Hawkey, R., Green, A. B. and Devi, S. (2009). The cognitive processes underlying the academic reading construct as measured by IELTS. In *IELTS Research Reports Volume 9*. London: British Council/IDP Australia, pp. 157–189.

10
a model for the development and application of a diagnostic test for trainee foreign language teachers

deirdre burrell, suzanne graham, dominique medley, brian richards and jon roberts

introduction

Foreign language teachers need a level of proficiency and subject knowledge appropriate for the courses they teach. In England, the official Standards for Qualified Teacher Status require teachers in all areas of the curriculum to "Have a secure knowledge and understanding of their subjects.... to enable them to teach effectively across the age and ability range for which they are trained" (Training and Development Agency for Schools, 2007: 9, Standard Q14). No further elaboration is given for individual areas of the curriculum, however, and what counts as appropriate or "secure" for language teachers is difficult to define (e.g. Barnes, 2002).

Student teachers following the Postgraduate Certificate of Education (PGCE) in the UK are frequently judged by their tutors and mentors to be lacking the necessary linguistic knowledge and skills to succeed in the classroom (Williams, 2009a). In fact, they are often evaluated much more critically by their mentors in schools than in their own self-assessments (Williams, 2009b), even though they tend to have low confidence and serious concerns about their subject knowledge right from the beginning of their course (Barnes, 2006). Such concerns are not confined to non-native speakers (Barnes, 2002; Richards, 2008; Williams, 2009b); subject knowledge is expected by tutors, mentors and school inspectors to include explicit grammatical knowledge, an area in which native speakers may feel particularly insecure. Inspectors have commented that explicit subject knowledge is lacking in native speakers.

While the precise nature of the relationship between L2 proficiency and explicit knowledge remains controversial (cf. weakly related in Alderson et al., 1997 versus strongly correlated in Roehr, 2007), they are undoubtedly interlinked, and both implicit and explicit grammatical knowledge predict language proficiency (Ellis, 2006). Quite apart from the top-down requirements of the Inspectorate, therefore, it is desirable that there should be a focus on both implicit and explicit knowledge in student teachers. Moreover, a conscious awareness of structure and an accompanying metalanguage are essential tools for those who need to deliver a pedagogic grammar, dispel misunderstandings in their students, identify, understand, correct and explain errors, and conduct a professional dialogue with colleagues.

This chapter describes how one institution in England addressed the issue of subject knowledge by incorporating a programme of formative assessment and diagnostic testing into its one-year PGCE course for postgraduate trainee teachers of modern languages. The focus is on teachers of French, but the model described is a further revision and elaboration of the process described elsewhere for German (Richards, 2008). The aim of the project was to develop procedures and instruments that would improve the quality of subject knowledge assessment in our PGCE French course. Specific objectives were to:

(1) Identify areas of grammatical, lexical and orthographic knowledge that are essential for teaching French to 11–18-year-olds, but which trainee teachers find difficult, or about which native speaker trainees may not have sufficient explicit knowledge;

(2) Develop a test of French language that provides diagnostic information about the areas identified and which would lead to high-quality formative feedback to trainees;

(3) Conduct a full-scale trial of the test and evaluate its effectiveness;

(4) Investigate the potential of the diagnostic test to monitor standards;

(5) integrate the diagnostic test and the feedback obtained into a programme of formative assessment that included target setting and systematic monitoring of progress;

(6) Evaluate the diagnostic testing and its place in the programme from the students' perspective.

diagnostic assessment

The point is often made that there are few diagnostic tests for a second or foreign language and that little research has been conducted in this area (Spolsky, 1992; Alderson, 2005; Huhta, 2007). There is even less literature relating to language teachers in training (Richards, 2008). Nevertheless, the area of formative and diagnostic testing in general has been given fresh impetus through the interest in "assessment for learning" (Black and Wiliam, 1998; Black et al., 2003). For languages in particular, publications by Ross (2005) on positive effects of formative assessment in EAP, Knoch (2009) on the diagnostic assessment of EAP writing, Lantolf and Poehner (2004) on dynamic assessment of L2, and Jang (2009) on cognitive diagnostic assessment in second language reading comprehension are indicative of increasing interest in the field of EFL. Recent action research conducted by Williams (2009a, b) on the reactivation of lapsed language skills demonstrates effective use of diagnostic assessment with PGCE modern languages trainees.

According to Huhta (2007), the term diagnostic assessment is one of the most difficult to pinpoint in the whole field of applied linguistics. The testing literature abounds with definitional anxieties: about the level of detail diagnostic assessment requires (e.g. Hughes, 2003); whether placement tests are truly diagnostic; the degree of overlap between the concepts of "formative" and "diagnostic"; whether "diagnostic" subsumes evaluation; and whether norm-referenced or summative tests can be used diagnostically (see Richards, 2008). The fuzziness of the concept is neatly characterised by Alderson's (2005: 10–12) review of the testing literature, in which he lists two alternative sets of features that are hypothesised to distinguish diagnostic assessment from other forms of testing, pointing out that some features contradict others. As Delandshere pointed out 20 years ago, diagnostic testing can be carried out in many different ways, and "If [it] is defined as providing feedback to teachers and students regarding their strengths and weaknesses, almost any test would be diagnostic" (Delandshere, 1990: 341). Huhta deals with the problem of overlap in terms of a two-dimensional model in which each axis is a continuum. The x-axis represents the extent to which assessment is based on courses, textbooks or curriculum versus theory, or a model, while the y-axis represents the level of detail of the assessment (Huhta, 2007: 2007). He places summative and formative assessment, placement testing, diagnostic assessment, proficiency testing and dynamic assessment in one of four cells (cf. Figure 10.1).

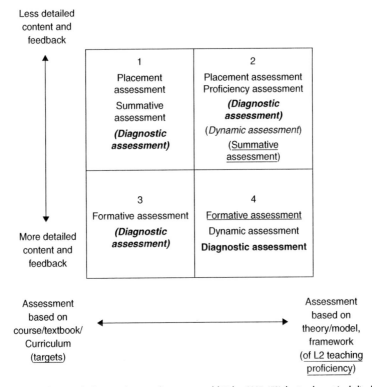

Less detailed
content and
feedback

	1	2
	Placement assessment	Placement assessment
	Summative assessment	Proficiency assessment
	(Diagnostic assessment)	*(Diagnostic assessment)*
		(*Dynamic assessment*)
		(<u>Summative assessment</u>)
	3	4
	Formative assessment	<u>Formative assessment</u>
	(Diagnostic assessment)	Dynamic assessment
		Diagnostic assessment

More detailed
content and
feedback

Assessment
based on
course/textbook/
Curriculum
(<u>targets</u>)

Assessment
based on
theory/model,
framework
(of <u>L2 teaching</u>
<u>proficiency</u>)

Figure 10.1 Adaptation of Huhta's two-dimensional assessment model (Huhta, 2007: 473) showing changes (underlined)

Given the proliferation of contradictory definitions of diagnostic testing, we will not add yet another attempt here. Instead we will identify our requirements for the particular context of postgraduate teacher education and then locate these in a slightly adapted version of Huhta's model:

- the diagnostic testing will be formative and an *integral* part of the learning process;
- it will identify strengths, weaknesses and students' confidence in their knowledge;
- it will provide *detailed* information;
- the information gained will lead to action by students and/or teachers;
- the formal test will lead to *immediate* feedback;
- it will be criterion-referenced;

- it will focus on individual students, but commonalities between students will feed into the planning of group teaching;
- it will be appropriate for all students, not just those with obvious difficulties.

Several points are worth noting in relation to the above. First, the above criteria would exclude test types such as placement tests, self-assessment for prospective students checking their suitability for courses, and some forms of norm-referencing that others might regard as diagnostic. They would also exclude the diagnostic approach of DIALANG (Alderson, 2005; Alderson and Huhta, 2005) on the grounds of insufficient detail and lack of information about how to improve in the feedback (Richards, 2008). Second, they relate to a formative process that covers the whole academic year (see below) and not just one specific test. Third, they are not in any particular order of priority except that the first five are those that correspond most closely with Alderson's (2005: 11–12) lists of features of diagnostic testing. The formal test described below displays further characteristics mentioned by Alderson, such as discrete-point testing, although these are incidental outcomes of the specification rather than part of the specification itself. One area where the overlap is less clear is to do with whether the test and other forms of assessment during the programme are "high stakes". According to Alderson, "Diagnostic tests are typically low-stakes or no-stakes" (2005: 11), and in our case the test is certainly intended to be formative and low stakes. This may not be how it is perceived by students, however, as their ultimate goal of gaining Qualified Teacher Status will depend on summative assessment of the required subject knowledge standard (Training and Development Agency for Schools, 2007: 9) by tutors and mentors.

Figure 10.1 shows an adaptation of Huhta's (2007) model. Huhta placed diagnostic testing in all four cells, but the italics in Cells 1 and 2 indicate that this kind of less detailed diagnostic assessment is more marginal. In terms of the needs of our PGCE programme, diagnostic testing is placed firmly in Cells 3 and 4. Initially, Cell 4 will be dominant, as new students are formally tested in accordance with the areas of knowledge identified in Objective 1 above. Individual feedback and target setting then leads to a more curriculum-based approach in Cell 3. One important difference from Huhta's version, apart from the labelling of the x-axis, is that we have put summative assessment in Cell 2 in addition to Cell 1. This is because the final assessment of the subject knowledge standard is based on general proficiency, the notion of "fitness to teach" rather than attainment or achievement.

The following sequence shows the place of formative, diagnostic and summative assessment in the 36-week PGCE course. New aspects that form the objectives of this project are enclosed in square brackets:

(1) Pre-course interview: speaking, listening and writing are tested. If applicants are accepted, they are set targets.
(2) Start of course (September): Subject knowledge audit (self-assessment). Students are set further targets. Tutors monitor previous targets.
(3) [First week of course: administration of the new formal diagnostic test[1] followed by immediate detailed feedback and group discussion of issues. Details of individual results fed to students' personal tutors. Further individual targets are set].
(4) Analysis of diagnostic test results feeds into regular language enhancement classes.
(5) Throughout the course, students keep an ongoing record of progress towards their targets. This is regularly monitored by university tutors and mentors in schools.
(6) [Students regularly update a self-assessment check list[2] based on the items in the diagnostic test].

phase 1: identifying gaps in essential knowledge (objective 1)

Criteria for identifying the areas to be tested were the frequency of error in previous students, expert judgements of tutors and mentors, and "usefulness", defined by reference to the Advanced Level syllabuses for national examinations used by schools. Analyses were conducted on 70 grammar tests completed by previous students, writing tests completed at interviews, written feedback given to students by tutors and mentors, interviews with five PGCE tutors, and the written record of a focus group meeting with the mentors from our partnership schools. The result was a set of 42 specific areas that were potential test items. These were predominantly grammatical and can be subsumed under the following broad areas[3]:

Negatives	Gerunds	Present participles
Tenses (various)	Conjunctions	Pronouns
Relative pronouns	Adjectives	Verbs
Subjunctives	Partitives	Appropriate usage
Passives	Time adverbials	Form of the imperative
Superlatives	Use of upper case	Transitivity and reflexive verbs

phase 2: constructing, piloting and revising the diagnostic test (objective 2)

From the preliminary work described above, it was clear that the main focus of the diagnostic test would be grammar. Other requirements were that it should access *explicit* knowledge, asking respondents to state whether they had answered each question according to their knowledge of rules or from their feel for the language, and allowing them to indicate their degree of confidence in their answers (see Figure 10.2). Traditionally, grammaticality judgement tasks (GJTs) have been used as discrete-point tests of both implicit and explicit knowledge (see Bialystok, 1979; Ellis, 1991). Although concerns have been expressed about the reliability and validity of such tests (Purpura, 2004: 47),

---

Name: ....   **Date:** ....

Course (delete as appropriate):   PGCE Secondary/PGCE Primary/
                                      Yr 1 Conversion Course/Yr 2 Conversion Course

Age: ....years

Are you a native speaker of French? ....

If not, how long have studied French at school/university, etc.: ....years

Time started test: ....   **Time finished test:** ....

For each set of four sentences:

    1.   circle the letter of the sentence that you think is the best French.
        *** circle one sentence only ***
    2.   show as a percentage how sure you are of the right answer (i.e. if you are **totally** sure put 100%; if your answer was a complete guess, put 0%).
    3.   underline to show whether you know the answer through your **feel** for the language or **explicit** knowledge of the rule (i.e. could you state the rule?) or if it was just a **guess**.

---

34.   a. Après s'être réveillée, elle s'est levée
        b. Après s'être réveillé, elle s'est levée
        c. Après s'être réveillé, elle s'est levé
        d. Après s'être réveillée, elle s'est levé

        Percentage sure = ... %
        "feel" / knowledge of the rule(s) / guess

Figure 10.2   The final test rubric and one sample question that assesses past participle agreement (Q34). The correct option is "a".

Ellis (2004, 2006) has argued convincingly that, whereas time pressure tends to give access to implicit knowledge, untimed tests access explicit knowledge. In spite of Purpura's claim (2004: 134) that GJTs are rarely used other than for SLA research, we are by no means the only group using them in teacher education (e.g. Williams, 2009a, b). In our case, the fact that the test was low stakes and a stimulus for individual feedback, target setting, and joint discussion between native and non-native speakers justified this approach. The disadvantage is that the usual method of presenting a single sentence to be judged correct or incorrect provides little or no diagnostic information. This was therefore replaced by multiple-choice items, where the use of three distractors was designed to identify the area(s) of weakness more precisely. The test was to be untimed, but designed to be completed comfortably in less than 45 minutes.

The difficulty of writing grammatical multiple-choice items containing convincing alternative sentences is considerable (Dávid, 2007). And, for French, Anderson (2007) has recently drawn attention to the consequences of discrepancies between pedagogic prescriptive grammars and authentic native speaker texts. These problems cannot be overestimated, and it was only with the assistance of two native speakers and French language corpora such as Beeching's (undated) Corpus of Spoken French that the team succeeded in producing 44 candidate items to test the 42 areas identified.

A rubric was added to the resulting draft (Figure 10.2), which was submitted to a scrutiny panel consisting of two native speakers (both university lecturers in French), two mentors in partnership schools, two university PGCE tutors, and one Professor of Linguistics with expertise in language testing. Following this, half the questions (22/44) and a quarter of the multiple-choice options (43/176) were revised in some way.

Piloting was carried out on 52 French speakers with a wide range of proficiency. These included 11 native speakers, five year-13 (final year) students in a grammar school, 12 PGCE secondary students at the end of their one-year course, six PGCE secondary students at the end of the first year of a two-year course, three PGCE primary students without a degree in French taking the French specialism, five qualified teachers of French, and members of an adult French conversation group. Written comments were invited from participants.

Responses and background information were entered into a statistical package (SPSS). For each test item the following was recorded: correct/incorrect, percentage confidence, "rule" or "feel", and, where appropriate, the incorrect distractor chosen. The internal consistency for the total score out of 44 was high (Cronbach's alpha = 0.932). Mann–Whitney tests showed that there were statistically significant differences between native speakers and non-native speakers on their total score (native speaker mean = 41.4, SD = 1.4; non-native speaker mean = 30.8, SD = 9.4) and on their average confidence across questions (native speaker mean = 96.8 per cent, SD = 3.5 per cent; non-native speaker mean = 76.2 per cent, SD = 15.7 per cent) ($p<0.001$). They did not differ significantly on the proportion of questions answered by rule or feel (native speaker mean = 34.3 per cent; SD = 36.7 per cent; non-native speaker mean = 45.42 per cent; SD = 26.2 per cent). As indicated by the large standard deviation, however, the native speakers showed much more variability in the way they responded. Native speakers took significantly less time on average to complete the test (22 minutes as opposed to 31 minutes for non-native speakers).

Item analysis identified eight items with low item–total correlations whose removal would either improve or, in one case, not reduce the alpha coefficient. Other candidates for removal included three items with item facility of over 0.9 and one item with a surprisingly low item facility of 0.5 for native speakers. As this is primarily a criterion-referenced diagnostic test, however, for which monitoring standards from year to year is only a secondary function, it is important not to make decisions purely on the kind of statistical criteria that are used to validate norm-referenced tests. For example, because the test addresses knowledge that, in theory, PGCE students ought to have already, we would not be expecting a normal distribution, or a facility index of 0.5. We therefore re-examined the pedagogic usefulness and formative potential of each doubtful item and finally decided to omit only four, leaving a test of 40 items. The four items that were removed were all suspect on statistical grounds, but were also either confusing or over-complex. Further revisions at this stage included adjustments to the rubric (Figure 10.2); starting the test with the question with the highest item facility; and amendments to the wording of eight items.

phase 3: full-scale trial (objectives 3 and 4)

The test was administered to 186 people, including native speakers, trainee French teachers, undergraduates and a small number of A level candidates. Details of the sample are given in Table 10.1. The trainee French teachers attended four English universities and the

Table 10.1 Sample of respondents in the full trial

	Native speaker	Non-native	Total
Secondary PGCE and GTP[a]	27	60	87
Fourth-year undergraduates	2	18	20
Second-year undergraduates	4	55	59
Two-year PGCE course	0	2	2
Primary PGCE course	0	7	7
A level students	1	7	8
Lectrices in French Depts.	3	0	3
Total	**37**	**149**	**186**

[a] Postgraduate trainees following an internship programme

undergraduates were working towards first degrees in French at two of these.

data analysis

Data were entered into SPSS as in the pilot study and three summary scores were calculated for each participant: total correct answers out of 40; the average confidence level across all 40 items; and the percentage of items answered by rules rather than feel. For these three summary variables, reliability (internal consistency) was estimated and item analysis was conducted taking into consideration the item–total correlations, the facility index and possible effect of the removal of each item on Cronbach's alpha. We also assessed how well the three summary scores discriminated between the subgroups in the sample.

results

For the total score out of 40, reliability was high. Cronbach's alpha was 0.920 (0.839 for native speakers; 0.884 for non-native speakers). The mean facility index was 0.64, ranging across items from 0.34 to 0.88. Item–total correlations ranged from 0.03 to 0.672. Two items had particularly low item–total correlations, but they were judged to be testing important areas and their removal would only have raised reliability to 0.922. They were therefore retained in the test.

The results in Table 10.2 show a highly predictable pattern, with the highest mean score for the native speakers, followed by the trainee secondary teachers, undergraduates and A level students. The native speakers were a much larger and more heterogeneous group compared with the pilot, and this is reflected in the larger standard deviation.

Table 10.2   Mean total score out of 40 and standard deviation for each subgroup in the sample

Subgroup	M	SD	Nᵃ
Native speakers	36.2	3.9	37
Secondary PGCE and GTP (excluding native speakers)	29.8	6.1	40
Fourth-year undergraduates	23.3	7.1	18
Second-year undergraduates	18.7	6.7	55
A level students	16.6	6.2	7
Total sample	26.1	9.4	157

ᵃStudents from the two-year secondary PGCE course and the primary PGCE were omitted from this analysis. There were also some missing data.

Nevertheless, they are once again the group that shows least variability. There were 10 questions on which none of the native speakers made an error, even though, as can be seen from Figure 10.3 , a small number obtained scores of under 30.

Figure 10.3 shows strikingly large ranges, overlapping distributions and some very low scores. With 40 questions and four multiple-choice options, test takers might be expected to obtain a score of 10 purely by chance, and there are five scores below this. A binomial test tells us that, to score significantly better than chance ($p<0.05$), 16 or above out of 40 is required. In total 25 students fail to do so, of whom two are A Level students, 17 are second-year undergraduates, one is a fourth-year undergraduate, and, worryingly, five are trainee secondary French teachers with degrees in modern languages. Nevertheless, a Kruskal–Wallis test confirmed that there were statistically significant differences between the groups (Chi-square=88.9; d.f.=4; $p<0.001$), and pairwise comparisons using Mann–Whitney tests with the alpha level adjusted for multiple comparisons showed that six out of a possible ten comparisons were significantly different ($p<0.005$). There were no significant differences, however, between PGCE students and fourth-year undergraduates, between fourth-year and second-year undergraduates, between fourth-year undergraduates and A level students, and between second-year students and A level students. Note that the small size of the sample of A level pupils makes it difficult to detect reliable differences, but, even so, they do surprisingly well in comparison with the second-year undergraduates. This can be explained by that fact that they attend a selective school and form a fairly homogeneous group of gifted pupils who had received a large amount of grammar-focused instruction. The undergraduates, by contrast, came from much more varied backgrounds.

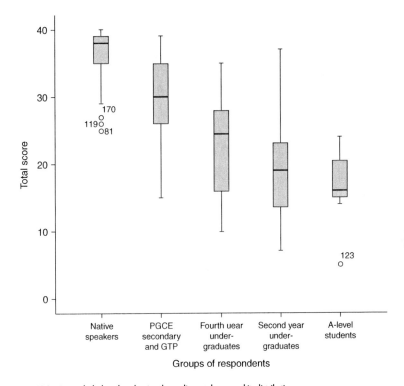

Figure 10.3 Box and whisker plots showing the median total score and its distribution

Similar analyses were conducted for the mean confidence scores and the proportions of questions answered by rule. Both variables showed high internal consistency (all coefficients ≥ 0.85). For confidence, the average rating per question ranged from 60.4 per cent to 83.2 per cent, and item–total correlations from 0.53 to 0.85. Figure 10.4 shows how the groups compare. The results for the native speakers, PGCE students and fourth-year undergraduates follow a predictable trend. The extremely high ratings and the homogeneity of the native speaker group are particularly notable. However, the high ratings for the A level students and second-year undergraduates are surprising, as their total scores did not justify such confidence. A Kruskal–Wallis test shows significant differences among the groups (Chi-square=91.8, d.f.=4, $p<0.001$). As Figure 10.4 suggests, post hoc tests show that native speakers and PGCE students differ significantly from each other and from all other groups, but that the two groups of undergraduates and the A level pupils form

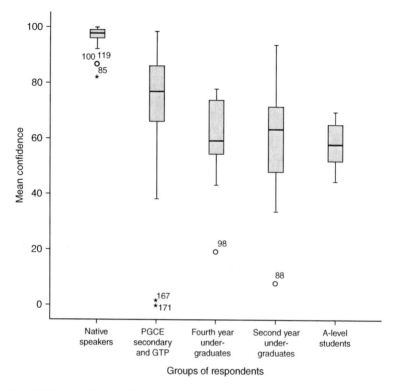

Figure 10.4 Box and whisker plots showing the median confidence and its distribution

a homogeneous cluster, suggesting that university teaching and students' year abroad does not improve their confidence.

For percentage of questions answered by rule, item–total correlations range from 0.10 to 0.54. The percentage of respondents claiming to answer by rule ranged from 78.4 per cent to 24 per cent across questions. Figure 10.5 shows the group comparisons. The pattern is similar to confidence in that there is a trend towards being less rule-based from the native speakers down to the fourth-year undergraduates, but with higher scores than this trend would predict for the second years and A level students. Concerns that native speakers do not have access to explicit knowledge of their language do not appear to be justified. On average, they claim to be answering well over 90 per cent of questions by recourse to rules. Nevertheless, there is more variability among the native speakers on this variable than on the previous summary variables.

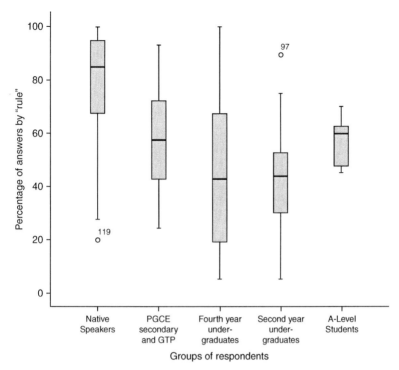

Figure 10.5   Box and whisker plots showing the median for percentage of questions answered by rule

Again, there are significant differences between the groups (Chi-square=45.2, d.f.=4, $p<0.001$). Post hoc tests show that the native speakers score higher than all other groups and that PGCE students score higher than the second-year undergraduates. No other pairwise comparisons are statistically significant.

The high average for the A level students and the lack of difference between the fourth-year and second-year undergraduates deserve some comment. A combination of relatively formal teaching in their grammar school and lack of experience of interaction with native speakers may well account for the former, while for the undergraduates it is important to recall that most spend six months to a year in a francophone country between their second and fourth years. There may, therefore, be conflicting factors at work for the fourth years, whereby an additional year of university teaching has furthered explicit rule knowledge while time spent in the country of the target language has facilitated the acquisition of procedural knowledge, allowing conscious rules to be bypassed.

Further analyses show that the three summary variables are strongly intercorrelated ($r > 0.64$; $p<0.001$). The amount of time taken to complete the test varied from 15 minutes for the native speakers to 34 minutes for the A level pupils. There was no correlation between the amount of time taken and the three summary variables. Finally, for a very small subgroup of non-native speaker PGCE students at our own University ($n=11$) we were able to investigate the relationship between their self-rating of accuracy in their subject knowledge audit at the beginning of the course and the three summary variables. There was a significant relationship between accuracy and percentage of questions answered by rule (Spearman's rho = 0.55, $N=11$, $p<0.05$).

integration of the test into the PGCE programme and students' perspectives (objectives 5 and 6)

The diagnostic test was incorporated into our own PGCE programme during the academic year 2007–2008 according to the sequence outlined above. The analysis of results showed that, as well as revealing individual strengths and weaknesses and further diagnosis of the distractors chosen, profiles of each student comparing his or her scores on the three summary variables were highly informative in identifying those who were over- or under-confident, and in relating scores and confidence to explicit rule knowledge. This information was passed on to personal tutors and students' mentors for subsequent follow-up and monitoring during tutorials and school visits.

Further analyses identified problematic areas that were common across students, and these were used to inform the syllabus of the intensive sessions in the language enhancement programme. For example, a simple cross-tabulation can reveal questions that have a low facility but high mean confidence separately for native and non-native speakers. This can then be related to the extent to which these questions were answered by rule or feel and an analysis of the distractors undertaken. An example of how this could proceed is provided by Q23 (use of the partitive after a negative) in the full trial. For non-native speakers in the full trial, Q23 was one standard deviation above the mean for confidence, but 1.37 standard deviations below the mean for the proportion of respondents who got it correct. Further examination shows that for this item 49 per cent of test takers claimed to answer according to explicit knowledge of the rules and that just over two-thirds of those who got it wrong chose the same distractor. This provides an indication of how the error can be addressed in language classes.

With regard to student evaluation, as part of the full trial, respondents had been invited to supply an open-ended response of their impressions of the test and 27 did so, providing information that fed into questionnaires and interviews of our own students. For example, one issue that had emerged was that some test takers had difficulty in deciding whether they had answered by rule or feel. A small number of our own students were interviewed in depth after they had taken the test in autumn 2007, and a questionnaire[4] was then designed focusing on the perceived effects of the test on personal subject knowledge, subject teaching and confidence. It was returned by 10 students in February 2008. The test was also discussed in plenary and one-to-one sessions with tutors.

The feedback suggests that students found the test beneficial:

It's definitely necessary for trainee teachers;

It helped me a lot. It makes us aware of problems we might have to face.

In general, it seemed to build their confidence whether their choices were correct or not, perhaps because it enhanced their sense of personal control not just over grammar knowledge itself but also over the means to improve it. The format of the test seemed to help them assess themselves:

Particularly useful to identify my knowledge and confidence gaps;

Helpful to think how I arrived at an answer;

It has an impact when you are asked "how do you know it?"

This seemed to direct them as they looked for clarification and explanation:

I looked up grammar books and analysed why I made the choice;

Finding explanations for what had been correct by feel;

I looked up my mistakes.

It also seemed to help them frame personal targets for development:

The four near sentences showed how exact we have to be;

I could set myself specific targets for French.... otherwise I wouldn't know where to begin.

Some feedback suggested that, while the forced "feel/rule/guess" choice led to useful processes of reflection and self-assessment, the three constructs were not necessarily viewed as mutually exclusive. A considerable number of test takers wanted to underline both choices for certain questions, and there were interesting comments that "feel" and "rule" were not experienced as separable:

> Feel prompted reasoning to knowledge of rule and vice versa.... Difficult to conclude whether it was "feel" or "knowledge of the rule" answer;
>
> Sometimes decision was taken on a mix of "feeling" and knowledge. However, I usually trust my gut instinct.

Often some knowledge of the rules combined with guesswork!

> "Feel" rules out some answers (and gives me the one I choose) but I can also recite the grammar rule - so I have selected "knowledge of the rules";
>
> My husband is a French speaker. I try to think what I'd hear him say and use my knowledge of the language.

Also, reasons for choosing feel suggested differing personal criteria of choice. Sometimes the choice of "feel" anticipated a "classroom standard" of knowing a rule:

> I didn't want to kid myself. I put feel if I could not have explained it well;
>
> I chose feel when I wasn't totally sure...if I could not convince them when I explain.

while for others it was a means to eliminate distractors:

> Usually I could eliminate more easily than say why I came to my answer.

Thus, while these responses provide evidence that the test gave a positive impetus to developing subject knowledge during the course, it also suggests the need for a more detailed understanding of strategies test takers use when making their choices.

conclusion

Using the approach described above we have identified areas of knowledge crucial to teaching French to 11–18-year-olds that require monitoring in trainee teachers. This domain is tested in a specially developed diagnostic test that provides formative feedback to tutors, mentors and the students, and assists with target setting, checking progress and syllabus design for language enhancement classes. A full-scale trial of the diagnostic test was conducted on 186 respondents. This provided evidence of reliability and validity through its internal consistency and the ability of its summary scores to discriminate between different proficiency groups and correlate with self-rating of accuracy. These results suggest that, in addition to its specialist function as a criterion-referenced diagnostic instrument, it also has potential for norm-referencing; it can be used in monitoring standards across successive cohorts of students, providing an indication of the average and range of scores to be expected of PGCE students and other groups. This test has become an integral part of our PGCE programme in combination with self-assessment and regular monitoring of subject knowledge. Data from questionnaires and interviews, and comments from respondents, suggest a very positive response to the diagnostic test. PGCE students felt that it promoted more precise target setting, enhanced their confidence and motivation, and contributed to their learning.

There is a human need to develop familiar routines in thought and action. As Thomas and Harri-Augstein (1985) put it, for efficiency we "manufacture our own robots" (ibid: 188), which can, however, obstruct our further development unless subjected to self-examination. For this reason they view self-assessment to be "the vehicle of all self-organisation and control" (ibid: 193). We suggest that our programme is such a vehicle, in that it helps prospective teachers monitor their personal knowledge of target language grammar. This is not only by getting things right or wrong; it is also by reflecting on the choices forced by the item format, which can then be explored and resolved privately and in conversation with others.

acknowledgements

This project was funded by the Higher Education Academy: Pedagogical Research Fund for Languages, Linguistics and Area Studies in Higher Education. We would also like to express our gratitude to Sara Poole and Brian Sudlow of the Department of French Studies, University of Reading, colleagues in three other universities, Helen Bradley of the Holt School, Jeanine Treffers-Daller of the University of the West of England, Bristol, and all those who completed the test. Special thanks are due to Rod Ellis and his colleagues at the University of Auckland for making their Grammaticality Judgment Test for English available to us.

notes

1. The final version of the test, self-assessment check list, correct answers, detailed description of the areas tested and the questionnaire can be obtained from http://www.llas.ac.uk/projects/2631 (accessed 1 March 2011).
2. Ibid.
3. Ibid.
4. Ibid.

references

Alderson, J. C. (2005). *Diagnosing Foreign Language Proficiency: The Interface between Learning and Assessment*. London: Continuum.

Alderson, J. C. and Huhta, A. (2005). The development of a suite of computer-based diagnostic tests based on the Common European Framework. *Language Testing, 22*, 301–320.

Alderson, J. C., Clapham, C. and Steel, D. (1997). Metalinguistic knowledge, language aptitude and language proficiency. *Language Teaching Research, 1*, 93–121.

Anderson, B. (2007). Pedagogical rules and their relationship to frequency in the input: observational and empirical data from L2 French. *Applied Linguistics, 28*, 286–308.

Barnes, A. (2002). Maintaining language skills in pre-service training for foreign languages teachers. In H. Trappes-Lomax and G. Ferguson (Eds), *Language in Language Teacher Education*. Amsterdam: John Benjamins, pp. 199–217.

Barnes, A. (2006). Confidence levels and concerns of beginning teachers of modern foreign languages. *Language Learning Journal, 34*, 37–46.

Beeching, K. (n.d.). *Corpus of Spoken French*. http://www.llas.ac.uk/resources/mb/80 (accessed 8 July 2009)

Bialystok, E. (1979). Explicit and implicit judgements of L2 grammaticality. *Language Learning, 29*, 81–103.

Black, P. and Wiliam, D. (1998). *Inside the Black Box: Raising Standards Through Classroom Assessment*. London: King's College London.

Black, P., Harrison, C., Lee, C., Marshall, B. and Wiliam, D. (2003). *Assessment for Learning: Putting it into Practice*. Maidenhead: Open University Press.

Dávid, G. (2007). Investigating the performance of alternative types of grammar items. *Language Testing, 24*, 65–97.

Delandshere, G. (1990). Diagnostic assessment procedures. In H. J. Walberg and G. D. Haertel (Eds), *The International Encyclopedia of Educational Evaluation*. Oxford: Pergamon Press, pp. 340–343.

Ellis, R. (1991). Grammaticality judgements and second language acquisition. *Studies in Second Language Acquisition, 13*, 161–186.

Ellis, R. (2004). The definition and measurement of L2 explicit knowledge. *Language Learning, 54*, 227–275.

Ellis, R. (2006). Modelling learning difficulty and second language proficiency: the differential contributions of implicit and explicit knowledge. *Applied Linguistics, 27*, 431–463.

Hughes, A. (2003). *Testing for Language Teachers* (2nd edition). Cambridge: Cambridge University Press.

Huhta, A. (2007). Diagnostic and formative assessment. In B. Spolsky and F. Hult (Eds), *Handbook of Educational Linguistics*. Oxford: Blackwell.

Jang, E. E. (2009). Cognitive diagnostic assessment of L2 reading comprehension ability: validity arguments for Fusion Model application to LanguEdge assessment. *Language Testing, 26*, 31–73.

Knoch, U. (2009). Diagnostic assessment of writing: a comparison of two rating scales. *Language Testing, 26*, 275–304.

Lantolf, J. P. and Poehner, M. E. (2004). Dynamic assessment of L2 development: bringing the past into the future. *Journal of Applied Linguistics, 1*, 49–72.

Purpura, J. E. (2004). *Assessing Grammar*. Cambridge: Cambridge University Press.

Richards, B. J. (2008). Formative assessment in teacher education: the development of a diagnostic language test for trainee teachers of German. *British Journal of Educational Studies, 56*, 184–204.

Roehr, K. (2007). Metalinguistic knowledge and language ability in university-level L2 learners. *Applied Linguistics, 29*, 173–199.

Ross, S. J. (2005). The impact of assessment method on foreign language proficiency growth. *Applied Linguistics, 26*, 317–342.

Spolsky, B. (1992). The gentle art of diagnostic testing revisited. In E. Shohamy and A. R. Walton (Eds), *Language Assessment for Feedback: Testing and Other Strategies*. Dubuque, IA: Kendall/Hunt, pp. 29–41.

Thomas, L. F. and Harri-Augstein, E. S. (1985). *Self-Organised Learning. Foundations of a Conversational Science for Psychology*. London: Routledge & Kegan Paul.

Training and Development Agency for Schools (2007). *Professional Standards for Teachers. Why Sit Still in Your Career?* London: TDA.

Williams, J. L. (2009a). Use it or lose it: retrieving lost language skills from the dusty corners of memory. In M. Edwards (Ed.), *Proceedings of the BAAL Annual Conference 2008*. London: Scitsiugnil Press, pp. 125–126.

Williams, J. L. (2009b). Reactivating lapsed language skills: a study to examine the reactivation of language skills in a PGCE Modern Foreign Language programme. Unpublished EdD Thesis, University of Wales Institute, Cardiff.

11
developing affordable "local" tests: the EXAVER project

adriana abad florescano, barry o'sullivan, carmen sanchez chavez, david ewing ryan, esperanza zamora lara, luis alejandro santana martinez, maria isabel gonzalez macias, mary maxwell hart, patricia evelyn grounds, patricia reidy ryan, roger anthony dunne and teresa de jesus romero barradas

introduction

In 1999, the Rector (Chancellor) of the Universidad Veracruzana, Dr Victor Arredondo, initiated a project which would allow the university to offer its students the opportunity to certify their knowledge of English by means of a series of standardised tests (Dunne, 2007).

These tests were to be designed by members of their own institution, working in close collaboration with external advisers from Mexico and the UK. The local team was to be drawn from the teaching staff at the University's language centres, with no previous experience of academic research into language testing or of language test development.

This was where the project began – a collaborative, cross-cultural project which would empower our team to create a new, much needed series of test products according to international standards. These tests would belong to us from the beginning and, in the longer term, we would become responsible for their sustainability. In this chapter, we reflect on the process of training and development that underpins the tests. In doing this we are, in effect, telling a story of professional and personal growth and development, and in this way the chapter differs significantly from the others in the volume.

the context

The University of Veracruz was inaugurated in September 1944, and since that time it has grown to meet the needs of the people of Veracruz province and of Mexico. In recent years the University has undergone a period of exponential growth. It now offers 224 different courses (60 undergraduate and 61 postgraduate), and every year some 10,000 new students enrol in undergraduate and postgraduate courses alone. English is taught throughout the university in different contexts: the School of Languages (which currently offers two postgraduate courses in ELT), the Language Centres located on six separate campuses throughout the state, and at a separate language centre, known as DELEX, which offers courses to the general public under the auspices of the School of Languages.

Although many graduates, especially from the School of Modern Languages, achieved a good level of English in the past, there were few options open to them to certify their knowledge and skills. Students commonly complained that the cost of reputable international English language examinations was prohibitive for them, bearing in the mind that, at the time of the project's inception, 60 per cent of the students at the University of Veracruz came from large families with a monthly income of approximately 1600 pesos per month (approximately US$150) per family. So extreme was the situation that it had actually become common for the university, and, indeed, even for some of the teachers themselves as individuals, for instance at the Faculty of Modern Languages, to award special grants for those students who could not even afford to *eat* and study, let alone buy books or pay for other *luxuries* such as international language examinations (Grounds, 2001).

Another significant driving force behind this project was the growing demands of the professional marketplace over recent years. An increasing focus on international exchanges for both academic development and commerce contributed to a common belief among potential employers in Mexico that the better qualified their employees are, the more successful their organisation will be in its business transactions. At the same time, employers began to look ever more favourably on prospective employees with recognised mastery of a foreign language, particularly English. This, in turn, contributed to an increasing demand for valid and reliable ways of certifying such knowledge in the interests of the students and the community.

the project

In order to ensure that the proposed project was developed on a solid basis, the University signed an agreement with the British Council, under the auspices of which a team of committed university EFL specialists was appointed to undertake training in foreign language examinations design, development and validation, in a process which is still very much evolving at the time of writing (nine years later). The test would be designed by this group, working in close collaboration with highly specialised advisers from the British Council, Mexico and, in the initial stages, Cambridge ESOL.

the aims of the project

The aims of the project have evolved in tandem with the extending vision of the possible roles and functions of the tests. By 2004, the broad aim was defined as follows:

> To provide a single rigorously validated certification system for the various EFL needs of the Universidad Veracruzana as a result of recent internal curricular change, according to which accreditation on English is to be compulsory for all undergraduate programmes. (Abad et al., 2004)

In fact, each test had been envisaged in response to a somewhat different aim; these were:

- The initial aim of EXAVER 1 was that it should meet the accreditation needs of students on completion of the two semesters of General English that became a curriculum requirement for all undergraduates in 1999;
- EXAVER 2 would then satisfy entrance requirements for aspiring MA candidates in some departments, as well as BAs at the Faculty of Administrative and Social Sciences and Accounting in the future;
- EXAVER 3 would become an accreditation requirement for students completing the BA in language teaching at the School of Languages and other MA programmes.

As time went on, EXAVER 1 became a minimum requirement for public primary school English teachers in Orizaba City, and numerous university exchange programmes now include an EXAVER examination as an application requirement. At the time of writing, EXAVER has "graduated" from the university context and is serving a range of accreditation needs in the community.

an overview of the EXAVER development and validation project

In this section we describe the extent of the project from a number of perspectives, bearing in mind that under each of the subheadings the processes described implied preparatory, pilot, formal administration and analysis stages.

governance and structures

The University of Veracruz authorities had already started studying more effective ways of certifying knowledge and skills in English by 1999, when drastic changes were being implemented in the syllabuses of the different faculties to include English as a second language in all undergraduate degree courses, regardless of the subject being studied.

Even before any agreement had been signed with outside agencies, an internal English examinations development and validation committee, known internally as *Commisión para la evaluación y el seguimiento de alumnos del Nuevo Modelo Educativo* (The Committee for the Evaluation and Follow-up of students of the New Educational Model), had been appointed and commissioned to write new, standardised exams for English as a second language. This *commission* consisted of English teachers currently working at the University English Department of the School of Modern Languages, Language Centres and Self-access Centres on the various campuses throughout the state. It was the responsibility of this body to collaboratively develop the English course syllabuses, exam specifications, glossaries and exams for the English component of the *Nuevo Modelo Educativo* (New Educational Model) for the institution.

In collaboration with the British Council and the other advisers, it was decided that a suite of exams would be developed at three levels (Figure 11.1). In our efforts to follow internationally recognised

EXAVER level	CEFR	Council of Europe
1	A2	Waystage
2	B1	Threshold
3	B2	Vantage

Figure 11.1   Planned levels of the EXAVER tests

	Paper 1	Paper 2	Paper 3
EXAVER 1	Reading + Writing	Listening comprehension	Speaking
EXAVER 2	Paper 1	Paper 2	Paper 3
	Read + Writing	Listening comprehension	Speaking
EXAVER 3	Paper 1	Paper 2	Paper 3
	Read + Writing	Listening comprehension	Speaking

Figure 11.2   The components of the EXAVER tests

standards and models, the team studied the *Waystage, Threshold* and *Vantage* level descriptor documents and then adopted the Common European Frame of Reference (CEFR) and the Association of Language Testers of Europe (ALTE) guidelines and looked to the Cambridge ESOL (then known as UCLES) main suite for examples of best practice in the area. At the time of writing, we are engaged in a major CEFR linking project, and hope, through this, to be able to substantiate our view of the general levels of the EXAVER tests as shown in Figure 11.2.

The new *commission* was formed specifically to meet this objective and to develop the following batteries of tests:

As indicated above, the *commission* consisted of qualified university English language teachers with different profiles:

- Four native Anglophones
- Six Mexican English teachers from the state of Veracruz
- External consultants

The team structure is shown in Figure 11.3.

The role of General Coordinator was taken by one of the Mexican teachers, while that of Chief Editor was taken by one of the native English speakers. There are two item writers at each level, with a further two members of the team dedicated solely to logistics, design and computing. The minimum professional requirement to join the team is a Bachelor's Degree in English Language Teaching, and some have a MA or PhD degree in the same field.

Together with our consultants, we have now developed specifications for batteries of tests at the three proposed levels, word lists to accompany each set of specifications, pilot versions and a significant number of live tests. The project continues with an ongoing process of re-editing and improving according to statistical analysis results and updating of specifications. Thus, we have a well developed item bank containing piloted/trialled and updated items for the future, and continue to produce new versions based on the amended specifications. In addition,

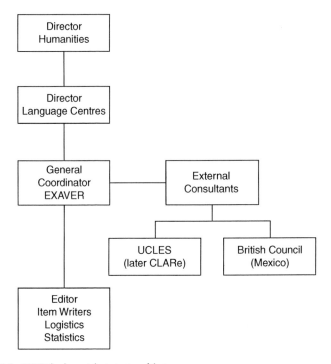

Figure 11.3   EXAVER development: basic structure of the team

we have developed an EXAVER webpage to promote and describe our experience and our tests.

The earliest version of the EXAVER specifications, sample examinations and first two versions of live tests were all written by an external consultant, with local editing from the project team. In this way, the team began to build confidence and the skills necessary to produce consistently high-quality test papers. By 2003, the process for the development of new versions looked as shown in Figure 11.4.

While this procedure worked well in the early stages of the project, once the local team began to grow in confidence, some issues emerged. The most notable of these related to the perception of appropriateness of content. The experience of the external advisers was almost entirely with large-scale international examinations, in which topics are deemed taboo across the entire population even though they may offend only a portion of that population. In a test context such as EXAVER, the situation is quite different. Here the intended population is essentially

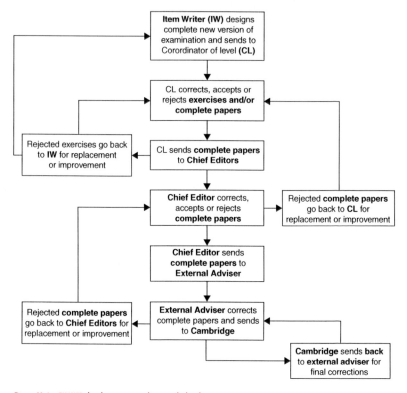

Figure 11.4   EXAVER development: initial materials development process (2003)

homogeneous, sharing a first language and culture. Moreover, the developers share those same features and are therefore better situated to make this type of decision than an external consultant who is not familiar with the context. For this reason, when the UCLES involvement with the project was due to end, the EXAVER team began to look for an alternative partner who would help develop a more "localised" system. After a period of overlap, in which UCLES and CLARe worked closely together, the latter group took over the role as chief external consultant for the project. By now we had examinations at three levels: CEFR A2, B1 and B2.

the project evolves

The new partners brought some changes to EXAVER. The first of these was the respecification of the three examinations using Weir's frameworks as a guide (the frameworks were developed by Weir and O'Sullivan at Roehampton and later published by Weir in 2005). The respecification was done for two reasons. The first was to familiarise the project team with every aspect of each examination (the weakness of working to a set of specifications developed by an external consultant is a lack of ownership by local testers and a subsequent tendency to drift from the intended level and focus). The second reason for undertaking this respecification was to ensure that the EXAVER tests were built on a sound theoretical basis, so that subsequent validation could be facilitated.

The next major change affected the development process. The final decision on all papers now rested with the Chief Editor in Mexico (see Figure 11.5). During annual training sessions held in Jalapa at Veracruz University, CLARe staff interacted directly with the EXAVER team in a series of test review and development sessions. In this way, we worked to develop the skills of the team even further and attempted to build a sustainable local system. In time, the contribution of the CLARe team grew increasingly less as more and more control was taken at a local level. At the time of writing, all procedures are carried out and monitored locally.

The final major change to the system was the training of a local teacher to undertake all of the complex classical and IRT-based statistical analysis, which had initially been undertaken by external consultants. We were very fortunate to find a person with real flair and

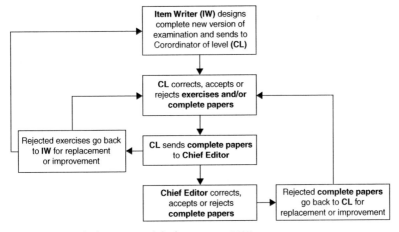

Figure 11.5 EXAVER development: materials development process (2009)

ability to undertake this difficult work. Many smaller-scale examinations are expected to perform systematic analysis of their tests, but lack the resources and personnel to do so; failure to do this means that they are seen as less professional and find it difficult to gain acceptance for their examinations (Grounds, 2007).

research and training

Training in task and item writing was considered an ongoing and iterative process, so staff received constant updating, feedback and training over the years. The decision to consider linking the three EXAVER examinations to the CEFR was taken to establish empirical evidence of the level and overall quality of the examinations but also to consolidate the professional development of the EXAVER team through the introduction of a research element to their work. Much of this work was undertaken under the guidance of Dr Pat Grounds (then working as Senior ELT Projects Manager at the British Council) and of Professor Barry O'Sullivan of CLARe, though all EXAVER staff actively participated in the process through their own research and through regular meetings. The current plan is to publish a formal report on the process for relating EXAVER 3 to CEFR level B2 by the end of 2010.

Two other aspects of the training and research element of the project should be mentioned at this point. As indicated above, EXAVER is fortunate to have a fully trained statistical analyst working on the project. Following every administration of the examinations a detailed statistical analysis is undertaken. The focus of this is twofold:

(1) EXAVER uses a series of anchor tests to maintain equivalence of level across the different test versions. Data from the administrations are first anchored using IRT, and the pass/fail boundary established. Following discussion with the relevant group, grading and awarding proceed.
(2) Full test, testlet and item analysis is undertaken to ensure that the papers are of the highest possible quality year on year. These analyses are used by the team to reflect on their work and to constantly improve the EXAVER papers.

The other major effort that has contributed to the improvement of EXAVER has been the word list project. The Chief Editor, Roger Dunne, has taken on the huge task not only of committing to edit the lists, but also of carrying out the necessary research to validate these lists, through comparisons with other sources and elicitation of feedback from colleagues on the project. As a result of these endeavours, EXAVER now has detailed word lists for each of its three levels.

The work described in this section has been a major contributor to the localisation of the EXAVER suite of examinations. We see localisation as referring to the degree to which the test papers take into account characteristics of the test population and contribute to its validity. For instance, if we look to the contribution of the word lists in this regard and we consider the use of the more internationally recognised lists, there is an obvious benefit from taking the first language of the candidates into account.

EXAVER recognition

The accreditation process required by the Mexican National Educational Standards Institution (CENNI), the institution responsible for the setting and moderating of foreign language standards, has been successfully completed. As a result, as from 29 October 2009, Universidad Veracruzana became the first Mexican institution to be placed alongside reputable international organisations on the table of accredited language test developers. By including EXAVER in its list of approved language certificates, the Mexican federal government has given the green light for other universities (both national and regional) to look to EXAVER as a model for meeting their own internal language certificate needs at affordable rates. This achievement has fulfilled hopes that were expressed in the early days of the project, namely that the impact of our project could become a major step towards Mexican national standards for language proficiency testing.

developing systems

We have developed not only examinations, but also a series of manuals for administrators and examination centre managers (actually, the coordinators of the respective university language centres). We have also developed a course to train Oral Examiners (OEs) systematically, and have a large cadre of some 116 examiners who are able to administer all papers, including the speaking test, all over the state in any one of our seven official examination centres at the different major campuses of the university: Xalapa (two centres), Veracruz, Orizaba, Córdoba, Poza Rica, Coatzacoalcos. OEs are carefully recruited on the basis of teaching qualifications and experience as well as previous examinations experience. They are then trained according to standardised procedures and receive a standardised trainers' manual, which has recently been updated and improved. Each OE receives a detailed manual for future reference with his or her induction package. To enhance inter-rater reliability, OEs are regularly monitored by trainers and annual standardisation meetings are held across the state, though it would be honest to say that these have not always been held as frequently as we would have liked, due to practical constraints.

the growth of EXAVER

Since one of the main aims of the whole project was to develop tests that were affordable to the broad population, we have worked very hard to keep the costs down. While this is not always easy, the fact that we rely less and less on external support means that we can offer these examinations at an average price to the candidate of between US$20 and US$30, according to the level. In this regard, the project has been a huge success. Candidate numbers have, over the past few years, begun to grow (see Figure 11.6). This growth is very important, as the test needs a growing population if it is to survive financially and rely less on the support of the University.

Perhaps the most important thing to have been gained from the project is a general increase in professionalism among the team. In terms of professional development, the group involved in the project has come a long way over the past decade, having progressed to the stage where a major nationally recognised suite of examinations is now regularly administered to an internationally recognised level of quality. In order to make this happen, there has been a high level of prolonged

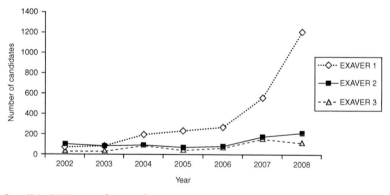

Figure 11.6   EXAVER test population growth

commitment on the part of the members of the group (in terms of professional development) and on the part of the University (in terms of the provision of resources).

what has been gained from the process

Beyond the development group, the project has had a definite impact on the participants at different levels, for example:

- the Institution within which the project operates;
- the Candidates, who represent the project's clients;
- the Teachers, whose classroom curricula and activities have become more thoughtful and varied as a result of the project (positive washback effect);
- prospective Employers.

the institution

The University of Veracruz has gained considerable prestige by having met the challenge of writing standardised exams for the certification of English, following international standards and guidelines and with international consultants of the highest possible quality. As mentioned above, the University has become the first in Mexico whose English language tests have been officially recognised at the national level.

In October 2003, in Xalapa, the EXAVER team instigated the first of a series of four National Conferences on the Evaluation of Foreign Languages in Mexican universities, and, we believe, in this way contributed to a new level of academic thinking about language test construction for foreign languages in Higher Education. In addition, articles on the project have appeared in the MEXTESOL journal, while team members have given academic presentations at major national and international conferences.

It is important to note also that the direct participants have not been the only people to benefit from heightened levels of professionalism. Because of the development, training and administration work undertaken over the years, a very large number of individual teachers and administrators in the University and across the province of Veracruz have benefited greatly from the training they received and from the experience of administering a high-quality test in their own locale. They can now transfer the expertise gained through participation on this project to their own assessment contexts.

the candidates

The candidates are now able to certify their knowledge and skills in English for a range of purposes, including certification and employment, through exams that are much more affordable than most international exams but are still recognised at the national level.

the members of the EXAVER examination board

The consultants, the general coordinator, the item writers, the statistician and the examiners have had the satisfaction of working on a project that may be, at least in some ways, unique in Latin America, if not the world. Among other things, this hard work has included meetings, workshops and information-sharing sessions three to four times per year with our external consultants.

The team has produced detailed specifications, word lists for each level, examiner and administrator training manuals, batteries of exams for each level, sample test papers and an EXAVER webpage. Moreover, the item writers have been able to take their new knowledge and skills to their respective workplaces and train colleagues, other teachers, how to write better exams. The oral examiners have also used their new-found knowledge in their own language centres and have used it to improve assessment of speaking there.

In October 2009, the vital stage of training and recruiting new members for the EXAVER development and validation group began with a one-week intensive training course for aspiring item writers, given by our local external consultant. Each new item writer will be assigned a mentor from the existing team, and together they will collaborate on producing new examination materials until such time as the new members are considered fully competent to work alone. Succession management is a vital element of the sustainability of any innovative project, and we plan to ensure that properly inducted and trained professionals are ready to join the team when needed.

future employers

People in the business world need employees who can use English sufficiently well to communicate, at various levels of ability, in order to compete in the global marketplace. One of the prime motivators for the project from the beginning was the awareness of the University that valid and affordable measures of language ability were urgently required to meet this need. In the past, candidates for jobs could not demonstrate their levels of English because they had no official document, since local, affordable tests did not exist and international exams were beyond the reach of our students. All this has changed, thanks to EXAVER. Gaining national recognition means that Mexican-based employers can now look to these locally developed tests as a source of accreditation of their prospective workers' language ability.

the current outlook

The formal Research Agenda that the team drew up and committed to in 2007 covers a three-phase research plan. The goal of the first phase is to formally link EXAVER's suite of three batteries of tests to the Common European Framework of Reference for Languages (CEFR). At the time of writing, the Board has finished the familiarisation and specification segments of this first phase, and will be moving on to the standardisation segment in the autumn of 2009.

For the second phase of the research, a series of general questions that relate to all EXAVER levels in relation to Cognitive, Context and Scoring validity have been designed and documented for future action. The third, but by no means final, phase includes a detailed agenda of research activities for each level concerning the same three aspects of validity.

Finally, we have been examining the possibility of including a direct test of writing at each level. So far, this has entailed a comparison with the ways in which writing is dealt with in a range of recognised exams at similar levels, trialling items and comparing results with those of other parts of the paper and with other measures of writing ability at the levels of the EXAVER papers. However, to date the results remain inconclusive and no decision has yet been made with regard to when and how this innovation will be introduced to the examination.

conclusions

The way in which this project came to life, through an ongoing process of collaborative planning, implementation and evaluation at an institutional level, has made it significant. Perhaps most of all, this is due to the fact that, despite the years that have passed since its inception, most of the founder members of the board are still actively participating in all stages of the development and validation process, and are now beginning to train our successors. This has lent, and will, in the future, lend, continuity to the activities. Also, the examination developers were, and continue to be, able to propose changes that the test may require as a result of the item analysis process and our knowledge of the context and to move forward in the development process together. This combination of increased professionalism, when considered in light of the general feeling that in this case "local" is good and stands for quality, marks the true value of the project, namely, in establishing a model for others to follow. Tests do not have to be international or expensive to be "good".

recommendations for similar projects

While a project such as EXAVER is designed to provide a series of high-quality affordable tests for a specific population, any prospective developer should consider a number of points before even thinking of starting out. These include:

- This is not a short-term project – we have spent nine years to date developing the EXAVER examinations and the support materials that make them possible.
- This is not a "cheap" solution – the length of time and resources employed show that such a project requires considerable long-term investment.
- Quality is never guaranteed – even with good specifications, test quality and level can drift over time, so we need clear and well-defined quality assurance systems (with external monitoring at least until the test matures).
- You are not writing a test – we learnt early on that we needed to develop an entire test system, from quality assurance boards, to websites, to item writer and examiner selection, training and accreditation, to the development of administrative structures and, of course, to the tests themselves, ensuring that the different versions are equivalent and that the outcomes are reliable and valid.
- Good teams don't just happen – it takes time and energy to build effective teams and even more energy to maintain the enthusiasm and effectiveness of such a team.
- Aim for excellence from the start – probably the key issue in the EXAVER project has been the recognition of talent and the constant push to develop the professionalism of the team so that it can now be seen to have reached international standard.
- Think local – we never lost focus on the individual test taker. From the inception of the project we wanted to build something that would recognise the culture and language of the prospective

candidates and provide them with a means to success in their society.

One final comment. Perhaps the most important factor to repeat is that all this has been achieved with a team of dedicated teachers, all of whom spend at least half of their working hours on other academic responsibilities, such as teaching, tutoring, and research and development projects. Additionally, two members of the team have completed their PhDs during the project. So, finding the right people and keeping them is vital to the success of any such project.

references

Abad, A., Dunne, R. and Grounds, P. (2004). A local alternative to international proficiency tests: the EXAVER project. In J. Pender (Ed.), *Ten Years of Collaboration in ELT: Accounts from Mexico.* Mexico City: British Council.

Dunne, R. (2007). The EXAVER project: conception and development *MEXTESOL Journal, 31*(7): 23–30.

Grounds, P. (2001). *Project Progress Report prepared for Dr. Victor Arredondo.* Internal Report. Veracruz, Mexico: Universidad Veracruzana.

Grounds, P. (2007). *Discovering Dynamic Durability: Beyond Sustainability in an English Language Curriculum Project.* Unpublished PhD Thesis, University of Kent at Canterbury.

12

the development and validation of an online rater training and marking system: promises and pitfalls

annie brown and paul jaquith

introduction

Advances in recent years have led to a proliferation of technology-based solutions to testing needs (see, for example, Chapelle and Douglas, 2006; Douglas and Hegelheimer, 2007; Chapelle, 2008). While the use of computer technology for the delivery of tests, including web-based tests and computer-adaptive tests, is perhaps the most visible of these, computers are also used for authoring tests, for the management of test and administration data, for automated scoring through speech recognition and natural language processing, and for the training of raters and delivery of test data to them for scoring. In this chapter we focus on the last of these through the description of the development of an online training and marking program for the assessment of second language writing.

There is some research pertaining to the online training of raters, and, while most of it focuses on the affective responses of raters (e.g. Hamilton et al., 2001; Elder et al., 2007), some also evaluates the effectiveness of the training (Brown and Jaquith, 2007; Knoch et al., 2007). In contrast with this research interest, however, has been a lack of description of operational software and of issues in software development and deployment. In addition, there is no published research to date on the online marking of second language writing tests, nor is online marking of essays addressed in key papers on the use of technology in language testing (e.g. Douglas and Hegelheimer, 2007; Chapelle,

2008). Therefore, the main aim of this study is to present to the reader a chronological walk through the development and subsequent refinement of one online marking and training project in order to illustrate the design issues that must be considered in such a development.

benefits and efficacy of online training and marking

Online rater training and operational marking are both said to have advantages over the more traditional method: face-to-face training and paper-based marking. Face-to-face training has been criticised on the grounds that large rater training sessions can be intimidating and therefore have limited efficacy (Charney, 1984; Hamp-Lyons, 2007) or that raters will vary in the amount of time they need to read and judge the quality of certain writing samples (Elder et al., 2007), so that forcing them to work at the same speed in training sessions might have a negative impact. However, the main reason for introducing online training is the practical advantage it has when it is difficult to bring raters together at one time for the training. For example, the distribution of raters over a wide geographic area was the reason behind the introduction of online training for the Simulated Oral Proficiency Interview (SOPI) in the United States (Kenyon and Stansfield, 1993), and the inability to bring busy faculty together at one time for training was the reason behind the introduction of online training in the case of the Hong Kong Polytechnic University Graduating Students' Language Proficiency Assessment (Hamilton et al., 2001). In addition, as Elder et al. (2007: 37) point out, online training "facilitat[es] access to training materials and rating samples and allowing raters to re-orient themselves to the rating scale and self monitor their behaviour at their own convenience".

A number of studies have investigated attitudes to, and the effectiveness of, online rater training for language tests. In general, responses to the use of online training have been favourable. Hamilton et al. (2001) report strong support among those who used it for an online training program developed for an end of course English for Academic Purposes (EAP) assessment in a Hong Kong University, although it was optional and only one-third of the markers accessed it. Of these, more than 90 per cent found the program useful, with paper saving, time saving and flexibility, and time for reflection cited as advantages. Twenty-five per cent reported some difficulty in using the programs, with problems including technical issues such as incompatible browsers and the occasional server breakdown, and "human responses" to page colour, layout and the need to scroll through essays. Similarly, most of the raters in a study by Elder et al. (2007) responded positively to an online training program in the context of a diagnostic test used on entry to a university in New Zealand, again citing the ability to work at a convenient time, the ability to self-pace, and privacy to be the main advantages. As in the study by Hamilton et al., the major disadvantages reported were having to read online and the need to scroll through the scripts. Given that scripts were marked using a number of ana-lytic criteria, and feedback was provided on all of these for each script, there was also a sense of information overload. Studies by Knoch et al. (2007) and Brown and Jaquith (2007) compared responses from two groups of raters: those who completed face-to-face training and those who completed the training online. Knoch et al. found that raters who participated in online training liked it because it was convenient and because the lack of interaction with other raters precluded the oppor-tunity for stronger personalities to dominate the training and for shy ones to feel uncomfortable. Disadvantages cited were the impersonal nature of the training, and difficulty or strain reading the scripts. In Brown and Jaquith's study, raters were allocated to either face-to-face or online training. All were positively oriented to their training, although there was marginally stronger support for paper-based training. Some participants in the online training complained about some technical difficulties as far as script loading speeds and familiarity with the inter-face were concerned.

As Elder et al. (2007: 40) point out, investigations of raters' attitudes to online training need to be accompanied by empirical data recording its impact on test scores and its effectiveness in reducing the various forms of scoring variability. In particular, they note that:

> It cannot be assumed that individualised feedback will have the same impact as peer pressure, which may be what produces convergence in rater judgements in a group training context. In addition, the suc-cess of online training may vary with regard to other factors such as raters' background characteristics (Reed and Cohen, 2001), including computer familiarity, as well as technical considerations related to the design of the training program.

Three of the studies described above did, in fact, also investigate the value of online training in improving reliability. Elder et al. (2007) asked eight raters to mark a batch of writing samples before and after participating in the online training. While raters who were more positive about the program generally showed more improvement than raters who were not, there was little improvement in severity, intra-rater consistency, and bias overall. Elder et al. attribute the minimal impact of the training to negative reactions to technical aspects of the training program, such as having to scroll through texts, eyestrain, and feedback overload. The lack of opportunity to engage in discussion is not, surprisingly, cited as a reason for the low level of improvement.

The study by Knoch et al. (2007) compared the efficacy of online training with face-to-face training. Sixteen raters scored a set of 70 scripts over a one-week period. Eight of the raters subsequently participated in face-to-face training and eight in online training. Both groups subsequently marked the 70 scripts again. The study found that both types of training resulted in improved reliability, with the online training being marginally more successful. This contrasts with the findings of Brown and Jaquith's (2007) much larger-scale study, involving 202 raters, in which the online raters performed less well. A Many-facet Rasch (MFR) analysis revealed that in terms of severity and leniency the most extreme raters were mainly those working online, as were the most misfitting raters. In addition, most of the unexpected responses came from the online trained raters.

In contrast to the attention paid to the acceptability and efficacy of online rater training, there is, surprisingly, a dearth of literature on the impact of the marking mode on operational rating quality. We say surprisingly as we cannot help but wonder whether the linear nature of online marking – the difficulty in going backwards and forwards and in comparing scripts – might somehow have an impact on scoring reliability. We argue that the studies cited above focusing on raters' reactions to the training medium highlight the need to examine the marking medium as it impacts raters' ability to apply assessment criteria.

In the remainder of the chapter we focus on the description of the evolution of an online training and marking program, for use in the assessment of the writing component of a university admissions and placement exam in the United Arab Emirates (UAE). We focus particularly on design issues, and on the identification and resolution of problems in the development and implementation of the program.

background to CEPA online marking development

The Common Educational Proficiency Assessment (CEPA) began as a joint venture between the National Admissions and Placement Office

(NAPO) in the Ministry of Higher Education and Scientific Research and the three higher education institutions in the United Arab Emirates: the United Arab Emirates University (UAEU), Higher Colleges of Technology (HCT) and Zayed University (ZU). While there are two elements in the assessment, mathematics and English language, here we focus only on the system devised for the writing component of the English language test.

CEPA English is a two-hour exam, which consists of three sections (Grammar and Vocabulary, Reading, and Writing) and is administered in two formats: paper-and-pencil, and computer-based. There is no formal break between the three sections in either format, though it is recommended to candidates that they spend 45 minutes on Grammar and Vocabulary, 45 minutes on Reading and 30 minutes on Writing. In the writing section, students are given a prompt and asked to produce a short essay between 150 and 200 words in length. The quality of students' writing is assessed on a six-point scale by trained markers in terms of a rubric that focuses on grammar, vocabulary, spelling, organisation and content.

In 2002, the first year of the CEPA English exam, the writing component was conducted along traditional lines. Fifteen thousand higher education applicants completed the test at one of 15 campuses across the country. They were given a test booklet and recorded their answers to the Multiple choice questions (MCQs) on a separate optical mark reader sheet (known colloquially as a bubblesheet) and wrote their essay in the back of the test booklet. At the end of the exam, the bubblesheets were collected and sent to the Ministry of Higher Education to be processed centrally. The booklets were collected in packets with two score sheets for recording scores (one for the first marker and one for the second marker) and were then distributed to the markers. At this stage all English faculty across the three institutions were required to undertake some CEPA marking as part of their regular duties, and their training was carried out by selected faculty at each institution. When the first marker returned a pack, the score sheet was removed and the scores entered into a prepared Excel spreadsheet. The packet was then marked by a second marker at the same institution. When the second marker's scores were entered into the spreadsheet, the scores were checked for agreement and differences of greater than one band were sent to a third marker for arbitration.

While the scoring system worked quite well in terms of operational practicality, it was time-consuming, and there was always some concern with regard to the accuracy of the final test scores for the writing component. This was because it was not always certain that the different centres shared a common interpretation of the rating scale or performance standards. In order to remedy this, it was planned that MFR would be introduced to allow the relative harshness and consistency of the raters to be taken into account when estimating final scores or grades. However, the fact that the raters were so widely spread across the Emirates meant that we needed to consider the possibility of operational online rating of scripts. At the time, no major examination had attempted to do this, so we were forced to develop a workable system from scratch.

Several advances in technology converged to make online marking of written work possible:

- High-speed document scanners had become readily available, with supporting software that allows automated writer identification, through either a barcode reader or using optical mark reader (OMR) technology which is used to automatically read candidate responses made on bubblesheets. These scanners also allowed image capturing of specific parts of a document. These images (i.e. the essays) could then be saved into a database for storage and later distribution.
- Dramatic increases in bandwidth available through most providers and over the intranets supporting most campus communities made it possible to send images of student writing to markers with sufficient speed and resolution that the validity of the ratings was not affected.

early developments

CEPA online marking began in 2003 with the purchase of an *ecabinet* and the development of the prototype marking site. The *ecabinet* was a dedicated document management system and was designed to interface smoothly with a variety of high-speed document scanners. This piece of hardware enabled us to capture the student writing sample from the back of the bubblesheet as a "jpeg" (a common image storing format), index it, and store it centrally on its hard drive. The *ecabinet* then provided an on-demand, web-based system for delivery of the images to markers all across the country.

In the first year of the project we used an *ecabinet* attached to a Gestner high-speed document scanner. This was a duplex scanner that would scan and archive both sides of the bubblesheet. Student information was read directly from the bubblesheet, but was also keyed in by hand to screen for bubbling errors by the students. This process was very time-consuming, but necessary given the high error rate of students inputting their personal information (student ID, name, etc.).

The marking site itself required raters to log in with a username and password, sent to them in an email. Once they entered the marking site, they commenced marking their allocated set of scripts. A facility was set up whereby marking could be monitored, in order to ensure that all marking was completed by the closure date. As there was no pressure to report scores early at this time, raters were given two to three weeks to complete their marking. Each script was randomly assigned to two raters.

technical problems encountered

Once the marking system was implemented, a few problems emerged. First, the use of high-definition images meant that for some raters the script upload speed was frustratingly slow. The IT team addressed this issue by reducing the resolution of the scripts and adding a button that would allow raters to call up a higher-definition script only when needed (e.g. with particularly small or faint handwriting).

Other early problems were associated with multiple browser configurations and different operating systems in use by the markers, in addition to variations in campus intranet configurations. This variety in the infrastructure made it impossible for the IT team to model and plan for all situations, and led to a number of unforeseen local system crashes and hangs. Interestingly enough, most of these problems were not actually resolved by the IT team; rather, they simply went away with the increase in standardisation across browsers, network configurations and services.

Server crashes were not infrequent in the first two years of the program because of instabilities in the early versions of the *ecabinet* and an inability of the servers to deal with peak volume traffic. As illustrated in Figure 12.1, server demand varies considerably throughout the day, with peak marker volumes occurring at around 12 pm, 2 pm and 4 pm. The down times created by these crashes were not long, usually less than a couple of hours, but the result was that all marking ceased during those times. Most markers would then move on to other activities and many would not return to marking that day. Hence, even an extremely short crash could add a day or more to the marking process. In the second year we added a second *ecabinet* to accommodate the heavy load experienced during the peak marking period. These problems were further reduced with increases in server speed and capacity, as the IT team began to better understand the daily traffic patterns of script marking. In recent years, the IT team has migrated the entire system to a pair of servers that can accommodate

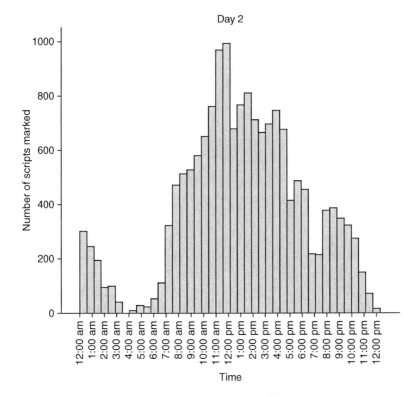

Figure 12.1 Daily volume of scripts being marked

much higher volumes through load balancing. It is interesting to note that, although peak volumes typically occur in the middle of the day and early afternoon, markers are active across the system 24 hours a day, with a surprising number of scripts being marked between midnight and 3 am.

In addition, local bandwidth limitations at some campuses caused considerable difficulties in the early years of the program, particularly during peak times, when an individual script might take as long as a minute to load. This situation led to high levels of frustration among the markers and encouraged many markers to multitask while marking.

other problems

Early in the process, we discovered that some students wrote their scripts with the essay sheet upside down, which meant that after being scanned into the database these scripts would be presented to the marker upside down. The reason for this seemed to be the fact that the bubblesheet side of the sheet was in landscape orientation while the back – the essay side – was in portrait orientation, so that some students, when they turned the paper over to begin the essay, placed it upside down in front of them. To deal with this we added an "invert script" button, which allowed raters to rotate the screen image. We also changed the orientation of the bubblesheet from landscape to portrait, which almost completely eliminated the problem.

Another problem that emerged was the use by some students of ink rather than pencil in writing the responses to the writing task. The issue here is that the bubblesheet scanners are designed to treat ink as a "drop out" colour. This allows them to "see" the marks made by pencils when students fill in the bubbles and ignore the ink of the printed bubbles themselves. This extends to the writing section as well, and responses written in ink do not appear in the jpeg images, so the scanned script appears blank to the reader. In fact, this was a problem that emerged several years after the program was initiated rather than at the beginning, due to a change in the administration procedures. In 2007, the CEPA English exam became the final exam for English in all UAE government secondary schools, and, because the testing population increased dramatically from just over 15,000 to nearly 35,000, we began using high school teachers as invigilators in some of the venues. These teachers came from a system that required all exam essays to be written in ink, so, when the time came for students to work on their essays, some teachers told students to write in ink, even though invigilator training sessions specifically stated that students were required to respond with the pencils provided. We had never seen an ink script before; suddenly we had hundreds scattered throughout the system. As ink script is not visible to the markers, we had to comb through all 35,000 scripts and score the ink scripts by hand.

Each year since, the number of ink scripts has declined as a result of more aggressive invigilator training. In addition, we now screen and sort all answer sheets as they come in. The word "Blank" is written in pencil on any blank answer sheet so we know that it was a true blank and not an ink script that slipped through. Blank scripts are also tagged in the database and are not sent out to markers. If a marker encounters a blank script, he or she flags it as blank in the marking scheme, and we double-check the original script at our end.

background to the online training module

In the context in which the program was developed, as the CEPA exam began to be used not only for placement into English programs but also, from 2006, for university admission, the shift from low to high stakes meant that it was important to ensure high inter- and intra-rater reliability in essay marking. In order to promote high standards, it was decided that marking should be scheduled as an optional, paid activity rather than a unpaid additional duty as was currently the case, and that potential raters should be required to undertake a program of training, as training is known to increase the reliability of ratings (see, among others, Weigle, 2002; Rethinasamy, 2006). At the same time, it was not feasible to carry out training in a face-to-face mode, as potential raters – English faculty of the three institutions – were scattered across 15 campuses across the seven emirates, and potential trainers – the examinations staff of the Ministry – were too busy in the period leading up to the exam administration to carry out such training. Therefore, the decision was taken to add a training module to the existing online marking program. It was planned that the module would consist of two parts, a training element and an accreditation element. Only those markers who were able to demonstrate a required level of accuracy in marking the accreditation scripts would be allowed to proceed to live script marking. An additional perceived advantage of an online training module was that raters would be able to access it to re-standardise at subsequent smaller administrations throughout the year.

format of the online training module

It was decided that the training module would replicate standard practice in face-to-face training, whereby raters review benchmarked scripts in order to reach a common understanding of the standards (Alderson et al., 1995; Elder et al., 2007), by providing sample scored scripts and scripts on which raters would practise scoring. While it was not possible to incorporate the interactive component of face-to-face training in which raters discuss their ratings, it was felt that this could be modelled to some extent by including comments provided by experienced, expert raters, for both the sample and practice scripts, which gave their reasons for awarding the benchmark scores.

The training module was therefore set up to replicate the normal process of face-to-face rater training. Figure 12.2 shows its organisation. Each rater enters the site using a personal login ID and password. The homepage contains information on the structure of the site, the

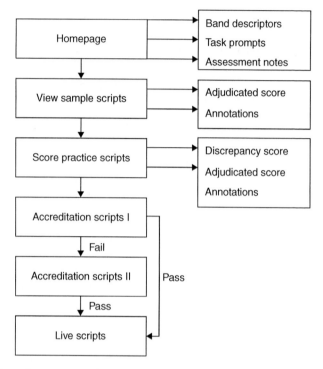

Figure 12.2   Website organisation: online rater training program

training and accreditation procedure, and the procedure for live marking. It has links to portable document format (PDF) files of the band descriptors and the essay prompts, and to assessment notes, which provide the raters with general guidance regarding the rating process. It also has buttons that link to the sample and practice scripts and, eventually, to the accreditation scripts and live scripts.

Trainee raters first view ten writing samples, presented in ascending order of proficiency. Each script is accompanied by its score (an adjudicated score derived from the ratings awarded by a set of expert raters) and a set of comments which explain why this score was awarded. (Raters can also return to these scripts when they are doing their operational script marking.) After the raters have viewed all the sample scripts they progress to a set of ten practice scripts, which are presented one by one in random order. For each script, after the rater submits a score, the adjudicated score is shown alongside the rater's score, together with

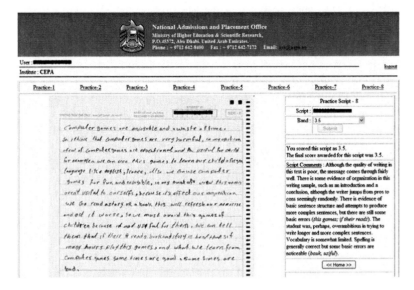

Figure 12.3 Practice script

comments explaining why that adjudicated score was awarded (see Figure 12.3). The raters can go back at any time and re-rate any or all of the practice scripts, but they must rate all of them at least once before progressing to the accreditation scripts.

The accreditation scripts are a set of eight scripts with adjudicated scores. Raters are required to assess the scripts within a specified discrepancy level. If they fail, they are advised to work through the sample and practice scripts once more and to mark a second set of accreditation scripts. If they succeed in marking the scripts with the required accuracy this time, they are allowed to proceed to operational marking.

operational marking

Markers are recruited from the professional EFL faculty at the three federal higher education institutions. They register their interest online by supplying their name, email address, mobile phone number, and institution and campus affiliation. They are also required to detail their qualifications (a master's degree in TESOL, or equivalent, and three years' experience). Their qualifications and affiliation are submitted to their institutions for confirmation.

Once the scripts have been uploaded into the marking site, an email and SMS are sent to all registered markers, notifying them that they can commence their training, and reminding them of the closure time of the marking period. Reminders are sent periodically by SMS in order to ensure that all marking is completed on time. In the early years of using the program we found that raters needed ongoing technical support during the marking period, so the phone number and email address of a technical support person were provided, in order to ensure that there were no delays in the completion of the marking. But as computers became more powerful, and the software became more sophisticated, problems arose less and less.

In the first model, all scripts were allocated to markers at the beginning of the marking period, and those allocated to markers who subsequently failed the training were reallocated. However, as some raters failed ultimately to complete the training or to complete their marking assignment, a number of scripts remained unmarked at the closing date. A subsequent change minimised this problem: scripts are not allocated to markers until they have passed the accreditation, and even then there is a limit to the number they can request at any one time. Raters can quit a session at any time and log in again later, at which time the system will present only the remaining unmarked scripts. In order to avoid fatigue, there is also a limit to the number of scripts each rater is allowed to mark each day. Once that number is reached the rater is automatically logged out, but can re-enter the next day to continue his or her allocation. Once a rater has completed the original allocation he or she can request a further set of scripts, if there are any available.

In the original version of the program, each script was randomly assigned to two different markers. However, complaints that they did not like constantly switching from one topic to another led us to modify the script allocation. In the revised versions, once the scripts have been scanned, they are sorted into batches of 25 of one version, and allocated to raters by batch. (The program is able to identify version number from the booklet number indicated on the MCQ side of the bubblesheet, although, as this is filled in by students, errors do occur. However, safeguards against scoring the student against the wrong key include having the marker indicate the presence of a script within a bundle responding to the "wrong" prompt and comparison of scores produced when the MCQ section is scored using all keys from the particular date of testing.)

In the first round of marking all scripts are rated twice, with scripts being allocated batchwise randomly to two raters. Once the first round of marking is complete, scripts with a predetermined score discrepancy for the two ratings are allocated to a subset of raters for a third rating. A many-facet Rasch measurement program, FACETS (Linacre, 2003), is used to produce scores, and also to produce feedback for the raters at the end of the marking round on their severity and consistency.

In the first model, there was no option for markers to review or change their scores, and occasional messages were received that a wrong score had accidentally been entered. (Scores were selected from a drop-down menu.) Two changes were subsequently made to the program: first, raters were required to confirm their score before moving on to the next script and, second, the option was provided for markers to return to previously scored essays.

monitoring the marking process

As part of the development of the online rater training program, a management site was set up to allow us to monitor progress from training to accreditation to operational rating, and thus to ensure that marking deadlines were being met. In a context where there are strict deadlines to be met in reporting scores, as was the case here, at least while CEPA English was being administered as part of the high school exit exams, it is important to ensure that all scripts are marked by the deadline, whether first round (first and second rating) or second round (third rating).

The management site allows an administrator to monitor the marking and to download data for processing of final scores. It has links to a page containing marker information, a site that shows the progress of the marking, and Microsoft Excel sheets of score data. All of these have been customised to the requirements of the particular context, and are described in more detail below.

markers full details

This link opens a page that displays the personal information requested from each marker at registration, including institutional affiliation, teaching and assessing qualifications and experience, and phone and email contact details (Figure 12.4).

The screen also shows whether the marker has passed or failed the accreditation, and allows the administrator to tag a marker as active or inactive, which allows for a selected set of raters to be granted access for the small administrations that are held throughout the year, or (although this has never occurred) for accredited raters to have their access to the site rescinded during a marking period. The data can also be downloaded into an Excel file.

258   language testing: theories and practices

Figure 12.4   Marker information

scripts upload

This allows the administrator to upload scanned scripts and divide them into batches based on versions.

marking status

This allows the administrator to monitor the progress of the marking by marker and total. For each marker the number of scripts requested, allocated, marked and pending is shown (see Figure 12.5).

microsoft excel export report

This link exports an Excel file with data arranged on one line per student in order to allow comparison of the two raters' scores and determine which scripts require a third mark. The same file is accessed after the third mark, and edited for import into the FACETS program, which is used to estimate fair scores.

current developments

Pressure from the universities to provide regular test administrations throughout the year has necessitated a move from paper-based to

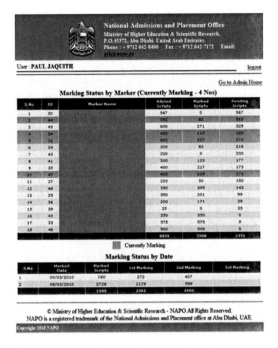

User : PAUL JAQUITH   logout

Go to Admin Home

Marking Status by Marker (Currently Marking - 4 Nos)

S.No	ID	Marker Name	Alloted Scripts	Marked Scripts	Pending Scripts
1	30		567	0	567
2	44		592	82	510
3	45		600	271	329
4	34		400	115	285
5	52		600	327	273
6	24		300	82	218
7	43		200	0	200
8	41		300	123	177
9	35		400	227	173
10	47		400	229	171
11	27		200	50	150
12	48		350	205	145
13	25		300	201	99
14	36		200	171	29
15	39		25	0	25
16	42		350	350	0
17	33		575	575	0
18	46		500	500	0
			6839	3508	3151

Currently Marking

Marking Status by Date

S.No	Marked Date	Marked Scripts	1st Marking	2nd Marking	3rd Marking
1	09/03/2010	780	373	407	
2	08/03/2010	2728	2129	599	
		3508	2502	1006	

Figure 12.5   Screenshot of an in-progress marking period (rater names obscured)

computer-based testing. This was implemented in the current academic year and has led to one change that affects the marking: essay scripts are now word-processor-mediated rather than handwritten. This has two advantages. First, essays are produced as text files, which can be imported directly into the marking program, thus removing the need for scanning of scripts and shortening the processing time. Second, the text files are much smaller than the scanned scripts, produced as jpegs, which has speeded up the load time. However, anecdotal evidence suggests that markers find it more tiring to mark the computer-mediated texts, which supports comments made by raters in a study by Dempsey et al. (2009) that handwritten essays include additional semantic markers that reveal the writer's process and impact on raters' perceptions of the students' identities and their writing abilities.

Although there was concern early on that some students may be disadvantaged by being forced to write on a computer, preliminary results indicate that the opposite may in fact be true: that students exiting high school these days are more comfortable writing on a computer than on paper, and that they produce longer responses of higher quality. This is in keeping with current scholarship in the area (Russell and Haney, 1997; Bennett, 2002; Goldberg et al., 2003), which indicates that students who are accustomed to writing on computers may be significantly disadvantaged when asked to write on paper. The move to word-processor-mediated writing is particularly important in our context, where the students are applying for admission to English-medium laptop-environment institutions.

discussion and conclusions

So, what has been the main value of the system? Within a national testing system where raters are geographically distributed, the online training and marking program has allowed us to ensure that marking is of a high standard and that the process of marking is carried out efficiently and completely within a very tight schedule (a turnaround time of three days is the norm for each round of marking), something that was not possible in the days of paper-based marking.

This paper has described how one testing system designed, developed and refined an online marking system, which was subsequently modified to include a training and accreditation module. The aim here has been to show how, in the (then) absence of any model that could be drawn on in its design, the program was very much tailored to the local context and needs, and very much a process of trial and error. On the way we learned from the problems we encountered, and over the years were able to refine the program to meet our developing needs.

From its inception in 2003, CEPA has been committed to the appropriate use of available technology, and we have prided ourselves on being at the cutting edge of modern language testing. Any system will be constrained by the available technology of the time. Advances in technology continuously provide potential opportunities, and we are constantly looking for opportunities to improve our existing systems and to exploit new technologies. Organisations taking this approach must be committed to a cycle of ongoing improvement and innovation.

References

Alderson, J. C., Clapham, C. M. and Wall, D. (1995). *Language Test Construction and Evaluation*. Cambridge: Cambridge University Press.

Bennett, R. E. (2002). Inexorable and inevitable: the continuing story of technology and assessment. *The Journal of Technology, Learning, and Assessment*, *1*(1), Available at http://escholarship.bc.edu/cgi/viewcontent.cgi?article=1012&context=jtla (accessed 15 March 2010).

Brown, A. and Jaquith, P. (2007). *Online Rater Training: Perceptions and Performance*. Barcelona: Language Testing Research Colloquium.

Chapelle, C. (2008). Utilizing technology in language assessment. In E. Shohamy and N. H. Hornberger (Eds), *Encyclopedia of Language and Education, 2nd Edition, Volume 7: Language Testing and Assessment*. New York: Springer, pp. 123–134.

Chapelle, C. and Douglas, D. (2006). *Assessing Languages Through Computers*. Cambridge: Cambridge University Press.

Charney, D. A. (1984). The validity of using holistic scoring to evaluate writing: a critical overview. *Research in the Testing of English*, *18*(1), 65–81.

Dempsey, M. S., PytlikZillig, L. M. and Bruning, R. H. (2009). Helping preservice teachers learn to assess writing: practice and feedback in a web-based environment. *Assessing Writing*, *14*(1), 38–61.

Douglas, D. and Hegelheimer, V. (2007). Assessing language using computer technology. *Annual Review of Applied Linguistics*, *27*, 115–132.

Elder, C., Barkhuizen, G., Knoch, U. and Von Randow, J. (2007). Evaluating the utility of online training for L2 writing assessment: how responsive are ESL raters? *Language Testing*, *24*(1), 37–64.

Goldberg, A., Russell, M. and Cook, A. (2003). The effect of computers on student writing: a meta-analysis of studies from 1992 to 2002. *The Journal of Technology, Learning, and Assessment*, *2*(1), Available at http://collaboration.pwsd76.ab.ca/file.php/4/Research_ATL/computersforwritingsummary.pdf (accessed 15 March 2010).

Hamilton, J., Reddel, S. and Spratt, M. (2001). Teachers' perceptions of online rater training and monitoring. *System*, *29*, 505–520.

Hamp-Lyons, L. (2007). Worrying about rating. *Assessing Writing*, *12*, 1–9.

Kenyon, D. M. and Stansfield, C. W. (1993). A method for improving tasks on performance-based assessments through field-testing. In A. Huhta, K. Sajavaara and S. Takala (Eds), *Language Testing: New Openings*. Jyväskylä: Institute for Educational Research, University of Jyväskylä.

Knoch, U., Read, J. and von Randow, J. (2007). Re-training writing raters online: how does it compare with face-to-face training? *Assessing Writing*, *12*(1), 26–43.

Linacre, M. (2003). *FACETS – Rasch Measurement Computer Program*. Chicago, IL: Mensa Press.

Rethinasamy, S. (2006). *The Effects on Rating Performance of Different Training Interventions*. Unpublished PhD thesis, Roehampton University, London.

Russell, M. and Haney, W. (1997). Testing writing on computers: an experiment comparing student performance on tests conducted via computer and via paper-and-pencil. *Education Policy Analysis Archives*, *5*(3), Available at http://epaa.asu.edu/ojs/article/viewFile/604/726 (accessed 15 March 2010).

Weigle, S. C. (2002). *Assessing Writing*. Cambridge: Cambridge University Press.

13

uses and impact of test scores in university admissions processes: the language test as the "hard" criterion

pauline rea-dickins, richard kiely and guoxing yu

introduction

The role of language tests in decision-making has a very long history, for example the Chinese Imperial Examinations dating back to over 3000 years ago. Even with this early example, given the stringency with which it functioned as gatekeeper to entry to the Chinese civil service, we can detect a notion of "certainty" in the message it conveyed to candidates, that in passing this test a candidate will be de facto a successful and fully functioning member of the elite civil service. Jumping ahead to this century, we also evidence ways in which our major international language proficiency tests have also acquired this "aura of certainty" in their interpretation and use. In the research we report here we found much evidence to show how this interpretation of a test score was important for admissions decision-making and how IELTS results – the measure used for our research – were largely constructed as certain and safe, especially in this context where decisions that affect people in negative ways may be challenged and have to be defended. In other words, those involved in student admissions for university study tended to perceive a student's score as a "true" account of that individual's language achievement and abilities and, relative to other available admissions data, interpreted the test score as "hard" and accountable evidence. This contrasts with the mitigated claims that the test providers themselves make with reference to score interpretation and use. The guidance on using the test score below notes the importance of taking the sub-test profile as well as the overall score into account, and relating these to the language demands of a specific programme and the other admissions requirements.

> The level of English needed for a candidate to perform effectively in study, work or training varies from one situation to another. That is why each individual organisation can set its one minimum IELTS score for applicants, dependent on specific requirements. Organisations using IELTS may consider the overall band score as well as the individual scores recorded for the four components of the test. [...] It should be noted, however, that many diverse variables can affect performance on courses, of which language ability is but one. (IELTS, 2009)

Test providers also recommend that institutions make subject-specific decisions about the appropriate cut-off score(s) for any given university programme. The IELTS guidance for stakeholders distinguishes between "academic" and "training" programmes, and in each case suggests further characterisations such as "linguistically demanding" or "linguistically less demanding". Thus, use of IELTS as an admissions tool, in the implicit framework here, includes some analysis of language demands of a programme itself, as well as consideration of factors other than language ability. This characterisation of test use might be considered proportionate to the stakes involved for both applicants and host institutions. The inherent flexibility called for in the use of IELTS scores requires both knowledge and interpretive skills, so that the decisions taken by admissions administrators and tutors regarding each prospective student are part of a multifaceted complex assessment.

In this chapter, we explore the role of IELTS in the very complex decision-making that surrounds international student admissions to universities. Such decisions are made by individuals, many of whom have very limited knowledge about the test itself, the language proficiency issues, and the nature of the various high stakes for students studying in higher education institutions through the medium of a second language. We look at the way the language test is used in conjunction with other admissions criteria, in order to understand the construct of "readiness" for the programme, and the ways the language proficiency result contributes to this. We present the findings from case studies from one institution conducted in two different social science departments in the UK admissions context. We first provide the background to our research through a review of the relevant literature

and summarise the design of our study. This is followed by our findings, contextualised around three themes. The first analyses the way
in which admissions tutors and others work with and interpret IELTS
scores in arriving at decisions about student admissions. Our second set
of findings focuses on the understanding of IELTS by these admissions
staff and the implications these have for assessment induction of these
non(language)-specialists. Our third theme analyses some of the ambiguities and ethical issues that are raised through discussions with staff,
in particular the way in which "international students" – once they
have successfully negotiated the IELTS hurdle and gained university
admission – are positioned in these discourses in relation to programme
participation, learning and progression. Our conclusion highlights the
ways the admissions decision-making process in our case study tends to
privilege the language score as the "hard" criterion, which is not in line
with the more flexible, integrated basket of criteria recommended by
IELTS and which we feel is required by programmes.

background

IELTS impact studies have employed a range of methodologies, including predictive validation studies of academic readiness or outcomes (e.g.
Cotton and Conrow, 1998; Hill et al., 1999; Kerstjens and Nery, 2000),
the use of a survey to identify how IELTS is used in managing admissions (e.g. McDowell and Merrylees, 1998; Coleman et al., 2003) or a
more ethnographic approach to uncover both student admissions and
learning experiences, most notably Banerjee (2003). In our research, we
align with Banerjee's study in two ways. First, she focused on two major
themes, which our research design also addressed: the admissions process and the students' learning experiences; in this chapter we present
data relating to the first of these themes. Second, highlighting the limitations of correlational and questionnaire-based studies, she chose to
work closely with two programmes and 25 students in one British university, thus achieving a close and fine-grained analysis of how undergraduate admissions are achieved when a language proficiency score is
part of an applicant's portfolio. A second study that also informs on the
research we report here is O'Loughlin (2008). He, too, investigated how
the IELTS, as a high stakes test, was used in the selection of international
postgraduate students in one large university in Australia. In addition,
he examined the knowledge and beliefs that students and staff (including administrative and academic) had about the test. Three main sources
of data informed his study: institutional documents on selection policy

and procedure, questionnaires and interviews with staff and students on their knowledge, experience and opinions about the test and its use. that is,

> Source 1: institutional documents on selection policy and procedure
> Source 2: questionnaires and interviews with staff on their knowledge, experience and opinions about the test and its use
> Source 3: questionnaires and interviews with students on their knowledge, experience and opinions about the test and its use

In her case study, Banerjee (2003) observed that the guides available to inform the admissions process tended to concentrate on procedural issues, such as documentation on each application and the interpretation of academic qualifications presented, with very little on the actual interpretation of language proficiency scores (p. 376). O'Loughlin (2008) also evidenced the use of clear guidelines about – in his case, minimal – English language requirements. In Banerjee's study (2003), the interpretations of test scores by admissions staff appeared to be restricted to a judgement of the score provided in relation to the minimum criteria set for the degree in question (p. 379), whereas O'Loughlin (2008) reports a range of views from considerable scepticism to "unrealistic expectations of the power of the test" (p. 184).

The admissions personnel in Banerjee's study (2003) demonstrated awareness of language issues in the admissions process: they were familiar with and used the University's published language proficiency criteria, and they were aware that they should take into account total test scores as well as sub-test profiles in processing applicants. They were also aware of the linguistic demands of postgraduate studies. On the other hand, it was not clear whether admissions staff understood what a particular score implied in terms of what a student can or cannot do in English. O'Loughlin (2008), by way of contrast, found variable levels of knowledge about IELTS, in terms of the test, the scores and what they imply about students' readiness for study and their future English language development needs.

In relation to the actual international student selection process, Banerjee's (2003) research evidenced a greater balancing out of factors as influential in the admissions process, with a reliance on data other than test scores, such as timing of the application, a recommendation from agents, or whether the student was in receipt of a scholarship. She also found that, if a risk were to be taken in the selection process, it was more likely to be in connection with the language test score than with another part of the applicant's case. O'Loughlin (2008: 182), however, uncovered a more unmitigated positioning of the language test, which emerged as a dominant procedure in selection processes:

> English language proficiency scores including IELTS are assumed to be definitive sources of evidence about a student's language ability and readiness to undertake study in an English medium institution.

In our findings reported below, we return to these issues: the role of the "language test" in the admissions process and the nature of staff knowledge about the tests; and we also evidence the impact that understandings of "language" levels have more generally on framing the way in which international students are positioned by their programme tutors in their learning and progression.

the study

aims

The overarching aim of the study – Student Identity, Learning and Progression (SILP) – was to investigate the possible affective and academic impact of IELTS results on students once they are accepted by an institution, with specific reference to their learning experiences and academic progress and achievement, and a number of specific research questions were formulated (see Rea-Dickins et al., 2007). In investigating how IELTS might impact on student learning and progression, three research questions relevant to this chapter are as follows:

- What use, if any, is made of IELTS scores (individual skills and aggregated score) by different participating stakeholders, in particular programme admissions staff and tutors?

Addressing this research question provides for a discussion of Theme 1 on the role of this test: the ways IELTS scores are interpreted and used by admissions tutors, and the ways they shape the admissions decision-making process and outcome.

- What is the level of awareness of the different targeted stakeholder groups of IELTS scores and the implications for student learning and progression?

Here we focus on Theme 2: the knowledge base relating to IELTS and language proficiency testing more widely among admissions tutors, and some issues involved in enhancing their assessment literacy.

- With reference to data obtained, how may we frame the stakes for post-IELTS student-as-stakeholder groups?

The focus on "stakes" here frames a discussion of Theme 3: the discoursal ambiguities and ethical dilemmas which arise within the programme and shape the learning experience of successful applicants.

participants

This study was situated within two university departments in a UK university: Politics and Education. This chapter draws on data from admissions staff and tutors, five of whom were from Politics and 11 from Education. In this chapter they are anonymised as EA/ET/PA/PT01-16: E for Education, P for Politics, A for admissions administrators, and T for admissions tutors.

procedures

We gathered data from subject tutors and admissions staff on their use and interpretation of IELTS scores through extended one-to-one interviews and a tutors' focus group. Our perspective on learning as identity development and the process of establishing membership of a community of practice provided our conceptual frame (for full details of this and the research design, see Rea-Dickins et al., 2007). In collecting and analysing the views of admissions staff, we sought to capture their understanding of readiness for the programme, both in terms of language requirements and levels and in terms of how this related to other, non-language entry criteria, such as educational achievements and work experience for the different postgraduate programmes. All interviews and focus group discussions were either video- or audio-recorded, subject to usual consents for both the recording and the subsequent use of the data. In most cases, our research participants also had an opportunity to comment on their transcribed interview data.

findings and discussion

theme 1: the role of the "language test" in complex and high stakes decision-making

The decision-making process in postgraduate programmes admissions is a complex one in which three sets of factors are taken into account. First, there are aspects of educational attainment in terms of prior achievements in learning, normally evidenced in first degree classification or grade profile. Second, there are contexts of learning other than formal education, such as work and related activity, to be taken into account. The postgraduate programmes in this study have a distinct interface with the professional world and value experience in work, consultancy or research contexts. Third, individual factors such as commitment and learning purpose are important. References constitute significant evidence here. In addition to these in the context of international applicants whose first language is not English, there is the issue of readiness for learning in a second language, as evidenced in the IELTS profile or similar test results. A Politics programme admissions tutor explained in interview how admissions decisions were informed:

> If there was a problem with the IELTS I might look at it more closely but pretty much as a benchmarking score [...] I'm not sure we have a clear balance, it's very much a qualitative exercise in terms of making judgements. But I think that the first, the decision would be taken largely on the basis of relevant qualifications to study in the Politics department and the secondly would be, well, the references and the IELTS English language ability. (PT07)

Another tutor commented on the overall interpretive frame of admissions decision-making:

> [the] academic elements of the application, the covering letter, the enthusiasm and interest and sort of around knowledge that the student has about the course.... (PT10)

Table 13.1 illustrates how the decision-making is informed in each of these areas.

This analysis of decision-making suggests that the language assessment is a minor part of the process. It applies to one section of the population only – those for whom English is not a first language, and those with limited experience of study through English. However, the data (and our experience) indicate otherwise: the attainment, experience and individual factors constitute "soft" criteria, leaving the IELTS profile as a "hard" criterion. There are three reasons for this. First, degree profiles are difficult to interpret, given the number and varying quality of institutions in all countries. In addition, if the first degree was completed some time ago, the exit profile will be less important

Table 13.1   An overview of admissions decision-making

Readiness	Evidence
Attainment and potential	First degree exit profile, including overall classification or Grade Point Average, and disciplinary relevance to PG programme area
Experience	Work: range and duration of activities, as set out in CV, letter of application and references
Individual factors	Awareness and commitment, as set out in letter of application and references
Readiness for study in English	IELTS

and greater significance will be accorded to learning through work since then. Second, it is difficult to interpret the quality of learning from work and experience more generally. For example, in the case of education postgraduate applicants, teaching may involve in-depth analysis and problem-solving in professional contexts, or may be a more mechanical activity, the unthinking use of compulsory teaching materials. Work as a researcher for a non-governmental organization (NGO) as a preparation for postgraduate study in Politics may similarly involve creative engagement with complex issues, or it may be routine clerking, data inputting or administration. Third, individual factors present similar interpretation challenges, especially where applicants draw on professional support such as agents, and where the culture of referencing is one of untempered support. In the case of applicants who have been undergraduates in a university with which the admissions tutor is familiar, the interpretation task in each of these areas can be undertaken with confidence: he or she will know the scheme of degree classification, the institution (or even the department), and the messages between the lines in accounts of experience and references.

This is unlikely to be the case in applications from international students. These students include an IELTS profile which appears to represent a hard criterion in the midst of a range of soft criteria: in essence, IELTS may drive the decision-making process in admissions in a way the programme, institution and IELTS stakeholders have not envisaged. Evidence of the IELTS score as a hard criterion comes from its construction as an administrative requirement, a box ticked that the required level has been reached which requires no further interpretation. As one admission administrator put it:

> My guidelines are just very very straightforward, you know, they need to have 6.5. (EA04)

Another administrator described the IELTS requirement as:

> a University regulation that we have to put in place [...] We're just governed by the University...we get them from the Registry Office. It's just a list of what the equivalent is. So many points to say 3–4 weeks at the Language School, etc., etc. To be honest we just do the paperwork and accept the overall score. (EA01)

The IELTS profile becomes particularly visible as a hard criterion in programmes for which applicant numbers are high and entry competitive:

> Well the issue we have is that particularly for our MSc programmes they're quite heavily over-subscribed and so we in a sense can afford to be quite tough in terms of the criteria that we apply to the students that we select. So a student with a weaker application and a weak IELTS score would probably not get through the application process. (PT07)

There are two issues for language testing arising from the discussion of the admissions decision-making process investigated as part of the SILP study. First, the role of the language test result, the IELTS profile in this case, must be one of a basket of factors informing the decision (Banerjee, 2003). The fundamental requirement of fairness suggests that this is necessary in order to ensure parity in making the admissions decision-making process for home and international applicants, that is, those who do not submit a language test result and those required to do so. Second, there is evidence that the test result assumes a disproportionate role: as a reliable benchmark, it can be a determining factor for applicants required to provide it. It can play a role in the initial screening of applications, or, later, can be seen as central when the picture afforded by the more qualitative, interpretive factors is not decisive. There are three challenges for language testing here. First, it has, in Messick's (1989) terms, to incorporate accounts of test use in complex decision-making processes. Second, it has to engage with the issues of fairness when language test results are used for some applicants in such processes. Third, there is an information and education challenge for language testing: it needs to engage with the user perspective, and provide guidance for incorporating the "hard" criterion it provides with the softer, interpretive factors that are at the heart of decisions on admission to postgraduate programmes.

The construction of IELTS as a safe "hard" criterion in our study contrasts in some ways with O'Loughlin's study, which found that 10 out of 16 admissions tutors in an Australian university disagreed with the statement that the IELTS score provided "accurate evidence about an applicant's English language proficiency" (2008:169). However, the view of IELTS as providing a clear statement of readiness is only part of the picture.

In the next section, we examine where these admissions staff obtain information about IELTS and to what extent the decision-making about the language test results by these non-language specialists might be affected by their (lack of) knowledge about IELTS.

theme 2: decision-making about language test results by non-specialists: the case for "assessment literacy" of a different kind

The construction and use of IELTS test score profiles, whether total or sub-test scores or both, as a safe "hard" criterion by admissions staff demonstrate a rather routine, unthinking and largely unproblematised approach adopted by these non-language specialists in processing the IELTS data submitted by international students in their applications. Given the relative lack of information that the admissions staff had about IELTS, it is unsurprising to note this rather routine and rigid approach towards the use of IELTS scores. However, we were struck by the lack of knowledge about IELTS, and the low level of information to which admissions staff reported having access. One extreme case was that the admissions tutor who was even hesitant about the actual entry level:

And I think that our score is 6.5, if I'm right. (PT08)

This same tutor – not the only one – also confused IELTS with TOEFL:

I know that it's got three main components – the reading, writing and listening test with an essay score...And we've set a requirement as IELTS 6.5 plus 4.5 in the writing test. (PT08)

Other admissions staff also admitted that they did not know much about IELTS.

To be honest I don't think any of them would know what the breakdown meant...he just looks for the 6.5. (EA01)
And this is basically...well this is our borderline so that they have to be 6.5. I don't know what that means but you know for me that's the guideline, that's how I use it. (PT09)

In terms of where the admissions staff obtain knowledge about IELTS, we noticed some differences between the two departments. In the Education department, since the admissions staff had the opportunities to "rub shoulders" with the language specialist team (TESOL/Applied Linguistics), their decision-making was influenced by the language specialist team in the same department:

> Well I know that X [TESOL admissions tutor] is very interested that have good writing. (EA04)

However, in the Politics department, the first port of call for some admissions staff is the university's Language Centre, which has some responsibility for advising departments and schools across the university on language requirements in international student recruitment:

> This is what we got from the language centre basically about the score. (PT09)

We also noticed hierarchical structures in passing on knowledge and information about IELTS from the top-level administration of the university. For example, admissions staff in Education mentioned that they received a comparison chart from the university registry.

> We did have a chart some time ago which was put out with all the equivalents. (EA05)

And in the Politics department this same information was dictated from the faculty level:

> so we use these equivalents. These are agreed equivalents, they're not our departmental decision they're agreed with faculty. (PT10)

Other sources of information that the admissions staff used to develop their understanding and knowledge about the IELTS test were a bit idiosyncratic. For example, PT07 was influenced by her brother:

> Um, I don't know too much and some of what I know comes from outside the University through my brother who's an English language teacher and uses the IELTS himself…I think it's quite low 6.5 but that's a sort of inherited comment from my brother who works in the field who was horrified when I said 6.5. (PT07)

Influence from peers, not necessarily relatives, can also be strong, though gradual, as one admissions staff member in the Education department reflected on her own experience:

> *Interviewer*: Where did you learn about IELTS? How did you develop your knowledge about IELTS?
>
> *Response*: That's hard to say because I think it's something that was gradually...I can't remember when I first started it was quite so prominent. I think it's something that's gradually happened. And I think perhaps more so since you've [i.e. a language specialist] arrived as well. (EA01)

Both the above quotes seemed to demonstrate positive influence from peers – brother or language specialist. However, we also noticed that admissions staff did not always feel the need to "know more" about IELTS or access further IELTS information: this was not necessarily welcome or considered useful for the task of processing student applications and making decisions:

> at the level of administration I suppose our interpretation of the scores is fairly superficial to be perfectly honest. I'm not sure that having an in depth knowledge...would actually help us to do our job quite honestly. (EA05)

There was even some kind of resistance towards knowledge and information:

> I know very little of the detail because I've never felt any need to know any of the detail and we have so much information we're bombarded these days with, that my life is dominated by superfluous information. So it's very important that I don't know what I don't need to know. (PT10)

In summary, we observed that the admissions staff had surprisingly little knowledge or awareness of the IELTS test, in particular concerning issues of total and sub-score interpretation. Aside from the official comparative language test table and the scores accepted by the university, to our knowledge no other readily available IELTS documentation had been brought to the attention of, or was used by, admissions staff, except where the expertise and knowledge of IELTS were available within the same department (i.e. the TESOL/Applied Linguistics team). Furthermore, we noted that the majority of admissions staff by and large did not perceive a need to be any better informed. There seems, thus, to be a pragmatic and also minimalist approach towards admissions decision-making: get it done, with a safe and "hard" criterion. "Hard", however, does not appear to be synonymous with "challenging" in the admissions decision-making process, because admissions staff seemed able to make decisions quickly using their pragmatically minimalist approach.

In the next section we examine how, post-admission to the programme, the information embedded in the IELTS profile does not necessarily only shape support provided in the learning process but also constructs the "international student" in several ways that are different from his or her English L1 peers.

theme 3: discoursal ambiguities and ethical dilemmas

As seen above, it is assumed that, once the IELTS criterion has been met, students are then in a position to engage in academic study on an equal playing field alongside their peers who were not required to provide evidence of English language proficiency: for many admissions tutors, meeting the IELTS requirement amounted to eliminating language as a learning and progression issue. The discourse of academic tutors, however, suggests that this is not the case. We have also seen the limited nature of tutor and admissions staff knowledge about the test and the ways in which most apply the criterion in processing student applications. In relation, then, to fairness issues that arise from our findings, the interviews with admissions tutors were revealing in two main respects. First, inequalities in opportunities and support varied across the two departments in the study. Second, the identity of international students was constructed in two ways: (i) in relation to the nature of their struggles in learning faced in different subject learning contexts and (ii) in relation to their success, or their potential for success, referenced – largely – to their achieved IELTS scores and their status as English L2 speakers. These findings, in turn, raise unpredicted equity issues.

inequality in opportunities and support

Although we have observed that IELTS acts as a hard and inflexible entry criterion, there is evidence that some international students stand a better chance of gaining admission than others: in some they are encouraged and in others discouraged from taking up a place. On the one hand:

> provided people have appropriate postgraduate experience and they
> fulfil the entry requirements at other levels and their references

are satisfactory we will try and...accommodate them...if they fall slightly short of the appropriate score then maybe by suggesting that they attend...or saying that entry is conditional upon their attendance at a pre-sessional course. (EA05)

If there was an IELTS difficulty or a language difficulty you know there are ways that we would try and... you know we might make the offer with a pre-sessional or in-sessional training. (PT08)

On the other hand, PT07 (see earlier) explained that a student with a weaker IELTS profile would not make the cut in that particular programme:

and basically our set target was initially 8 [students]...so I was actually being quite selective...(PT09)

These equity issues, with acceptance on some programmes more likely than others within the same institution for students with similar IELTS profiles, are also reflected in the variable nature of accommodations for students with weaker language profiles. Once on a course, differences emerged in how students were supported. The prevailing view in our data was that, in spite of the constraints in their learning and struggles experienced in the process, students usually achieved success in the end. The extent to which staff supported students is part explanation for this "success":

because we try to support our students to the nth degree really. And we try and...we try and enable successful completion of the course....But we have lots of systems in place to help support students who seem to be failing. I think there are combinations of factors and I think English language is one of them and it is an important one. (EA05)

On the other hand:

because probably unlike many other tutors I actually make corrections to the English language...and I know that other tutors don't. They will make a[Query: delete "a"?] general comments about recurring faults and a general statement will be passed on to the student...I realise how important it is to have someone somewhere who's actually helping you with these sorts of areas, which otherwise you would continue to do for the rest of the year. (PT07)

Of their actual achievement, progression and success, one tutor observed:

> And we don't want to put too high a bar on students who come, [though they] might struggle for a few months... (PT08)

This suggests that there might be different treatment or expectations of their performance, although this same tutor (PT08) also observed that students "might struggle for a few months" but then find their feet and improve dramatically, with some achieving an excellent degree at the end. This raises the second issue of how the identity of students is constructed by tutors.

the "international student" as "different"

Three different facets of international student identity emerged in our study.

An identity of struggling in learning: Most of the tutor respondent group constructed international students as having difficulties in their subject learning on account of their English L2 status. Tutor observations included the need for international students to work hard, that studying entails a steep learning curve, and that the reading requirements are high:

> Well they're struggling for a start because they can't follow what's going on in the seminar classes. The way that we teach at MSc level is very active and participatory....So students have to do a series of some quite often...theoretically complex readings before they turn up for those seminars....They do four units in a term and so that is 12 readings that the students have to do a week, at a minimum, and that's before they start on their essays, before they start on their presentations. (PT08)
>
> And over time I would suggest that actually 90% of students with a second language whose English is not you know wonderful, by the end of the course their essays are up to scratch, they get through at MSc level and they have a sharp learning curve. But at this time of the year [i.e. first academic term] in particular it's quite difficult and there are every year one or two students who simply just do not manage to make that extra jump. (PT08)

These and other similar comments on the struggles in learning, extensive reading in particular, experienced by international students have also been linked by tutors with their learning progression and achievement and with what Torrance (2000: 178) suggests "endorses the construction of identity through discourses of "passing and failing", "knowing and not knowing", defining who becomes one sort of person and who another". While the majority of international students will pass their programmes, their chances of obtaining a distinction are unlikely.

A glass ceiling identity for the "international student": This discourse, therefore, running throughout the data evidences a perception by staff that, although international students may pass their courses, they may not achieve their potential:

> We are taking on a higher number of students who struggle and because of their language struggles perhaps do not get the grade that their abilities merit, but you know overall most of them will come out with an MSc and some of them will really turn around and come out with a distinction. (PT09)

The data suggest that tutor construction of student identity by and large conveys the notion of students "just managing" to get a pass, and "getting through the programme". The approach to learning thus appears more analogous to factory throughput than one that values growth and depth in student learning. In this account there is the implication that, although international students may pass, they may not actually achieve their potential: for them – rather inevitably – a glass ceiling may well exist in terms of their ultimate performance. Although there are some conflicting views in our data – students may make it in the end with an "excellent" outcome (PT09) – a strong current in the discourse is that it is highly unlikely that this will be possible:

> Getting a pass is um…pretty much everyone will do, if they're an individual who's prepared to accept the advice and support that's on offer. But getting a distinction is noticeably harder if you're a student who's coming here especially having taken pre-sessional English language training. The chances of getting a distinction are low…(PT10)
>
> it's blatantly obvious that if you're reading slowly and covering a limited amount of material that you're going to struggle to get a distinction which requires you to get a grip of an extremely large amount of material. (PT10)

The fact that this construction of "international student" identity is framed as "unlikely that an international student will gain a distinction" raises an equity issue of two kinds: (i) a glass ceiling on their overall achievement exists and (ii) the international student is constructed as significantly different from the home or English L1 speaker, with an unspoken assumption that the struggles in learning and in programme progression are in some way unique to the English L2 speaker.

A three deficit identity: In our data, language ability is portrayed as one of three deficits, with "language deficits", irrespective of IELTS attainment, linked to deficits in "critical thinking abilities" and appropriate grounding in an "academic culture". This alignment of language with a cultural dimension and lack of critical engagement and thinking with subject learning was expressed, alongside weak language proficiency, as a factor that tutors consider impedes subject progression, thus perpetuating the view of the "international student" as different:

> The bigger problem I think with language is...more one associated with how you write critical social science essays. And part of that is not just a language issue but it's an academic culture issue. There are certain things that we are very clearly looking for as tutors in terms of how we mark and how we assess essays, and critical analysis is one of the things that we look for in our essays. Analysis more generally....And there are a significant proportion of the students who have come here from other countries or non North American or European countries. (PT09)

This last point evidences the construction of student identity with the co-occurrence of language, cultural and critical thinking challenges and problems. The merged constructs here may constitute an explanation for the operation of the glass ceiling and self-fulfilling prophecies elaborated above: the highly visible features (evidenced elsewhere in our data-sets) of a student's text, such as problematic word choices and infelicitous sentence structure, may be viewed as indicators of less visible qualities, such as a critical perspective in analysis and discussion. The perceived lack of impact of language and academic skills programmes provided by the university may in turn accord permanence to such tutor perceptions of students' ability, and the inevitability of completing the programme with the minimum M-level grade. The patterns here are important for an understanding of the consequential validity of the IELTS test: where IELTS 6.5 or 7 is used to admit students to a programme, the very features of students' use of English, particularly in writing, may set them on a track where a high level of achievement in learning is unlikely. It also raises issues of equity in relation to significant others in a programme who do not have a language assessment requirement, for example: do they have a different learning experience and achieve better levels of engagement in their programmes of study? Further, irrespective of their language profile, from "high" to "low"-risk students, although most will succeed in their courses we need to know whether they successfully achieve academic community membership.

conclusions

In this chapter, we have evidenced the following. First, we have examined the nature of the admissions decision-making process, which tends to privilege the language score as the "hard" criterion. This is not in line with the more flexible, integrated basket of criteria recommended by IELTS, and as required by programmes. The construction of international student identity following successful admission to the postgraduate programmes reveals some problematic consequences of this aspect of admissions management: the hard criterion leads to a hard landing. The picture we present suggests that the appropriate support mechanisms, including tutor expectations, are not always aligned to enabling students achieve their full potential. Rather, there is a readiness to accept comparatively low levels of achievement in the programme as the norm. Alongside this glass ceiling and deficits in academic culture and capacity for critical thinking discourses, another explanation may be relevant: the students gaining entry to the programme through the hard criterion of IELTS may not be ready for or suited to the programme in terms of the other criteria. Their educational achievements, experience of related professional domains, and personal capacity and commitment, which may not match programme requirements, are obscured by the message in the IELTS score in a manner that would not happen with students who do not require a statement of language ability.

Second, as a backdrop to the above, we observed that the admissions staff demonstrated very partial knowledge about IELTS, with limited access to the information "out there" about IELTS. Of concern is that they also showed little need or desire to be better informed: many were of the view that it was sufficient for them to know the IELTS cut-off band for their specific programme and to then apply this as a "hard" criterion. To some extent, this unproblematised task-focused minimalist approach is understandable, but it does raise wider ethical issues in relation to admissions decision-making processes as well as to the effects on the "successful" applicants who are accepted onto their programmes.

Third, these ethical dilemmas and fairness issues are evidenced in relation to the study support and opportunities for international students. Different chances of getting admitted to a university department for students with similar IELTS profiles, and varying support and constructive qualitative feedback for students with weaker language profiles, suggest that the language element of the learning experience introduces additional risk factors for students. And the discourse that constructs international students as unlikely to achieve their potential and/or obtain a distinction, and defined by deficits not only in language but also in academic cultural experiences and critical thinking capacities, illustrates how they are on an unequal playing field with students who are not required to evidence their English language proficiency. Thus, the stakes and the consequences for university study, framed as significantly different depending on the language backgrounds of the students, are considerable for second or foreign language speakers.

We can relate the findings of this study to the more general context in which language tests serve access and gatekeeping purposes in education and other domains of social practice. The interface between the technical, specialist world of language testing and a range of other domains of decision-making where language test information is interpreted and used is one of growing importance in a globalised world characterised by mobility for study and work in second language contexts. Language tests, as statements of capacity and readiness used in managing this interface, have informational, procedural and ethical dimensions, which have to be investigated and understood as part of our developing theories of language testing and assessment. And the developments in the quality of tests and testing processes that have occurred over recent decades have to be matched by similar improvements in test use: at a time when the training of language testers is developing at an increased pace, the "assessment literacy" of decision-makers who use IELTS scores also needs to be enhanced such that "test use" is on a par with more established dimensions of test validity.

references

Banerjee, J. (2003). *Interpreting and Using Proficiency Test Scores*. Unpublished PhD dissertation, Lancaster University, Lancaster.

Coleman, D., Starfield, S. and Hagan, A. (2003). The attitudes of IELTS stakeholders: student and staff perceptions of IELTS in Australian, UK and Chinese tertiary institutions. *IELTS Research Reports*, Vol. 5. Canberra: IELTS Australia Pty Limited.

Cotton, F. and Conrow, F. (1998). An investigation of the predicative validity of IELTS amongst a sample of international students studying at the University of Tasmania. In S. Wood (Ed.), *IELTS Research Reports 1998*, Vol. 1. Canberra: IELTS Australia Pty Limited, pp. 75–115.

Hill, K., Storch, N. and Lynch, B. (1999). A comparison of IELTS and TOEFL as predictors of academic success. In R. Tulloh (Ed.), *IELTS Research Reports 1999*, Vol. 2. Canberra: IELTS Australia Pty Limited, pp. 52–63.

IELTS. (2009). IELTS Website. http://www.ielts.org/pdf/IELTS%20Guide%20for%20Stakeholders%20March%202009.pdf (accessed October 2009).

Kerstjens, M. and Nery, C. (2000). Predicative validity in the IELTS test: a study of the relationship between IELTS scores and students' subsequent academic performance. In R. Tulloh (Ed.), *IELTS Research Reports 2000*, Vol. 3. Canberra: IELTS Australia Pty Limited, pp. 85–108.

McDowell, C. and Merrylees, B. (1998). Survey of receiving institutions' use and attitude to IELTS. In S. Wood (Ed.), *IELTS Research Reports 1998*, Vol. 1. Canberra: IELTS Australia Pty Limited, pp. 116–139.

Messick, S. (1989). Validity. In R. L. Linn (Ed.) *Educational Measurement* (3rd edition). New York: Macmillan, pp. 13–103.

O'Loughlin, K. (2008). The use of IELTS for university selection in Australia: A case study. In J. Osborne (Ed.), *IELTS Research Reports*, Vol. 8. Canberra: IELTS Australia, pp. 145–241.

Rea-Dickins, P., Kiely, R. and Yu, G. (2007). Student identity, learning and progression: the affective and academic impact of IELTS on "successful" candidates. In P. McGovern and S. Walsh (Eds), *IELTS Research Reports*, Vol. 7. Canberra: IELTS Australia and British Council, pp. 59–136.

Torrance, H. (2000). Postmodernism and educational assessment. In A. Filer (Ed.), *Social Practice and Social Product*. London: Routledge Falmer, pp. 173–188.

14
assessment in the learning system

john o'dwyer

introduction

Much of the literature on the assessment of English as a second or foreign language rightly concerns itself with issues surrounding the ability of tests to measure what they set out to measure (e.g. Bachman, 1990; Hughes, 2003); in other words, with the five aspects of validity as defined by Weir (2004). However, language assessment takes place in many different types of learning system. For example, it is predicted that over the coming decades primary and secondary school systems worldwide, each operating within a distinct set of expectations and constraints, will progressively cater for more and more language learners (Graddol, 2006). English medium faculties and universities, some operating in cultures where the target language is spoken outside the institution, others where the target language is restricted in the main to use within the university, each have different realities with which to deal in setting language entry criteria, admitting students to their ranks and setting learning benchmarks.

Thus, given the variety inherent in the learning of English, it is to be expected that different learning systems will impact on assessment systems used to monitor and judge whether these same learning systems, and the students within them, are achieving the standards desired. A simple illustration of the implications of context is the use of a skills-based model for language assessment in a secondary school system. Although it may be deemed desirable to focus on language skills in terms of learning outcomes, teachers themselves may not have sufficient training or competence in the skill areas being assessed. Hence, the learning system might not be able to deliver the sought-after skills, and intermediate steps may be necessary prior to changes in testing practice.

The main focus of this chapter is a university school of English language in Turkey, outside the target language community, which prepares students for a wide range of university departments in which the medium of instruction is English. The school is large, with over 2500 full-time preparatory programme students, another 3000 plus faculty programme students taking credit courses, and over 280 teaching staff. The school went through a major renewal of its English language curriculum from 1993 onwards. Assessment changes brought in with a view to improving standards, or supporting a curriculum innovation, had major impacts on the learning system and represent a case that may be instructive for other contexts. The examples and discussion developed here reflect the experience and institutional learning of almost 20 years of assessment practice as part of curriculum development in this large-scale ELT operation. The hope is that the exploration of a different angle on assessment, more from an implementation perspective, will provide insights of value to those working on assessment in learning systems in a variety of institutional contexts.

dealing with expectations in the learning system

Changing habits can be difficult and long. Turkey is often exemplified as a test-driven society (O'Dwyer et al., 2010), and tests are a major means by which lives are realised. The Turkish national university exam is currently a 180 item multiple-choice test which assesses knowledge of the main subjects studied in grades 9–12. The two-hour exam decides the fate of over 1.5 million students yearly competing for some 200,000 university places, with those higher in the rankings acceding to quality university places. Such tests are elevated to a high stakes imperative (Bachman, 2004) for those who wish to progress to high-return occupations. National testing now also occurs in Grades 6 to 8 to regulate competitive entry to select high schools. Cram schools, called *Dershanes*, are common. A form of "test roulette" pervades test-taking, where entry to a test is seen to bring with it an element of chance, particularly prevalent in the case of multiple-choice testing. Due to its importance, therefore, assessment entails legal rights, and test outcomes may be readily contested in the courts. Governments may even enact legislation to declare national amnesties allowing multiple repeat opportunities to university students who have been unsuccessful in their departmental or exemption exams.

Exams such as TOEFL and IELTS are less prone to questioning in the courts, being externally set and graded, and having a worldwide distribution and reputation. This does not mean that their use is immune from validity concerns, however (EL Gazette, 2009: 1). By comparison, locally produced institutional tests might not have such a comfortable ride in the courts. A new test, particularly where it has major implications for the taker, places a heavy burden of responsibility on test developers. In the context under discussion here, the introduction of a new English exemption test called COPE (Certificate of Proficiency in English), the benchmark to entry into faculties, met with a flurry of litigation from individual students who had failed to meet its minimum language requirements. The test had to be robust enough, particularly from a scoring validity perspective, to stand up to independent scrutiny by court-appointed markers/arbitrators. Much administrative time was, and continues to be, invested in winning court cases, thus providing support, of sorts, to the exam's validity claim in the face of opposition to its introduction. Defending exam standards is associated with large costs, as, somewhat inevitably, court documents are not always secure and the exam has to be entirely rewritten each time a court case is instigated. Banking of items cannot be undertaken as they are effectively out in the open.

challenges in introducing a new local examination

Not only did the new exemption test, COPE, need to be robust in the face of potential external challenge in the courts, but it also had major consequences for the institution. New tests designed to benchmark standards for entry into a faculty impact on the number of students qualifying, particularly if the tests have been developed in response to prior poor standards. The desire for improved standards needs to take account of the effect of failure on the system within which the tests are operating. For faculties, a reduction in one fell swoop in student target quotas would have been difficult, as they are dependent on a flow of students, particularly if previous testing decisions had created expectations of a certain number of entrants.

The response to this dilemma in the current context was to maintain the COPE exam boundaries at the desired standards but to devise additional rules for entry to faculties, to alleviate the immediate negative impact of changing standards. The new rule, called the "D boundary", allowed preparatory programme students who were in the immediate fail zone to be reassessed, based on a complex formula, taking into account formative assessment during the previous semester(s). D was a fail grade in the exam. A, B, C were pass grades. The numbers passing into the faculties as a result of this modified system were not negligible, giving time for the learning system to readjust and work on improving standards across the board, while allowing the university departments to achieve their quotas. Learning system needs, therefore, have to be weighed relative to the validity constraints of exams: the latter are designed to ensure that only those who have met the desired standards are able to enter their departments. Learning system needs may encompass issues of organisational sustainability and take precedence in key situations. Test impact may have to be moderated by the context, a facility not easily provided with externally set international exams.

COPE was followed, three years later, by a newly developed skills-based curriculum, with associated regulations defining success. The curriculum was introduced in response to poor learning outcomes and high failure rates (O'Dwyer, 2008). Whereas, previously, the right to take the exemption exam was guaranteed at the end of an academic year for all preparatory students whatever their level of attainment, now access was granted only at the end of the final level. In other words, students first needed to complete successfully the five levels in the learning system. The change provoked a sharp reaction among a large number of students, who felt they had been disenfranchised by the new rules, as their previous rights had allowed them to sit the exemption exam irrespective of their performance. The open access policy had led to failure rates of 70–80 per cent in the past, not a positive statistic for the psychology of the student body, some 3000 in number at that time, with 60 per cent experiencing failure in the exemption exam at some point in the learning system.

It proved difficult to persuade students that the new assessment arrangements were well founded and would lead to positive gains in the longer term. Despite meetings at which the new learning and assessment system was presented and explained, a campaign was waged in a national glossy magazine to discredit the new system and standards. The university, an educational trust and the first private tertiary institution in Turkey, enjoys a high profile, and exposure of this type was unwelcome. The negative client reaction gave the relatively new school management a challenging time, even threatening its continuation.

Thus, the introduction of the new exemption exam and learning system was subject to external and internal questioning. However, the project held to its course. The new system reduced the numbers taking the exemption exam by only allowing entry at the highest course level, reduced the amount of time a student could stay in the learning system prior to dismissal from three to two years, and abandoned the D boundary system discussed earlier. To compensate, the exemption exam was offered after each semester, thus increasing the possibility of exiting the system early if language competence met required standards.

responding to the challenges

The first sitting of the COPE exam at the end of the first semester in the 1993–1994 academic year presented the school with an interesting quandary. Pass rates plummeted, which dampened the spirits of teachers, who were expecting better pass rates as a result of the learning system innovation. The management quandary was whether to respond through changing the test on the assumption that it was lacking in its validity argument, or assume what Handy (1994) calls the "Sigmoid Curve"; in other words, a dip in performance often seen in new systems prior to their picking up. At this early stage in the new system statistical data was lacking, as the underlying population characteristics had changed. The essential dilemma was to fathom the cause of the downturn from a variety of possibilities, potentially: a lack of familiarity with new systems on the part of teachers and students; substantial numbers in the learning system remaining from the previous order, who had not had the benefits of the new "treatment"; problems in the marking of the skills-based formative tests, which had changed to more open-ended formats; the concept of English for Academic Purposes being new to teachers, who were not teaching learners in a manner conducive to success in the system; a continued reliance on grammar teaching in the face of changed understandings of student needs.

The question as to how a school's management should deal with the Sigmoid Curve effect, that is, falling numbers of those passing the new exam against expectations, is a difficult one in the absence of solid data. Should this be construed as a problem with the test, or with the markers, or with the boundary setting, or with attainment levels? Should there be an immediate response by changing the test, or should the management sit it out in the knowledge that a downfall in output may be associated with the implementation of new systems? The final choice needs leadership skills, not mentioned often in testing annals, but of crucial importance in the management literature, in developing confidence in the new learning system and instituting evaluation procedures capable of pinpointing areas where support might be necessary. In the current situation the response was the institution of a wide-ranging evaluation, led externally but carried through internally, to look at aspects of the innovation in depth. In addition, meetings were undertaken across the school to sample teacher reactions and provide an opportunity for confidence-building around the solid foundations of the new learning system.

formative assessment in curriculum innovation

Formative assessment is an important element in any learning system that wishes to provide assessment for learning (Black et al., 2002); in other words, "provide immediate information to teachers who then adjust instruction accordingly to meet students' learning needs. In this way, assessment is simply a major component of instruction itself" (Grabe, 2009: 373); a complex task in that it assumes an even level of skill in testing on the part of all teachers in a system, not always reflective of reality. Another issue that deserves attention, according to Grabe (ibid.), is the relationship between informal and formal assessment in the classroom and the question as to whether all assessment activities can become learning activities. Even skilled assessors, with many years of teaching experience, may disagree as to the need for formal formative testing, preferring their own informal brand.

formative assessment in the learning system

In the case under consideration here, the new learning system adopted a formal to less formal formative assessment mix, consisting initially of:

- five classroom assessment tests, called cumulative achievement tests (CATs), covering content over an eight-week course and set independently by a testing committee, taken by all students at a level;
- six project-based Independent Study Components (ISC), requiring students to carry through a specified learning task in their own time, submitted to deadline, subject to teacher feedback based on criteria, with the option to improve the score by resubmitting based on the feedback.

Continuous assessment contributed 60 per cent to the final course grade, that is, CATs (25 per cent) and ISC tasks (25 per cent), plus 10 per cent awarded by teachers for in-class work. The end of course assessment

(ECA) contributed the remaining 40 per cent, with the pass boundary set at 60 per cent overall.

The formative system was designed to motivate students to perform. Therefore, those who achieved between 50 per cent and 59 per cent overall at the end of a level, although considered a failing score, had the opportunity to continue to the next higher level, with the proviso that they did an extra number of hours in courses in the higher level. These extra hours were over and above the course load of students who had achieved 60 per cent and more. The view was that the extra course time would compensate for performance lacks and allow borderline students to continue on their path of progress. The reality now was that a student who earned, say, 20 per cent from ISCs and 10 per cent from in-class assessment needed to score only a further 20 per cent from the CATs and ECA combined in order to progress; in other words, 20 per cent out of a maximum of 65 per cent (25 per cent CAT + 40 per cent ECA). This represented a poor performance in the more formal elements of the assessment. De facto, formative assessment was given the central role as the mainstay of the learning system, the motor for student progress.

issues with the new formative assessment system

The new formative assessment system proved problematic for many reasons. First, the introduction of the six new concept ISCs, aiming to promote a more English for Academic Purposes (EAP) curriculum, required a steep learning curve on the part of teachers. They were unfamiliar with the task types and marking criteria used, developed independently by the curriculum committee. Teachers needed to mark and give feedback to students within tight deadlines, spending substantial time dealing with the novel ISC concept itself and maintaining assessment standards across the programme. Pressure mounted, as did complaints from teachers related to the number of assessments, task quality, the criteria, amount of marking and so on. Second, as the assignments were incorporated into the overall pass grade for a course, the pressure mounted on classroom teachers to modify grades in response to students quibbling over points awarded. As pointed out above, the assignments for which the class teacher was the arbiter for grades were particularly important in the decision to move to a higher level. Variation ensued in marking standards of ISCs, which proved difficult to monitor across such a large teaching population, aggravated by the tendency for teachers to give the full 10 per cent for class work.

Third, instances of plagiarism and cheating, particularly on ISC tasks, became more common, given that advancement was determined in the main through continuous assessment. In addition, a thriving market developed outside the institution for the writing of ISCs. Fourth, grading the more formal classroom assessments (CATs) provided a further source of variability. The new tests put more emphasis on open-ended answers and marking standards had not settled, as institutional skills and understandings were developing in tandem. Furthermore, although double marking was in place for the more formal CATs, class teachers were involved in the grading to help corroborate and validate student performance, as well as making use of the performance data for ongoing teaching.

The outcome of this commitment to formative assessment as the means of motivating students to perform through feedback on learning was problematic at an institutional level. First, unreliability had entered the system, through pressure exerted on staff, or a lack of familiarity with test types in the new emphasis on EAP, or not fully developed professional skills, or attempts to defraud the system. As a result, a number of students advanced to higher levels who had not met the barrier criteria as judged by the end of course exam, considered a relatively independent measure of a level. On top of this, allowing borderline students through to the next level with a heavier tuition load proved problematic, as the assumptions about their being able to catch up rarely materialised. The overall outcome was a crowding of students at certain levels, unable to realise the objectives of that level, creating frustration for teachers and necessitating an investment of additional resources to deal with the fallout. The problem was perpetuated into the next level, with impact on the whole delivery system. In a sense, encouraging students to earn their way through the system, through faith in the motivational benefits of advancement, impacted negatively on the ability of the learning system to respond to their needs.

The solutions were incremental. The scores to be achieved on the formal end of course assessment (ECAs), which regulated passage to the next level, were gradually increased because of the variability in formative assessment. Two years into the curriculum innovation, the rule allowing those achieving lower than 60 per cent overall to continue to a higher level was abandoned. Three years in, the ISCs were reduced in number to three and percentage grading abandoned, with students receiving either "satisfactory" or "incomplete". Satisfactory then became an eligibility requirement, along with 90 per cent attendance, to access the ECA for a level. The latter reduced grade pressure and allowed for variation in teachers' appreciation of students' work, but still attached importance to coursework and maintained the desired EAP focus. By the beginning of the sixth year of the innovation, the summative end of course system (ECA) was disconnected from the formative system and students were required to obtain 60 per cent on formative assessment in order to access the ECA. The latter test became the sole decider of the right to progress to the following level.

managing the formative system

The formative assessment focus in the learning system entailed challenges and was modified over time. In addition, assessment for learning presupposes the ability to diagnose individual learning needs and adjust instruction accordingly (Black and Wiliam, 1998; Black et al., 2002). In a large teaching operation, however, with class sizes up to 22 students at certain points in a year, where courses run to 30 hours a week and teaching schedules reach 25 hours per week, the capacity of teachers to detect and respond to students' specific needs may be reduced. Furthermore, patterns across an institution where groups of students are not performing to level, for a variety of reasons, would not be immediately apparent to individual classroom teachers. Hence, data from formative assessment, unless aggregated and used in the broader learning system, may be less effective than it could be at dealing with overall learning needs. In order to compensate for this lack of whole system perspective, a computerised data aggregation system was developed. Information posted on the system about a student's previous performance was immediately accessible to a new course instructor, with comments if needed. The computer system also prompted teachers to estimate each student's predicted performance in the ECA two weeks into an eight-week course.

This ability to look at learner performance after about 50 hours' teaching became an integral part of the formative assessment system. Teachers predicted student performance, pass/borderline/fail, against criteria, in this case their expected performance in ECA in the skills of writing, reading, listening and speaking. The estimate in the computer database created a picture of learner profiles at all levels and allowed institutional resources to be shifted to deal with underperformance. A second estimate, further into a course, corroborated or allowed adjusted teacher perceptions in response to action taken. These estimates are accurate predictors of student performance in the ECAs, with variation reduced substantially by the second estimate. Inevitably, in the early days of the curriculum innovation when teachers' perceptions of level were not firmly established, variation was greater. However, through reflecting on data coming back at the end of each course, teachers' abilities to predict improved considerably.

This system changed the ECA into a truly formative tool. It still retained its role as the deciding factor in the reshuffling of students at the end of a course. However, the ECA had become more a corroboration of the formative perceptions of teachers made during a course. Teachers were able to accurately predict the performance of students using the ECA as a measurement rod. As a result, effective action took place in the learning system well before level decisions were taken at the end of a course. The ECA thus assumed the role of validating teachers' prior decisions, rather than simply being summative. Establishing a solid validity argument for the ECA was crucial, but the logic had changed. If the ECA was the yard-stick by which teachers decided whether students' in-course performance was up to standard, ensuring it gave an accurate picture of the desired attainment at the end of a level became of paramount importance.

moving to a single exit measure

An added difficulty experienced with the formative course assessment system became apparent at the highest level in the learning system. A pass in the final level's ECA entitled students to sit the exemption exam and, if successful, exit the program. Students were passing the ECA, constructed around an EAP perspective, but were failing the exemp-tion exam, despite both tests being theoretically pitched at the same level. The expectation that those who displayed the requisite EAP skills would be able to pass the exemption exam was not borne out in prac-tice. About five per cent of students failed to pass the second exam out of a yearly exam-taking population of around 2000, which meant at least 100 students who passed the end of level exam being consigned to repeating the level. This difference in results was difficult to explain to the university administration and student body. Under pressure, the exemption exam, COPE, became the only exam for the highest level.

The decision to have a single exit exam for the whole school also entailed the creation of two separate cut scores in COPE. Associate Degree students, who made up a small portion of the school's popu-lation, were required to achieve a lower English level for entry into their departments than four-year degree students. The university now requested, in the interests of clarity, that each COPE exam provide exemption for two separate exit levels. This solution was less than ideal from a testing perspective, but practicalities won out.

challenges in direct testing of performance

A final point relates to the difficulties of implementing direct testing of speaking and writing in institutional settings, even though the validity arguments for skills-based language assessment are clear. In formal assessment situations writing may be handled through specialist teams trained for the purpose, with reliability strengthened by the disassociation of ECA from ongoing assessment. However, the introduction of widespread oral testing raises issues of a practical nature, such as the large-scale training of all teachers to undertake reliable direct assessment, whether this is feasible and fair, and the time it takes to submit a few thousand students to an oral interview when turnaround time may be crucial. Substantial assessment of oral production also raises once more the fear of variable grading, thus detracting from standards in a large system. Each context needs to find its solution to such tensions, through either reducing the grade impact of oral testing as a part of overall assessment, making oral assessment a contributory factor to requirements with no specific grade, or training specialist teams of raters. Again, a tension is apparent between a delivery system that would benefit from all teachers being an integral part of an assessment format, in order to increase organisational learning and skills thresholds, and the need to maintain a level of reliability that strengthens the claims made by an assessment format. Whichever the solution, an organisation is committing itself to a substantial investment of resources in order to enhance its validity argument.

organisational learning: assessment development and benchmarking

The introduction of a new language curriculum with new systems and assessment types presents a specific challenge for teaching organisations. In the case discussed here a new assessment system was developed by a specialist group, after consulting the teaching body. However, the skills needed to deliver the tests in a consistently valid way were not immediately apparent in all members of the teaching body. The challenge was how to ensure the development of the assessment system over time in response to everyday experience in the curriculum delivery system. The testing literature suggests monitoring test implementation through, for example, questionnaires and statistical procedures (Bachman and Palmer, 1996). However, such measures may not be responsive enough in real time, particularly, but not exclusively, at the outset of an innovation, to pick up on some of the challenges being experienced. This is especially relevant for formative assessment systems. Summative assessment allows delayed post-test analysis prior to the next sitting, generally taking place at a course end and not affecting a course in progress, whereas formative systems may need to be rectified quickly. In this system they contributed to in-course outcomes, with immediate impact.

A management information system was instituted to give regular feedback on the progress of the new assessment system. For example, the ISCs, discussed above, were a formative assessment tool which had never been tried before, devised to focus students on acquiring academic skills. These were produced independently by a curriculum and testing group, based on a redesigned curriculum specification. A feedback cycle, centred on teachers' weekly meetings in 12 separate teaching units (the way the preparatory program is structured managerially), sought to collect process data on the implementation of the ISCs. Data from questionnaires filled in by teachers while implementing ISCs were discussed, with a curriculum and testing specialist present. Results were brought back to the curriculum and testing group to inform the design of the next formative assignments and so on, cyclically. Initially, feedback comments received related more to task complexity, the breadth of assignments and the quality of criteria. Comments led to immediate changes in these elements, based on the representativeness of the data. An interesting fact was that, as successive feedback loops were undertaken, the focal point of feedback changed. Initial concerns related to what might be termed cosmetic issues in design, changing over time to more conceptual issues to do with understandings, training needs and organisational requirements, as the system settled.

Such *Performative Evaluation* is a type of formative evaluation which is "an embedded evaluation process, entirely insider run, centred around decision-making structures and roles in an organization, in which data is regularly collected on a curriculum innovation and passed through the structures for decision-making and action" (O'Dwyer, 2008: 321). It recognises that developing assessment practice is a learning process and that an assessment system needs to be able to transform in response to feedback in an ongoing way, as experience develops. Challenges experienced with an assessment system may not be specifically related to the assessment format proper, but may relate to broad institutional issues to do with training needs, different understandings, or conflict of interests. A commitment to embedded evaluation can fundamentally alter the perceptions of implementers and innovators, and build a culture in a school in which regular feedback is sought and incorporated into developments as they proceed, thus also contributing to organisational sustainability. Teachers involved in assessment, although they might not be able to write a test to the same degree of desired validity as a specially assigned and trained assessment committee, will nonetheless be able to provide first-hand data as to how a test is performing in practice. Perceptions of teachers may be just as effective in securing gains, by virtue of their being in the forefront of the action, so to speak. Thus, the combination of data based on the validity considerations that characterise good testing, and knowledge from within the system, strengthens learning systems.

understanding level in an assessment system

An important aspect in any context is the interrelatedness of assessment within and between levels. It takes time for teachers to gain a sense of level; it is not something that one can assume is automatic. It seems reasonable to assume that those teachers who do not have a clear sense of attainment for different levels will be less effective in directing student learning to achieve those levels, particularly in relation to skills. Benchmarking of levels can be done internally through standardisation, and externally through benchmarking procedures such as those suggested by the CEFR. In this context, incorporating teachers into the test design system through working with testing specialists helped, over time, to produce a broader institutional understanding of level. When the end of course testing system was disassociated from the formative in-course assessment, standard tests were developed by a specialist group, which reflected the collective understanding of experts as to what performance at the exit of each level was. These tests were banked and reused. However, the lack of a clearly enunciated validation argument to support the level of the exemption exam (COPE), and the fact that the level exams were not benchmarked either, set the institution on a path to define these levels using the Common European Framework of Reference for Languages (CEFR).

The benchmarking undertaken in this context using the CEFR manual is reported elsewhere (e.g. Kantarcıoğlu et al., 2010). That study concludes that linking to external benchmarks, within a fully functioning school, is not easy. Training in the process takes time, even if a benchmarking team is carefully constituted. Substantial resources need to be devoted to the endeavour, including time and external expertise. The process is greatly underestimated in the CEFR benchmarking design, which could be reflected in the relative dearth of complete studies almost ten years since the publication of the CEFR, and six years after the Preliminary Pilot Manual (Council of Europe, 2003), a revised version of which appeared in 2009. It took two years of intense activity to develop a robust validation argument for the COPE exemption exam, and a similar time frame seems to be the norm for benchmarking other levels leading up to the COPE level. In addition, it seems that bench-marking lower levels, and levels above the COPE, is subject to specific challenges which institutions need to deal with independently. For example, the applicability of descriptors at these levels may be a fac-tor. Benchmarking, however, can add to the intellectual capital of an institution over time. It can ensure a realistic curriculum progression built on data, and allow an organisation to respond in its own time to shifting needs and level requirements. From experience and expertise gained through the process of constructing a validation argument, an organisation's ability to learn and sustain itself is enhanced.

discussion

The profile of an institution, its context and the aims it has set itself carry major implications for assessment in the learning system. The development of student competence can be a slow and difficult process, illustrated in this context by Figure 14.1. The graph shows success rates on COPE for each new cohort of preparatory programme students. Up to 1993, students had three years to achieve the target level, reduced

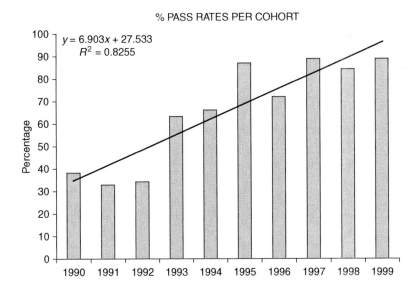

% PASS RATES PER COHORT

$y = 6.903x + 27.533$
$R^2 = 0.8255$

Figure 14.1   Per cent pass rates over the first seven years (start 1993) of the new curriculum

to two years from then on. The trend line shows a steady increase in real pass rates over ten years, validated through a Rasch anchor study (O'Dwyer, 2008). Gains are better represented, however, as a histogram. Each distinct platform was achieved after much process-based reflection over the course of the curriculum innovation, in which assessment was an important element. In the new millennium, not shown in the diagram, pass rates have remained high, with a mean of 86 per cent and a standard deviation of 5.2 per cent.

Our experience shows that testers may need to respond to exigencies arising from the operation of assessment in the learning system, particularly when innovating and changing client expectations. For example, the integrity of a high stakes test may be challenged externally. Therefore, specifications and data that allow a test to stand up to external scrutiny are essential. Validation arguments have become more widespread in practice over the past 10–15 years in response to criticism in the testing community (e.g. Alderson et al., 1995) and interest created through linking studies, notably to the CEFR. Explicative case studies of the linking and benchmarking processes are only slowly coming to light (Thomas and Kantarcıoğlu, 2009; Kantarcıoğlu et al., forthcoming). In the literature, validation arguments covering a whole exam are rare and, where claims do exist in the published reports of recognised exams, the specific evidence itself may be missing. Where rigorous linking to external standards is evidenced, then external challenge will be easier to defend. In turn, the ability to defend standards will add to the validation argument of an exam and enhance its quality in the eyes of the test-taking community.

Establishing credibility may encompass the need to go to court. Such vigilance costs administrative time and effort and needs to be factored into operations, but may well be worth the effort and associated costs, as was borne out in the context discussed earlier. Reliance on international exams for exemption purposes, although providing a convenience factor in cost investment terms, might deprive an institution of a learning opportunity which could have repercussions on the overall ability of the delivery system to define its standards and respond to its needs as they evolve. Such an institutional commitment, however, entails a commitment to in-house quality test production, including developing a team of writers, building an item bank based on Item Response Analysis (IRT), and constantly replenishing items when compromised, all expensive resources.

increasing the standards in a learning system

Where a learning system is trying to improve its standards, setting a valid exemption test at a distinctly higher level may spell internal problems for the system in which it is anchored. A solid argument exists for devising an approach that allows a gradual change from one standard to another. This is not easy to achieve, particularly where the test is the basis for regulating numbers through to a further level of study, as is often the case in EAP contexts. The simple reliance on cut scores that reflect the new level may prejudice the workings of a school by interfering with internal expectations, such as student numbers passing into departments. A solution might be employed such as the "D boundary" system discussed earlier, which does not compromise the validity of an exemption test but which recognises the interdependency of different parts of a learning system. Such solutions risk potential rejection by testing experts or external moderators, who might put validity concerns paramount. Although setting new standards and doggedly sticking to them may be deemed a plausible response to entry to an oversubscribed learning system, it is not acceptable in contexts where people are already bound to a system. Administrators need to be prepared to put the argument for the training of teachers, allowing skills levels to build slowly, and explaining that exemption testing, for example, is not simply a level argument, but has many factors dependent upon it. In other words, the delivery system needs to be fine-tuned before the impact can be rightfully measured by the test itself. A similar argument for progressive adjustment can be advanced for national assessment systems that wish to increase levels, or coverage, or focus. Alternatively, Rasch measurement techniques might be employed to allow average difficulty levels of exam papers to be put up gradually, but this represents a technically sophisticated solution, which might not be within the capacity of all institutions.

managing assessment for learning

Assessment is conceptualised in terms of its ability to deliver accurate information for the context in which it operates. Many discussions of testing appear to assume a structure already in place, ensuring available expertise in test design and delivery. For a number of reasons, such an assumption may not reflect the day-to-day reality of operating assessment systems in specific educational contexts. First of all, variation in assessment expertise is inherent in the range of skill levels of available teachers in any context, particularly when an institution is large, or across a national delivery system. For example, teachers new to a system or to the profession will have to learn the standards and expectations of the system, which takes time and may never be 100 per cent complete due to staff turnover, new initiatives, and so on. Secondly, an environment of change, in which new assessment understandings and concepts are being forged, needs time to settle and deliver more reliable results. Much responsive action on the part of schools will be needed to find ways of improving the accuracy and usefulness of assessment data. If the institution is constantly seeking to re-evaluate, in the manner of a learning organisation, the effectiveness of its delivery systems and assessment practices, then the system may never settle in the ways understood by professional testers. Institutions may wish to increase levels over time, or respond to exigencies in curriculum delivery, to which assessment will be subsumed. The important factor then becomes, not the assessment vehicles themselves, but rather the management systems in place, which allow changes in the assessment system in response to changing imperatives in the curriculum.

The practical experience recounted earlier shows that attempts to create a more valid learning system, based on formative principles, may work counter to traditional validity expectations in testing. Extending formative assessment and allowing teachers more control over formative grading, specifically in contexts where the formative grades count substantially towards a final grade, may cause problems for the system in which the testing is embedded. Eliminating formative assessment altogether would undermine an important part of a teachers' input into the learning cycle, but allowing cumulative grading, as was illustrated in this context, may be detrimental to the whole system, particularly in high stakes contexts. Disconnecting the grading of formative assessment from the final grade for a course reduces immediate pressure on teachers. However, maintaining an eligibility system in which access to final course assessment depends on formative grades in short, traditional-style tests, marked independently of a class teacher, coupled with a satisfactory/unsatisfactory grade system controlled by a class teacher, has merits. Any individual variability in grading would no longer affect final outcomes negatively, but there would remain an obligation on students to complete ongoing assessment requirements.

Some commentators agree that there is no real distinction between summative and formative (e.g. Levine, 2002) and that a test may be used for both purposes, reflecting to a degree, but for different reasons, the rationale behind Scriven's (1967) original dichotomy. The difficulty in practice of summative data used formatively, exemplified in many university student feedback schemes, is that the data do not always arrive during a specific learning process. It can only be formative for an indeterminate future use and lacks a performative feature (see above). It smacks of closing the stable door after the horse has bolted. So, although much effort and planning may go into producing end of course exams, the reality is that these data are generally used for pass/fail decisions and may not have a direct effect on the flow of learning.

In the case discussed here, by instituting a system that formally encourages teachers to estimate final exam performance at early stages in a learning programme, and by aggregating the data electronically, the final exam becomes a reliability check on earlier perceptions used to improve the course. Therefore, the final exam is not only seen as more formative in helping teachers improve the course in real time using the final exam as a criterion beacon, but it also helps professional development by honing this ability in teachers, over time, by force of repeated comparison with the final result. In this perspective the final exam becomes more meaningful in the learning system, as do validity constraints in designing the final exam, as they then set the strength of the beam on the beacon. In fact, with repeated use, teachers can become extremely proficient in estimation and gauge test performance to within close parameters. Responsiveness in the learning system may thus be increased by this development of in-house expertise through such institutional learning. The data are then available to the teacher and institution for individual action and resource reallocation, ensuring a more responsive learning system.

learning system validity versus test validity

The issue as to whether formal standardised assessment can cover all objectives is an important one in learning systems. Models of formative and summative assessment assume, in the manner of Scriven (1967), that formative is a gradual testing of intermediate objectives leading to a summative test covering achievement on objectives "referenced to the teaching syllabus. Or... to criteria external to the course" (Rea-Dickins, 1985: 28). Cronbach (1963), to whom Scriven was responding when coining his famous dichotomy, raised this crucial issue by pointing out that students may learn things other than what is prescribed in the curriculum, and therefore testing may miss learning. This logic may be extended to language testing in learning systems of which English language development is a part. An EAP context may wish to develop academic skills of which a test may be a poor reflection, as with the ISC system discussed above. A school context may wish to focus on a learner profile, as with the International Baccalaureate Primary Years Program (PYP, 2008), and subsume content to process. Both these examples rely heavily on types of formative assessment that may not be replicable in a traditional summative test. Ongoing assessment, therefore, plays a critical role in focusing on and achieving certain linguistic and non-linguistic goals which may have a crucial impact on long-term learning success in a university or school context.

Thus, the validity of a test is a part, but not the whole, of the validity of the learning system. Assessment systems and practices that may be less amenable to traditional testing validation procedures will, none-theless, add to the overall validity of the learning system. This tension between summative and formative is resolved to some extent by discon-necting the two, as discussed earlier. However, it is resolved with great difficulty where progress is determined entirely by success in formal high stakes assessment. A high stakes test of this type falls down in consequential validity (Messick, 1989) or ethical terms (Weir, 2004) if it is the sole arbiter of success, as it can mean that important learn-ing skills may be missing from the assessment. Thus, in consequential validity terms, a summative exemption test may be considered invalid, as it does not represent the full gamut of learning objectives targeted in the learning system. This mismatch between avowed learning aims and the backwash of high stakes testing requires a rethinking of assessment relative to educational mission. In contexts of innovation and change, in which assessment can play a major part, those responsible for assess-ment in the learning system need to take a position in the debate over what Westbury refers to as the "tensions between the notions of public control of standards and the curriculum and their professional control" (2008: 46).

standards in a learning organisation

The benchmarking of standards as part of the learning system was broached earlier in terms of an exemption exam, but, in reality, bench-marking is required at all levels in a learning system in order to build reasonably and logically on language skills development. This is easier said than done. Two aspects of test production that are crucial to bench-marking, namely trialling of items in a population and the establish-ment of a team with common understandings and experience of all levels, are achieved with difficulty in institutional settings. Pre-trialling means that items may be compromised, particularly in high stakes con-texts where takers remain in the delivery system for a while. In cases where items are given to parallel institutional populations, a lack of seriousness on the part of takers may also negate level data. Additional points exams have been used in the context discussed here and given to the population of students at a level. Extra points are given for strong performance; none are subtracted for less than average performance, and they are thus motivating for students. Levels can then be linked using population characteristics through Rasch analysis; again a technically difficult process requiring additional resources.

The benchmarking processes suggested by the CEFR are not easily transferred to institutions, or testing bodies for that matter, as contributions in this volume show. The CEFR Manual seems to underestimate the time needed to train specialists selected institutionally for their testing acumen (Kantarcıoğlu et al., forthcoming); regular non-specialist staff may require even more time. This underscores the need for sustainable testing systems which are integrated into a development plan for an organisation, which recognise that building up institutional expertise is a slow process requiring commitment to the development of testing skills at all levels. The EALTA guidelines (EALTA, 2006) emphasise the importance of training for testers, but, in educational institutions, this has to be part of a leadership model that fosters the development of skills through integrated training and professional assessment practices, which include: regular standardisation; feedback systems of a performative nature; and a recognition that tensions in the delivery system as regards the function of assessment need to be managed according to the context. The tail must not be allowed to wag the dog.

conclusion

This chapter has discussed systemic issues surrounding assessment in an EAP context with a view to developing a perspective on "applied testing", focusing on factors influencing day-to-day assessment practice in learning systems. The attempt to establish clear standards and establish the tenets of valid assessment as part of a learning system has to take account of the complex nature of running educational organisations. Establishing quality assessment procedures involves resolving the tensions apparent between realising and assessing worthwhile learning aims and the inherent characteristics of a system. These latter may include learners' prior expectations, staff training and development levels, resource and expertise availability, and the feasibility of realising learning outcomes through standard assessment procedures.

The implications of the above discussion for leaders are numerous and underscore the need for a continuous commitment to staff development, an intricate knowledge of the characteristics of the context, and a recognition that sustained organisational learning is dependent on, among other factors, a commitment to establishing feedback loops and decision-making which build on experience as it develops.

references

Alderson, J. C., Clapham, C. and Wall, D. (1995). *Language Test Construction and Evaluation.* Cambridge: Cambridge University Press.

Bachman, L. F. (1990). *Fundamental Considerations in Language Testing.* Oxford: Oxford University Press.

Bachman, L. F. (2004). *Statistical Analyses for Language Assessment.* Cambridge: Cambridge University Press.

Bachman, L. F. and Palmer, A. S. (1996). *Language Testing in Practice.* Oxford: Oxford University Press.

Black, P. J. and Wiliam, D. (1998). *Inside the Black Box: Raising Standards through Classroom Assessment.* London: King's College.

Black, P., Harrison, C., Lee, C., Marshall, B. and Wiliam, D. (2002). *Working inside the Black Box: Assessment for Learning in the Classroom.* London: King's College.

Council of Europe (2003). *Relating Language Examinations to the Common European Framework of Reference for Languages: Learning, Teaching, Assessment: Preliminary Pilot Manual.* Strasburg: Council of Europe, Language Policy Division.

Cronbach, L. (1963). Evaluation for course improvement. *Teachers College Record, 64*(8), 672–683.

EALTA (2006). *EALTA Guidelines for Good Practice in Language Testing and Assessment (Adopted 20 May 2006).* Available at www.ealta.eu.org/guidelines.htm (accessed 15 November 2009).

EL Gazette (2009). TOEFL test score forgery scandal. *EL Gazette, 348*, January.

Grabe, W. (2009). *Reading in a Second Language.* Cambridge: Cambridge University Press.

Graddol, D. (2006). *English Next. Why Global English may Mean the End of "English as a Foreign Language".* London: British Council.

Handy, C. (1994). *The Empty Raincoat: Making Sense of the Future.* London: Hutchinson.

Hughes, A. (2003). *Language Testing for Teachers* (2nd edition). Cambridge: Cambridge University Press.

International Baccalaureate (2009). Available at http://www.ibo.org (accessed 15 November 2009).

Kantarcıoğlu, E., Thomas, C., O'Dwyer, J. and O'Sullivan, B. (2010). Benchmarking a high stakes proficiency exam: the COPE linking project at BUSEL. In W. Martyniuk (Ed.), *Relating Language Examinations to the Common European Framework of Reference for Languages: Case Studies and Reflections on the Use of the Council of Europe's Draft Manual.* SILT Series. Cambridge: Cambridge University Press, pp. 102–118.

Levine, T. (2002). Stability and change in curriculum planning. *Studies in Educational Evaluation, 28*, 1–33.

Martyniuk, W. (Ed.) (2010). *Relating Language Examinations to the Common European Framework of Reference for Languages: Case Studies and Reflections on the Use of the Council of Europe's Draft Manual.* SILT Series. Cambridge: Cambridge University Press.

Messick, S. (1989). Validity. In R. L. Linn (Ed.), *Educational Measurement* (3rd edition). Old Tapan, NJ: Macmillan.

O'Dwyer, J. (2008). *Formative Evaluation for Organisational Learning: A Case Study of the Management of a Process of Curriculum Development.* Frankfurt: Peter Lang.

O'Dwyer, J., Aksit, N. and Sands, M. (2010). Expanding educational access in eastern Turkey: a new initiative. *International Journal of Educational Development,* 30(2), 193–203.

PYP (2008). What is the primary years programme (PYP)? Available at http://www.ibo.org/pyp (accessed 1 March 2011).

Rea, P. M. (1985). Language testing and the communicative language teaching curriculum. In Y. P. Lee, A. C. Y. Y. Fok, R. Lord and G. Low (Eds), *New Directions in Language Testing.* Oxford: Pergamon Press.

Scriven, M. (1967). The methodology of evaluation. In R. W. Tyler, R. M. Gagne and M. Scriven (Eds), *Perspectives of Curriculum Evaluation.* Chicago, IL: Rand McNally.

Thomas, C. and Kantaraçioğlu, E. (2009). Bilkent University School of English Language COPE CEFR linking project. In N. Figueras and J. Noijons (Eds), *Linking to the CEFR Levels: Research Perspectives.* Arnhem: Cito.

Weir, C. J. (2004). *Language Testing and Validation: An Evidence-Based Approach.* Oxford: Palgrave Macmillan.

Westbury, I. (2008). Making curricula: why do states make curricula, and how? In M. F. Connelly, M. F. He and J. Phillion (Eds), *The Sage Handbook of Curriculum and Instruction.* Thousand Oaks CA: Sage Publications.

index